Learn Xcode Tools for Mac OS X and iPhone Development

Ian Piper

Apress®

Learn Xcode Tools for Mac OS X and iPhone Development

ISBN-13 (pbk): 978-1-4302-7221-2

ISBN-13 (electronic): 978-1-4302-7220-5

Printed and bound in the United States of America 9 8 7 6 5 4 3 2 1

Distributed to the book trade worldwide by Springer-Verlag New York, Inc., 233 Spring Street, 6th Floor, New York, NY 10013. Phone 1-800-SPRINGER, fax 201-348-4505, e-mail orders-ny@springer-sbm.com, or visit http://www.springeronline.com.

For information on translations, please e-mail info@apress.com, or visit http://www.apress.com.

Apress and friends of ED books may be purchased in bulk for academic, corporate, or promotional use. eBook versions and licenses are also available for most titles. For more information, reference our Special Bulk Sales–eBook Licensing web page at http://www.apress.com/info/bulksales.

The source code for this book is available to readers at http://www.apress.com. You will need to answer questions pertaining to this book in order to successfully download the code.

To Caroline, Alice and Ben, at the centre of my universe

—Ian

Contents at a Glance

Contents

About the Author

Ian Piper has been developing software on the Macintosh, Newton, and iPhone since clapping eyes on his first Mac back in 1984.

Ian runs an information management consultancy based in the UK and his day job mostly involves picking apart and rebuilding taxonomies for complex information systems, and writing software for the Mac and iPhone. He spends as much time as is left over from doing this stuff climbing hills in the Lake District and Yorkshire Dales.

He lives with his wife Caroline, children Alice and Ben, and dog Meg in Warwickshire. Despite any indications to the contrary in these pages, he regards Marmite as, on the whole, the best thing on sliced bread.

About the Technical Reviewer

James Bucanek has spent the past 30 years programming and developing microprocessor systems. He has experience with a broad range of computer technologies, ranging from piano teaching systems to industrial robotics. James is currently focused on Macintosh and iPhone software development, where he can combine his knowledge of UNIX and object-oriented languages with his passion for elegant design.

Acknowledgments

President John F. Kennedy immortalized the phrase "Success has a thousand parents: failure is an orphan." To the extent that this book succeeds for you or any other reader, or for me as author, or for the publisher, I want to acknowledge the endless patience and tireless hard work of those wonderful people who have helped make it work. To the extent that it fails, I'll assume full parentage.

First and foremost, I want to thank my wife Caroline, who has made it possible for me to have the time I needed to write and kept the children out of my remaining hair when I needed to concentrate. I know the hard work it has taken on your part and will always be grateful to you for the sacrifices you've made. To my children, who came and bugged me anyway and thus kept me reasonably human and sane, my love and thanks.

This book wouldn't have got off the ground—at least not with me as the pilot—if not for Clay Andres at Apress. Clay's boundless enthusiasm and encouragement was incredibly valuable. It has been a privilege to work with him.

The coordinating editors Mary Tobin and Kelly Moritz, and the development editor Brian MacDonald, had their work cut out in dealing with my creative approach to syntax and over-use of diagrams. I found them a delight to work with and appreciate their continual patience, indulgence, support, and encouragement.

I want to make special acknowledgment of the help provided by the Technical Reviewer, James Bucanek. It was a wonderful boost to have someone of James's experience and eminence in the Mac development world looking over my shoulder, and he provided extraordinary help to me throughout the development of the book.

Preface

Apple's products have always had the reputation (richly deserved in my opinion) of providing the easiest to learn and richest working environment of any computer system. As Mac or iPhone users we are privileged: software that requires little time, effort, or documentation to become productive is the rule rather than the exception.

Unfortunately, that rule hasn't historically extended to the tools and technologies used to *create* such programs. Learning to write software for the Mac has traditionally involved a major investment of intellectual effort and time in new tools, technologies, and techniques. I have thought for a long time that this is an essentially artificial barrier. Delivery in the sophisticated environment of the Mac and iPhone takes a lot of effort behind the scenes, and there is no doubt that learning to write software that works in such environments involves taking on a significant burden of new technologies and concepts. However, I believe that, with suitably accessible tools, and some good, clear, written guidance, creating great Mac and iPhone software should be within the grasp of most competent developers.

With the latest release of the Xcode Developer Tools, the new developer has access to a formidable tool-chest for Mac and iPhone development that is easier to use than any previous version. The missing piece, to me, has always been a simple and clear description of the tools and technologies needed to write for the Mac and iPhone. That is why I have written this book.

I wrote this book with the idea that it would be a companion for the new developer. It's the book that I hope you will keep within reach as you learn to write software for the Mac and iPhone, because it's the book that I wish I'd had. It is intended to be a friendly guide to the environment, tools, techniques, and technologies that you will need to take on to be comfortable writing software for the Mac and iPhone. It will take you, I hope in a fairly rational way, from the basic developer tools through to more advanced technologies such as source-code management, performance analysis, and unit testing. Along the way you will be visiting some lesser-travelled roads to learn about usability and accessibility. Although there is a progression from simple to advanced topics, this is also a book to dip into where you need to, and to skip the areas you already know or don't need to know right now. It is, finally, intended to be fun—using a Mac is one of life's great pleasures, after all, so why shouldn't it be fun to write software on it and for it?

It's not intended to replace Apple's Developer Documentation, though it will take you a long way before you need to resort to the official word. It's not intended to be a course in Objective-C (the principal language underlying Xcode development) though you should pick up many of the core features from what you read here, especially if you already know a language like C, C#, or Java.

I hope that you enjoy the experience of reading this book as much as I have writing it, and that it turns out to be your developer's companion.

Chapter 1

Introducing Xcode Tools for Mac OS X and the iPhone

Since you are reading this, I hope that you are doing so on the way to the checkout at your bookstore! Or perhaps you have just opened a packaging from the mail. Either way, you have a great journey ahead of you, and I hope that this book fulfills the hopes you have for it.

When I learned the arcane rituals of Mac software development I found it difficult, in part because I needed to learn at least three new and difficult paradigms simultaneously. I needed a friendly helper to get me over those barriers. This is the book that I wanted to have at my fingertips, and I hope it becomes your friendly helper.

Software Development Choices for the Mac Programmer

Software development for the professional Mac developer has always had great support from Apple. For new developers and those who are doing it for fun, the situation has been less easy. For many years such developers had some difficult decisions to make if they wanted to build their own Mac software.

Mac OS X offers some great high-level tools for improving productivity and automation, such as Automator, Dashcode, and, of course, the venerable AppleScript. These are very useful in adding features to existing applications and in automating repetitive tasks, but you wouldn't use them to create real applications.

There have been pseudo-languages like HyperCard and its successors, taking a very modular building-block approach to building software. These let you put together simple applications quickly and easily, but can be limited in their features. So what if you want to create your killer application for the Mac?

It's worth mentioning REALbasic. This is a great tool for software development and has a loyal following of active programmers. It has a simple and easy-to-use integrated development environment (IDE) and uses the syntactically simple BASIC as its language. It also has the benefit of creating executables for Mac OS X, Windows, and Linux from essentially a single code base.

However, it has some limitations. REALbasic uses its own libraries, not Cocoa frameworks (at the time of writing the company has announced its intention to support Cocoa), and there is usually an indefinable air that tells you an application has been written in REALbasic. Executable files can be on the large side. Although it supports an object-oriented approach, REALbasic doesn't enforce it, and this, together with its short learning curve, can lead to products of indifferent quality. You will find that Xcode is quite different. It is what is known as *opinionated* software: while there is a lot of flexibility, there is a right way to develop in Xcode, and you will find life much easier if you follow it.

REALbasic is not a good grounding or a springboard for a subsequent move to Xcode. The paradigms are completely different, and when I made the move I essentially had to forget everything I knew. REALbasic is a commercial product, of course, in contrast to the free Xcode Tools. Finally, although you are able to target Windows and Linux as platforms, REALbasic cannot be used (at least, at the time of writing) to build iPhone software.

All in all, REALbasic offers a lot of fun and productivity to the developer, and for knocking out simple utility programs it's unbeatable. But as you develop more of an interest in serious software development, there is a good chance that you will begin to develop some curiosity about Xcode.

Why You Should Develop Using Xcode Tools

Given the number of alternative choices, it might seem easy to dismiss Xcode Developer Tools (which you'll often see referred to as just Xcode Tools) and Cocoa frameworks as a choice for developing software for the Mac. It is fair to say, too, that historically Xcode and its antecedent products have not been very accessible to the new developer. The first sight of the Xcode project interface can be daunting, Objective-C has a quirky syntax, the separation of design imposed by the MVC pattern is a conceptual leap too far for many, and the documentation, though comprehensive, has historically not been aimed at the learner.

The need to come to grips with all of these new concepts was the main thing that prevented me from learning to develop using Cocoa and Xcode. And that is a shame, because once you get past these initial barriers, a major benefit of Apple's tools and technologies is their ease of use. Really. That observation was the driving force for this book—many would-be developers have no doubt been put off developing using Xcode because of the multiple learning curves that need to be negotiated simultaneously. My sincere hope is that this book will help you past those learning curves, because once past them you will find Xcode an elegant, easy-to-use, and highly productive environment in which to work.

Of course, there is one very good reason for making Xcode your development platform of choice—the iPhone. At the time of writing, there simply is no other way to create iPhone software. If you are even thinking of writing iPhone apps, then you need to learn Xcode.

Xcode, Cocoa, and Objective-C

One aim of this book is to dispel some of the confusion surrounding terminology. The new developer has not only to learn a sophisticated and complex environment and toolset, but also a range of new concepts and terms. In particular, the three terms *Xcode*, *Cocoa*, and *Objective-C* are often mixed up in the minds of newcomers to Mac development. Let's nail this confusion right now.

Let's start with *Cocoa*. This is the name given to the complete object-oriented environment within which you are working when you create software for Mac OS X and iPhone. The most visible aspect of Cocoa is the collection of code libraries known as the Cocoa frameworks. These provide you with a consistent and optimized set of prebuilt code modules that will vastly speed up your development process. You'll learn a lot more about the Cocoa frameworks in Chapter 5. The Cocoa frameworks make extensive use of the Model-View-Controller pattern: this is a very popular design approach (or *pattern*) for creating modern object-oriented programs. We will cover MVC design in Chapter 6.

Objective-C is a programming language, like Java or C++ or Ruby. This book is not about learning Objective-C, for the very simple reason that there are plenty of great books already out there to teach you the language. Most of the software you write with Xcode Tools is likely to be written in Objective-C, but it doesn't have to be. Xcode supports a number of other languages. We're not going to cover any of these in this book, but there is plenty of information in the Apple Developer Documentation and on the Web to help you discover more. You'll learn much more about the Apple Developer Documentation in Chapter 8.

If you have developed software in Ruby on Rails, the above will be instantly familiar. In that case, Ruby is the programming language and Rails is the object-oriented, MVC-centered environment within which you create software.

So, to Xcode. *Xcode* is shorthand for the Xcode Developer Tools—the subject of this book. The Xcode Developer Tools provide one way for you to develop Cocoa-based software. You don't have to use Xcode Developer Tools—if you really want, you can develop your code using a text editor and compile it at the command line in a terminal. But what a missed opportunity that would be: the Xcode Developer Tools combine to give you a complete professional-quality development environment. It contains all of the tools you need for project management, code development, user-interface design, debugging, revision management, unit testing, performance monitoring, and packaging. Not only that, but the entire toolset is imbued with typical Apple build quality and usability. These tools are a pleasure to use: as well as accelerating your development, they will give you hours of fun! What's not to like?

I like to think of these terms with an analogy. In a sense, Cocoa is the world that you are living in while creating Mac and iPhone applications. The frameworks are pre-fabricated units that help accelerate your building and make your products meet the standards. The Xcode Tools are what you use to build your houses, factories, and roads. Objective-C provides your bricks and mortar. You might think of MVC as the building regulations or architectural standards that you use to make a safe and strong structure.

The Apple Xcode Developer Tools Family

The Xcode Developer Tools is a family of applications designed to work harmoniously together to provide most of the tools you need to create your software. The map in Figure 1–1 divides the Developer Tools into the core tools, companion tools and features, and supporting utilities. This broadly reflects the importance of the tools in terms of the amount of use you are likely to get out of each, but of course there are different ways of categorizing them.

Figure 1–1. *The Xcode Tools family*

The central components are Xcode and Interface Builder. Beyond this is a range of analysis and performance-management tools and technologies. There is also a variety of supporting utilities to help with refinement, usability, accessibility, and distribution of applications.

What You'll Find in This Book

Here is a brief introduction to each of the main Xcode-focused topics that I'll be covering in the book.

Part 1

The first part covers the core Xcode toolset. **Chapter 2** introduces the Xcode program itself, covering the Xcode Workspace and code-development tools. **Chapter 3** describes Interface Builder and takes you through examples of interface development for different types of applications. **In Chapter 4** you get your first look at the tools for iPhone development. I have already mentioned **Chapters 5** and **6**, on Cocoa Frameworks and MVC. In **Chapter 7** you will learn how to use the various debugging tools in Xcode. **Chapter 8** explores Apple's Developer Documentation and other sources of help and support. The final chapter in this core section, **Chapter 9**, allows you to put into practice much of what you have learned in the preceding chapters, when you build an entire Mac OS X application.

Part 2

This second part builds on the core tools to cover some more advanced and less-used features. **Chapter 10** introduces revision control with Subversion, a subject avoided by many developers (me included until I had lost one piece of project code too many) but that, with a little investment, will ensure that you never again lose track of your precious code. In **Chapter 11** we will be tackling another topic that is normally given a wide berth—unit testing. Very few developers build unit tests, yet properly done they can be a considerable timesaver. Ruby on Rails developers, used to having unit tests built into the environment, will be familiar with the benefits of this approach. **Chapter 12** takes covers performance monitoring and analysis tools—if you've ever wondered what Instruments is for and how to use it, this is the chapter for you.

Part 3

The final part of this book deals with some of the lesser-known supporting tools for the developer, focusing on adding that extra layer of polish to enhance your application. **Chapter 13** describes some of the support utilities available in the Xcode Tools, including the Icon Composer, Property List Editor, and File Merge.

Chapter 14 is all about usability and accessibility. Sadly, the mere fact that you are developing on the most usable computer platform in the world doesn't guarantee that your software will be usable. We'll be covering the Human Interface (HI) guidelines and run through some approaches to software design and features within Xcode Tools that will make your Mac and iPhone software stand out. A key partner to usability is accessibility—designing software that is usable for people with disabilities. Xcode Tools provides some excellent support for building accessible software, and you will learn about this here.

And so to the final chapter. **Chapter 15** deals with getting your software out the door. Most of your time within Xcode is likely to be spent creating software in debug mode, but eventually you will get to the point of release. This chapter covers the Xcode support for moving your software from debug to release. You will also learn how to use Apple's packaging software, PackageMaker, to create slick and appealing installation packages. We will also be covering the business of releasing iPhone software using the App Store.

What You Won't Find in This Book

I've mentioned it already, but it bears repeating. This book is not about learning to write Objective-C code. The focus is on introducing you to, and making productive use of, the Xcode Tools. Along the way, there will be many completely worked examples that are obviously written in the language, but there will not be extensive discussion of language syntax or structure. There are plenty of great books and other resources out there to help you with that.

This book is a learning book, and as such is not aimed at advanced developers. As a result, many of the topics are introduced and described to a sufficient level of detail to let you being to be productive, but no further. If I were to cover every topic in exhaustive detail, you'd be holding a book of over 1000 pages right now!

Summary

Well, that's what you have in store if you really are on the way to the checkout with this book. The journey begins here: it should be fun, and you will learn a lot! I hope you enjoy the journey, and I look forward to seeing the fruits of your labor when I buy your killer applications! Turn the page now, and let's get started.

Part I

The Core Xcode Toolset

Chapter **2**

Introducing the Xcode Workspace

OK, you're persuaded. Apple's world-class development tools are within your grasp, and Xcode is worth a serious look. It's time to set it up on your computer.

In this chapter, you are going to get Xcode (actually, you may already have it!), install it, and get to know the coding environment—aka, the Xcode Workspace. You will create, build, and run the simplest possible application.

Getting and Installing Xcode Developer Tools

Before starting, it's worth explaining some terminology. Though they are often used interchangeably, there's a difference between *Xcode* and *Xcode Developer Tools*. The Xcode application is your entry point to Xcode development, and it gives you access to the Xcode Workspace. This is your working environment—the place where you are going to do the bulk of your code development, and the focus of this chapter. The term *Xcode Developer Tools* covers the whole suite of tools, including Interface Builder (which is the subject of the next chapter), Instruments, Shark, the documentation set, and so on. You will learn more about these tools throughout the rest of the book.

Getting Xcode

You may already have the Xcode Developer Tools: Apple includes them in the installation media for every new Mac. In the Optional Installs folder, you'll find Xcode Tools, and within that folder, Xcode.mpkg.

Given the rate of change of Xcode features (Apple doesn't tend to rest on their laurels with any of their products, and Xcode is no exception) the chances are that the version on your disk is out of date, so it's a good idea to go and fetch the latest version from the Apple Developer Connection site, which this book will refer to as "ADC" for the most part.

You can't just go and download the tools, unfortunately; you first need to register as a developer on the site. The good news is that the process is easy, immediate, and—always a bonus—free. Let's walk through it.

Point your browser to the Mac Dev Center home page at http://developer.apple.com/ mac/. From here you can explore plenty of useful resources for Mac development, but for now follow the link to register for a free ADC Online Membership.

You have a range of options for ADC membership, and it's worth coming back to explore these later, but your aim now is just to get the tools. So find the button to register for ADC Online Membership, and then complete the registration form.

Once you have completed the form, you will find yourself back at the Mac Dev Center home page. Find the link to log in and use your freshly minted credentials. What you see on the resulting page depends on your membership level, but at a minimum there will be a link to download the latest version of Xcode. Follow this link and the download will start immediately.

You will notice that the installation kit is substantial—nearly a gigabyte for Xcode 3.1.2— so depending on your network connection it may take some time to download. Finally, though, you will have a file with a name like xcode312_2621_developerdvd.dmg. Double-click this to mount it on your Mac's desktop, and you'll see the installation kit. Note that this is also what you would see if you had started from the Install DVD with an up-to-date copy of the tools, so from this point on the process is the same whether you install from a download or from the Install DVD.

Installing Xcode

Installing Xcode Tools works in the same way as most Mac software. In the installation folder, find the file called Xcode.mpkg and double-click the icon to run it. The installer asks you to authenticate, and there is the usual license agreement stage, but there should be few surprises in the installation process. There are two places where you might be unclear about the installation: the location of the installed files and custom installation options. Let's deal with both of those now.

Installation Location

In earlier versions of Xcode, you had no choice about location: the files went into the Developer folder at the root of your main disk—that is, /Developer. Although Xcode 3 offers you much more flexibility about where to install Xcode, the default is still /Developer, and to be honest, unless you have a special reason to put it somewhere else, that's probably the best place.

Custom Installation Options

The installation process takes you through the custom installation options screen (quite a few Mac software installation programs have a screen like this, but most of the time you don't see it unless you choose to). Figure 2–1 shows what you will see here.

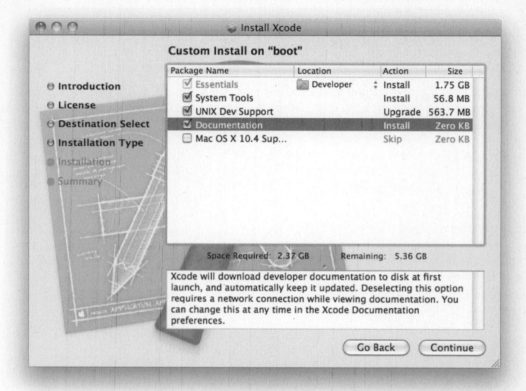

Figure 2–1. *Xcode installation options*

The options here simply give you a little more control over the installation. For example, if you want to create applications that use the Mac OS X 10.4 APIs, you can check that option. You may want to think about the Documentation option. If checked, *the default* Xcode will download—and keep up to date—a copy of the Developer Documentation. Unchecking this option means that you will need to be online in order to use Developer Documentation. You can change this setting in the Preferences (we'll be taking a closer look at this later in the chapter). If you are new to Xcode development and you just want to create applications for Mac OS X and iPhone, leave this screen as it is and choose the Continue button.

All being well, the installation will run without incident, and you will see the usual successful installation message.

What the Installation Added

Feel free to skip this section if you are not interested in knowing what goes where. Personally, I am always keen to know what software installations have done to my computer, and I'm just curious in any case. So here is what the installation has added to your computer:

- In /Developer, you will have a collection of top-level folders with child folders containing a vast number of application, documentation, and other files. This, for most practical purposes, is the whole of Xcode.

- In /Library/Developer, you will have a range of folders containing configuration and support files. You will probably never venture anywhere near these folders unless you need to uninstall Xcode (see below).

- In /usr/bin lives the gcc compiler (gcc is a UNIX-based compiler that is at the heart of Xcode software) and a variety of support files. You will probably never go looking for these either.

Removing Your Xcode Developer Tools Installation

Should you ever wish to uninstall Xcode (unlikely though that may seem), it's very straightforward. Open a Terminal, change to the /Developer/Library folder and run the uninstall-devtools script:

```
$ sudo ./uninstall-devtools –mode=all
```

By the way, there are a number of different options for running this script, giving you finer control over what you remove. Check out the documentation for this in About Xcode.pdf (which you can find in the same folder as the installation package).

Note that you need to run this script with root privilege, hence the sudo command.

It's worth checking that the /Developer/Library/ folder has been removed, and if not just move that to the Trash, too.

Getting to Know the Xcode Workspace

You start up Xcode just like any other Mac application: either click on the Dock icon (if it is there) or double-click on the icon in /Developer/Applications (you didn't install it there? OK, wherever you did install it).

PUT THE XCODE ICON IN THE DOCK

I am a great fan of the Dock in Mac OS X. It places the most common applications within single mouse-click range. Also, as the great Apple UI guru Bruce Tognazzini has observed, there is a great usability benefit to be obtained from having clickable objects at the edge of the screen, so that you are less likely to overshoot when you zoom the mouse toward them.

Be that as it may, I recommend putting the Xcode application icon in the Dock. To do this, just find the original Xcode application (if you have accepted the defaults, this is in /Developer/Applications) and drag its icon to the Dock.

The Welcome to Xcode Window

Your first sight of Xcode, at least the first time you run it, is the Welcome to Xcode window. This window is a bit of an orphan: most articles and how-tos tend to dismiss it with a brief "if you see the Welcome window, just uncheck the 'Show' box and you'll never see it again". That's unfortunate, because in fact this window provides a wealth of useful information for the new Xcode developer. It's easy enough to dismiss or minimize the window, and the benefits of having it there as a signpost to useful resources far outweigh the hassle of that one click. By the way, if you have been experimenting with Xcode, opted not to show this window at startup, and then change your mind, you can reset Xcode defaults—see "It's All Gone Horribly Wrong" below.

One really good reason to keep the Welcome window as an Xcode startup item is that it now (as of Xcode v3.2) has a list of recent projects, giving you simple single-click access to your work.

You are also one click away from a new project.

The "Getting started with Xcode" link takes you to the Xcode Documentation Quick Start window, and this is a good entry point to tutorials, articles, and reference documentation. You will return to the documentation in Chapter 8, but it is worth making a visit to this window your first port of call when you need to understand something in Xcode.

You are probably eager to get to Xcode itself, so let's leave the Welcome window there. My advice—at least until you are really comfortable with Xcode's features, tools, and environment—is to leave the "Show at launch" checkbox enabled. For now, though, minimize the window or close it.

The Xcode Clean Screen View

If you are accustomed to IDEs (Integrated Development Environments) like Eclipse or even REALbasic, you may be expecting a window crowded with panels, inspectors, and wizards. Having moved the Welcome screen out of the way, your first sight of the Xcode Workspace may be a little underwhelming. There is no immediately visible user interface—nothing beyond the menu bar. This is part of the philosophy of Xcode development, and you will see it time and time again as we move through the book; you tend to see just what you need to see at any point in the development. For now, you are not actually doing anything, so there is no user interface to manipulate.

In order to explore the Xcode Workspace, you are going to have to create a software project. You will learn a lot more over the coming chapters about what type of project to choose for the different applications you want to create, but for the purposes of exploring the environment you are just going to create and run a very simple application.

Starting a New Project

If you still have the Welcome to Xcode window up, you can start a new project using the link on that window. Otherwise choose the File➤New Project... menu (or use the keyboard shortcut Shift⌘N). As you can see in Figure 2–2, Xcode provides templates for a huge range of projects, though for most purposes you are likely to pick from only a few of these.

> **NOTE:** At the time of writing, the Xcode Tools and iPhone Tools come in two separate installation kits. If you have installed just the Xcode Tools so far, then you will see only options for creating Mac OS X development projects. However, it seems likely that the Mac OS X and iPhone Tools will soon be bundled together, in which case you will also see options for iPhone development. You'll do a lot more work on this in Chapter 4.

In this case, choose Cocoa Application (it is the default selection). You will notice that there are checkboxes for Document-based application and for using Core Data. We'll cover both of these soon, but leave the boxes unchecked for now. Just click the Choose... button.

You need to provide a name and location for your new project. For now, any suitable location and name will be fine, but for the purposes of this chapter, call it "My First Project" and put it in My Documents. This may seem a little undisciplined, and in later chapters you will see how a systematic approach to choosing where you install your projects will pay dividends. This is a disposable project, and you won't do anything with it beyond this chapter, so it doesn't matter where you put it or what you call it. Also, since the Welcome to Xcode window includes recent projects you will be able to find it again (not that that is an invitation to undisciplined storage habits!).

At last! We have a user interface that looks like it means business (see Figure 2–3). Welcome to the Xcode Workspace.

Figure 2–2. *Creating a new project*

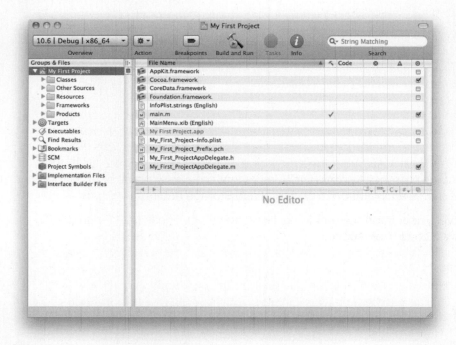

Figure 2–3. *Welcome to the Xcode Workspace user interface.*

There is an awful lot going on here, and in truth there are some parts of this sophisticated working environment that you won't need to visit for some time yet. However, you are reading this book because you want to create great software, and it's worth just showing one great feature of Xcode now: your application, running. Take a look at the toolbar and you will see a big green button with the label "Build and Run." Click that button.

That's right—you have a working application. Granted, it doesn't actually do anything interesting yet, but it has a resizable window, an About box, and placeholders for all of the main menus you are likely to have to use in your development work (see Figure 2–4).

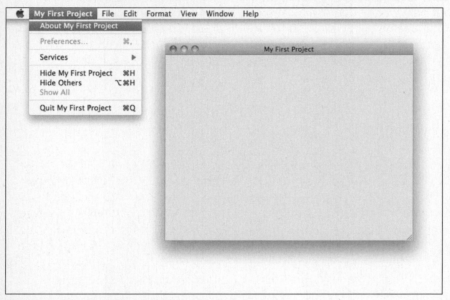

Figure 2–4. *Xcode projects compile and run out of the box.*

It's worth just noting that you have some useful information available as your application compiles and runs. The Status bar at the bottom of the Xcode Project Workspace window shows the current compilation task and then a Debugger message saying "GDB: Running..." confirming that the program is indeed running. To the right, the status bar shows a progress indicator (the whole process should take just a few seconds for this application, but can take a lot longer once your project gets more complex) and then an indication of whether the project has compiled successfully.

There's nothing more to see with this application just yet, so quit. Since this is a complete Mac OS X application already, you can use the normal File➤Quit or ⌘Q methods. However, you have another option. Because you built it from within Xcode in debug mode (lots more on this later), you can stop the application from the Xcode window using the big red Tasks button. Try this now. You will see the Status bar shows the message "Debugging terminated."

It's time to take a closer look at the Project Workspace. Let's start with the major items of interest and the things you need to know right now.

The Xcode Workspace Working Environment

The default layout for the Xcode Workspace (called the *Project Window*) has a simple three panel display (List, Detail, and Document) with a toolbar. If you have used Apple Mail or iTunes, then this interface will be familiar. I'm going to cover each of the major parts of the interface briefly, but I will come back to some of them in more depth later.

Xcode offers a number of different layouts, ranging from All-In-One (as the name suggests, all of the components are presented in one window) to Condensed (where a subset of the main features appear in separate windows). You can change between these layouts, but only when you have closed all open projects. Since you have only just created a project, it seems a little churlish to close it again, so let's park this topic for the moment (there is a section on Preferences later in this chapter if you want to know more right now). Each layout has its own advantages and, as usual, it comes down to personal choice. When you have settled on the one you like, you can make it the default by choosing the Window➤Defaults... menu.

Groups & Files List

The Groups & Files list provides an overview list of all components and assets in your software project. At the top of the list is your project name, containing *source groups* (also called the *Project Structure*) providing convenient storage locations for the classes and other components for your project. You are not limited to these, however; feel free to create groups that make sense for your working style and to move your source files around between groups. For example, you might want to have a custom classes group within your project. You can simply right-click (or Control-click) your project name in the list and choose Add ➤New Group from the popup menu.

Source groups contain your working code— .h header and .m class files if you are developing in Objective-C—and you will usually keep them in the Classes and Other Sources folder.

Under the source groups are a collection of *smart groups*. Most of these are empty when you start your project and content appears as it develops and grows. As a new developer (and maybe later on, too), you are not likely to need to explore the content of the Targets and Executables groups, which essentially contain instructions and other information related to the building of your application. Similarly you may not want immediately to explore the Project Symbols group, as this is a more advanced topic.

You can hide any unwanted groups; just right-click on any group in the list (or use Control-click), choose Preferences, and uncheck the group you want to hide. You will see a dialog asking you to confirm deletion, but don't worry—you will be able to put the group back in the list simply by repeating this process and checking the group again. I tend to hide the Targets, Executables, and Project Symbols groups simply because they don't hold much meaningful information for me as a relatively novice developer.

Finally, you can move groups around in the list to suit your preferences—just drag a group to a new location in the list.

I have picked some of the groups you are likely to find useful from the start for a closer look.

Find Results

Like most modern Mac software, Xcode provides a Spotlight-style search interface, which is very useful when your project grows. The Xcode stores these search terms here so you can come back to them as you need to.

Bookmarks

Xcode allows you to flag various locations as bookmarks, enabling you to get back to them quickly. Any bookmarks you create in this project will appear here. To create a bookmark, select the item you are interested in (say, main.m in Other Sources), then right-click or Control-click and choose Add to Bookmarks from the popup menu. You can also choose Edit➤Add to Bookmarks, or press ⌘D. To remove a bookmark, select it and press the Delete key. The confirm dialog may give the impression that you are about to delete the file. Don't worry, you're not; only the bookmark is deleted.

SCM

SCM stands for *Source Code Management*, more commonly known as *version control*. Xcode has powerful support tools for managing version control of code in your projects, and whether you are coding as part of a project team or solo, good version control will undoubtedly save your skin one of these days, so it's a good practice to adopt. You will learn all about Xcode's SCM tools in Chapter 9. The SCM section is empty and will remain so until you have put your project under source control; from then on you will see any project components that need attention from a source control point of view.

Implementation Files and NIB Files

As your project develops and you add more classes, user interface files, and other components, each of them appears here. These two groups behave differently from the others in that you can control what appears here using wildcards or regular expressions. So, for example, if you just wanted .m files to be displayed in the Implementation Files group, you could set ".m" as your wildcard. To see your options for customizing these two groups, simply select one of them and choose File➤Info (or use ⌘I).

WHY "NIB"?

The word "NIB" has a venerable history. Many of the UNIX underpinnings of Mac OS X can trace their ancestry to tools developed for the NeXT computer, which ran on an operating system called Nextstep. The NeXT had a comprehensive toolbox for software development, and Xcode is its direct lineal descendant.

As you work in Xcode you will see many references to objects with the precursor "NS", a reference to Nextstep that has somehow never disappeared (it always seems to me rather like the appendix in the body of Xcode). Similarly NIB stands for Nextstep Interface Builder, and NIB files, as they are known, are where you create and store the user interface components for Xcode applications.

Just to confuse things further, as of Xcode v3.0 NIB files have a .xib extension instead of .nib, reflecting their new XML-based structure. However they are still referred to widely as NIB files (perhaps because of the difficulty of pronouncing "XIB").

Detail View

The Detail view gives you an expansion of the currently selected group (or groups—you can select more than one and their contents will be displayed in the Detail view). This view is designed to give you detailed information at a glance across a collection of files. The columns display (where relevant) information such as an icon for the file type, the build status of the file, errors and warnings, version control status, and so on. You can configure this to your taste by right-clicking on the title bar in this view and setting the list as you want it (the popup list is shown in Figure 2–5).

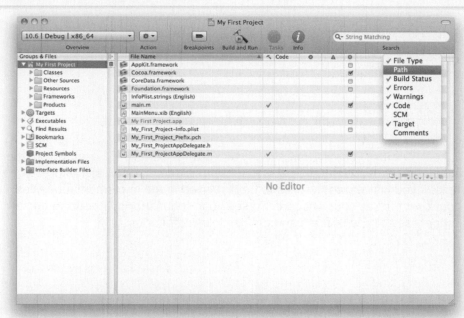

Figure 2–5. *Information available in the Detail view*

Editor View

The Editor view offers quick access to any editable files in your project. This means that when you select a file in the Groups and Files list, or in the Detail view, its contents will be shown in the Editor view.

Xcode offers you two overall ways to edit your code: within the main Project Workspace window or in a separate window. To see your code in a separate window, just double-click the filename in the Detail view.

Whether you choose single or separate window editing, what you see here and how you edit it depends on the format of the file you have selected. To see how this works, choose the Project Structure top-level folder in the Groups and Files list (its name will be the same as the name of your project—in this case, "My First Project"). The contents of this folder will show in the Detail view. If you select the first few items in the Detail view (various .framework files), you won't see any change in the Editor view because these files are not editable. In fact, the only editable files in this list are My_First_ProjectAppDelegate.h, My_First_ProjectAppDelegate.m, Info.plist, InfoPlist.Strings (English), Simple application_Prefix.pch, and main.m.

Selecting Info.plist will show you a tabulated view of the plist file for this project. This is essentially the same view you would see if you opened the file in the Property List Editor, but the Editor view is a convenient way to get access to such files. You'll learn much more about plist files and the Property List Editor in Chapter 14, but fundamentally they are configuration files holding key-value pairs and stored in a binary format (exactly why Apple made this change escapes me; until recently plist files were simple text-based XML files). The tabular display allows you to modify existing rows, usually by selecting from dropdown lists, or to add new ones.

Below the plist file entry you will see InfoPlist.Strings (English). On choosing this, the Editor view shows a text file (empty for now apart from a comment). This file is used to hold localized versions of string properties if you are creating applications for use in different languages. The most interesting files though are My_First_ProjectAppDelegate.h, My_First_ProjectAppDelegate.m, and main.m. Click on one of these and, at long last, you can see some code!

YOUR APPLICATION'S ENTRYPOINT—MAIN.M

The file main.m is created as part of every Xcode project, and while this book is not about the Objective-C language or writing code, it is worth a quick look at what this file is doing, as it will inform the rest of your software development.

If you have done any C programming, the structure of this file will hold few surprises. It is the formal entry point of the application, the main function. Having imported the Cocoa header files it simply instantiates a Cocoa application object and then quits. From this small acorn of a file, the enormous oak of your application springs forth. In later chapters you will see exactly how the application progresses from here.

Like most code development environments, Xcode offers color-coded editing, with keywords and symbols highlighted for ease of identification. You have complete control over the color-coding through the Preferences window (see the section on Xcode Workspace preferences later in this chapter).

At the top of the Editor view is a slim toolbar that allows you quick access to specific files, and functions within files, through a number of popup and dropdown lists. You can also use this to swap back and forth between file *counterparts*. Each .m file has a header or .h counterpart file. Clicking the little gray-on-white square icon at the right of the editor toolbar toggles the editor between the .h and .m files (if you have used the BBEdit code editor, this feature will be familiar to you).

The Editor toolbar also proves to be a really quick way to navigate your project. When a class file gets big, you can simply click on the functions popup and there will be a list of all of your functions. You can even add your own layer of organization to this popup list by using the Pragma mark option in your code. If you put a string like the following into your class code in the Editor view, then all of the methods below that point in your code window will show in the popup list as children of "My custom methods":

```
#pragma mark My custom methods
```

I find this an extremely useful way to organize my code projects. You will see a worked example of this shortly.

ABOUT THAT COPYRIGHT STATEMENT

When you create a new project or class file in Xcode, notice that there is a brief author and copyright statement in a comment at the top of each file; however, you will look in vain for an Xcode Preferences item that sets the values you see here.

In fact, these settings are managed completely outside Xcode, in the Mac OS X Address Book! Xcode will pick up your record (often called the "Me" record) from Address Book to provide the name (only the first and last names are picked up from this record by Xcode). If your record has a Company Name entry, that will go into the copyright statement. If you don't have a Company Name in your "Me" record, the copyright statement will read "Copyright __MyCompanyName__ 2009."

Toolbar

The toolbar in the Project Workspace provides expected shortcuts to many common functions. The shortcuts available depend on the layout you choose (see Figure 2–6 for the standard options), but as usual with Apple software you can customize the toolbar to have exactly the features you want (right-click on the toolbar and choose Customize Toolbar...).

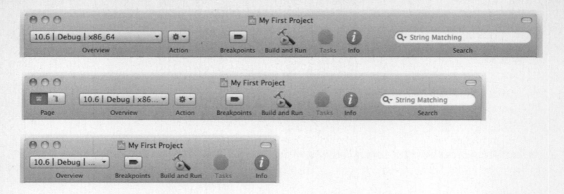

Figure 2–6. *Toolbar features in the Default, All-In-One, and Condensed layouts*

Note the toolbar in the All-In-One layout in particular. I like this layout because it keeps everything within the range of a single click, and this is illustrated nicely with the Page button group on the left. This allows you to switch between coding and debugging page views when you are running your application.

Another very useful button is the Breakpoints button. This allows you to turn all of your breakpoints on and off in one click. Note that the Build and Run button changes to Build and Debug when breakpoints are set; if you disable breakpoints, the appearance changes back to Build and Run.

This is all probably best illustrated with a quick example. Let's add some code, put in a breakpoint, and run the application. If you are not in All-In-One layout, close your project (as I mentioned a while back, Xcode does not allow you to change layouts while a project is open), go to Xcode➤Preferences... or use the keyboard shortcut ⌘, (that's Command and a comma), find the General Preferences panel, and choose All-In-One from the popup named Layout:.

Now open your project again and select the file My_First_ProjectAppDelegate.m (click on the filename in the Detail view). Listing 2–1 shows how the code looks in the Editor view.

Listing 2–1. *My_First_ProjectAppDelegate.m*

```
//  My_First_ProjectAppDelegate.m
//  My First Project
//
//  Created by Ian Piper on 23/08/2009
//  Copyright 2009 Tellura Information Services. All rights reserved.
//

#import "My_First_ProjectAppDelegate.h"

@synthesize window;

- (void)applicationDidFinishLaunching:(NSNotification *)aNotification {
    // Insert code here to initialize your application
}
```

@end

Don't worry too much about following the code for now. All you are going to do is to add a line of code to log a message in the Console. Add the line indicated in bold in Listing 2–2.

Listing 2–2. *Adding a logging statement*

```
[…]
- (void)applicationDidFinishLaunching:(NSNotification *)aNotification {
  // Insert code here to initialize your application
  NSLog(@"Application has initialized");
}
[…]
```

> **TIP:** The NSLog command is a convenient way to add debugging messages to your applications; the message is displayed in the console. You can use this to display variable values too, which can be useful when bug tracking.

Now you need to set a breakpoint. Click once in the gray border to the left of the line of code you just added. You will see a blue arrow in the border (see Figure 2–7). This is a breakpoint—an instruction to the compiler to halt execution when it reaches this point.

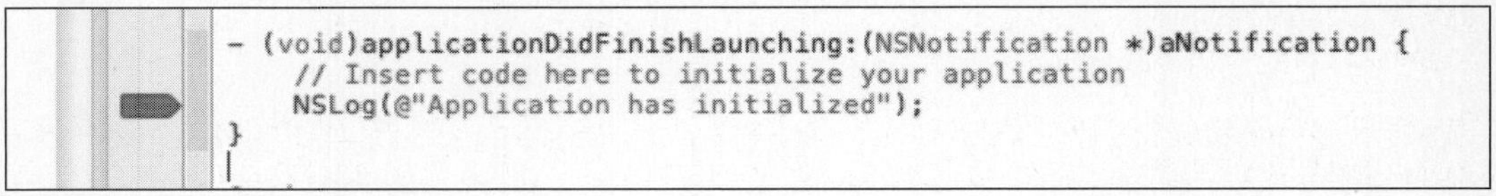

```
- (void)applicationDidFinishLaunching:(NSNotification *)aNotification {
    // Insert code here to initialize your application
    NSLog(@"Application has initialized");
}
```

Figure 2–7. *Adding a breakpoint*

You'll notice that the Build and Run button now reads Build and Debug, and the Breakpoints button is highlighted. The latter button toggles the breakpoint(s) on and off.

OK, click on Build and Debug. The program runs as before, but stops at the breakpoint. Click on the Debug button in the Page button group. This shows you the Debugging window for your running application (see Figure 2–8).

Figure 2–8. *The Debugging window in your running application*

We're going to cover debugging in much more detail in Chapter 7, but for now you can see that the window shows a code editor, a panel displaying current variable values, and the console. The console shows the gdb (GNU Debugger) prompt. Now click on the Continue button in the toolbar. The application window—which has been hiding behind the Workspace—comes to the front, and the NSLog message appears in the console (Figure 2–9).

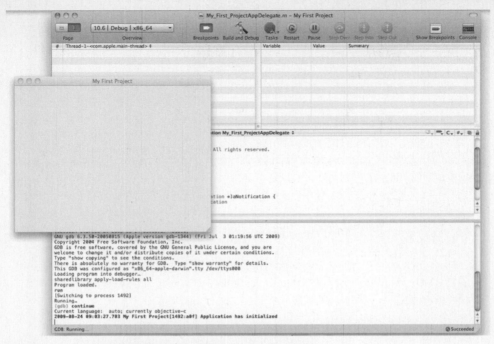

Figure 2–9. *The application after continuing past the breakpoint*

With strategic use of NSLog messages, the console can be an excellent place to follow the flow of execution of your application.

Favorites Bar

The Favorites bar is a little like the bookmarks bar in a browser. It is yet another way for you to organize your work: simply drag any object that you want to be able to get to quickly onto the bar. Of course, you need to show it first: choose the View➤Layout➤ Show Favorites Bar menu. To remove an item from the Favorites bar, just drag it off; I find this works most reliably if I just drag the item toward the toolbar, then release it and wait for the puff of smoke.

Status Bar

You saw the Status bar earlier, as a place for Xcode to give you messages about the progress of a range of activities, and there isn't a great deal more to say about it. If you don't find the Status bar useful you can hide it using the View➤Layout➤Hide Status Bar menu.

It's All Gone Horribly Wrong

Xcode is an incredibly rich and complex environment. It's easy to make changes, and consequently easy to make mistakes. Luckily, it's easy to reset the Xcode environment back to its defaults. If you need to restore the defaults, open up the Terminal and enter this command:

```
> defaults delete com.apple.Xcode
> rm -rf ~/Library/Application\ Support/Xcode
```

This will delete the plist file for Xcode and put everything back to default settings. Bear in mind that, if you do so, this will remove all of your Xcode preferences, default layout choices, file history, toolbar settings, and so on (interestingly, bookmarks are not lost).

Xcode Workspace Preferences

To finish up this chapter, let's take a look at the Preferences window for Xcode. To get to the Xcode Preferences window, choose Xcode➤Preferences... or press ⌘, (that is, command and comma).

The Preferences window has two parts. At the top is a scrolling toolbar of thirteen buttons, and for each of these there is a detail view below. This is quite unlike the Preferences windows for Apple's other software. It is also a very complex collection of settings, many of which you may never need to change, and so we're going to cover only the most important settings for now.

General

The General button is selected by default. The main thing to choose here is the layout, which you briefly used to look at the toolbar options. There are three layouts:

- **All-In-One**. This keeps all of your components in one window, with a Project page presented as three panels: Groups and Files list, Detail view, and Editor view. It also provides you with a page control in the toolbar that allows you to flip between the Project page and the Debugging page. You are still able to open an editor in a separate window by double-clicking on its name in a list.

- Condensed. This option gives you a simple view made up of a variation on the Groups and Files list. This list shows just the Source Groups by default though you can use the right-click➤Preferences popup menu to choose other items to display here. Unlike the Groups and Files display in the other layouts, however, the Condensed layout includes some detail information on the items (Build status, warnings, and errors by default, though a right-click on the header bar will allow you to change this). Editor and Debugger views open in separate windows.

■ Default. This is similar to the All-In-One layout except that the Editor and Debugger views open in new windows. This layout also allows you to collapse it to a more compact layout by double-clicking the little button that appears top-right in the Groups and Files list.

Code Sense

If you have used other software development tools you may have come across the concept of *code completion*, through which the editor monitors your keystrokes and makes (hopefully good) guesses about what you are intending to type. It then offers suggestions for whole words or phrases that you can select to complete the phrase. Code Sense in Xcode takes this a step further, by providing a continuous update that even allows you to tab through a complex method definition, adding in each parameter as you go along. Code Sense is turned on by default. You can turn it off here, but frankly the advantages of using Code Sense—mainly helping you write more accurate code— far outweigh any drawbacks, so you're probably best leaving it enabled. The normal behavior of Code Sense is that as you type, it offers its best guess as a grayed-out string of text completing your typing. You can accept it by hitting the Tab key. If it is the wrong guess, then you can either carry on typing or hit the Escape key, which will bring up a list of likely contenders.

This preference panel allows you to choose a variety of parameters governing this behavior. The main things you are likely to want to modify are whether the popup list includes variations on symbols showing different collections of parameters (for methods that have more than one form) and whether the editor waits before offering a suggestion.

Building

This preference panel allows you to choose where your project puts your compiled code. By default, the compiled application goes into a folder called Build within your Project folder. For most developers, this is a convenient place, but you can specify an alternative. You may want to alter the "For Unsaved Files:" option. The default value is "Ask Before Building," but I tend just to set it to "Always Save." Another useful option governs the Message Bubbles settings. When you compile an application with errors, Xcode shows colored bubbles within the editor close to the locations of the problem code. I like to set this to "On Errors" so I don't see the bubbles for warnings. You can also choose whether and in what circumstances the Build Results window appears. By default, this is set to "Never," but you can choose to have Xcode show the window on errors or warnings.

Distributed Builds

The settings in this window are aimed at developer teams or developers who have access to a number of computers for sharing the work of building the application. This is a fairly advanced group of settings, and it is unlikely that you will need to make any changes here, at least not initially (I have never modified any of these settings).

Debugging

You can use this panel to modify the appearance of the debugger prompt in the console, but it is probably advisable to steer clear of making any changes that you don't really need to make.

Key Bindings

Key Bindings refers to the shortcuts you use to access operations within the Xcode environment. These generally follow the norms for Mac OS X software, but there are specific key bindings for Xcode itself. If you have used another coding environment in the past, such as Metrowerks CodeWarrior or BBEdit, you can choose to keep the bindings from that product by choosing it here. Alternatively, you can create your own by duplicating one of the current options and modifying it to meet your needs.

Text Editing, Fonts & Colors, and Indentation

These preferences govern how the editor works for you. The options are very straightforward and need no any explanation to an audience of this caliber.

File Types

This preference panel lists all the file types you might expect to be working with in your Xcode software development and allows you to define how those file types are handled. For example, you can specify that image files in your application should be opened with Photoshop, PHP files with TextMate, and so on. In general, my advice with this panel is to leave it with the default mappings unless you have a very good reason not to.

Source Trees

This preference is aimed at development teams for which particular source files need to be in locations other than the project folder (for example, custom Objective-C classes that need to be shared among a group of developers). As a new developer in Xcode, you are not likely to need to make any changes here.

SCM

The SCM preference panel is where you set up access to a source code management or version control system. Later in the book, you will learn how to set up a Subversion repository and how to configure your project to use it. For now, just make a note that this is where it all happens.

Documentation

This preference panel lets you define how to manage the Developer Documentation. You may recall that this was an option during the Xcode installation. Selecting the checkbox ensures that you can keep the documentation up to date, or you can use the button to do this on demand. By default, you will have access to the Mac OS X Snow Leopard Core Library and the Xcode 3.2 Developer Tools Library, but you can also choose to get a range of other libraries. See Figure 2–10.

Figure 2–10. *The Documentation preferences panel*

Summary

So there it is. By now you should have a good picture of how to get around the Xcode Workspace and how to make it look the way you want. You'll have a growing sense of the powerful code development tools at your fingertips. However, you are probably also aware that there is something missing. A big part of Mac software is a great user interface—a compelling visual design that draws you into the application and is strongly focused on user experience. This being an Apple product, wouldn't you expect the Xcode Tools to include great support tools for creating that user experience? Of course you would, and you won't be disappointed. Interface Builder is the tool of choice for professional Mac and iPhone developers.

That's where you are going in the next chapter.

Chapter 3

Interface Builder

Professional User Interface Design—and More—for Your Xcode Projects

If you have used other software development systems like REALbasic, or written code on other platforms, chances are you have used a system that integrates the coding and interface design in one holistic, coordinated user interface (usually called an *integrated development environment*, or IDE). REALbasic and Visual Studio on the Windows .NET platform are good examples of this kind of system. One of the most engaging features of such systems is the way they link events on the objects in your user interface to the underlying code. For example, you may create a user interface in REALbasic that shows a window with a button, a textbox, and a label. Then you double-click on the button and type in the code for the Action method for that button. Lo and behold, you have a simple Hello World application. It all happens in one application—in one window, in fact. This approach can be a great way to get started on code development, helping you to connect the events occurring in your application with the visual objects that take part in those events.

Now it might seem odd to begin this chapter by talking about a completely different product (and that, by the way, was the last mention of other ways of writing Mac OS X software—there are plenty of other books around on those!), but there is a good reason. Development of Mac OS X software using the Xcode Tools is unlike using any other software development system, and nowhere is this uniqueness more evident than in the way in which you build the user interface and connect it to your application code. Forget most of what you know about other development environments: Interface Builder is different. This difference is one of the biggest hurdles to the new developer, and so this chapter will spend a lot of time going over how it works.

You will be spending the first part of this chapter entirely in Interface Builder. In order to focus just on Interface Builder, you will be starting it up directly from the Finder. (As you will see later in the chapter, your normal route into Interface Builder is from the Xcode Workspace.) You will then create a few disposable interfaces just to get the feel of the environment.

The second part of the chapter will cover the second major role of Interface Builder (and the part that gives new developers most trouble): the way in which Interface Builder wires up the different components of your application to work together. You will create a couple of simple but complete applications. Let's get to it!

Getting to Know the Interface Builder Environment

To start, open a Finder window at the location where you installed Xcode Developer Tools (the default is the top-level Developer folder on your main disk). Move to the Applications subfolder and start Interface Builder. You don't need the Xcode application for this section, by the way; if it is open at the moment, close out of it.

The first window you see is the Template Chooser, which provides template applications for most of the applications you are likely to want to create. Choose Application in the left panel, select the Cocoa Application template, and then click on the Choose button (see Figure 3–1).

Figure 3–1. *Template Chooser in Interface Builder*

Interface Builder opens up with a collection of five main windows (see Figure 3–2). Two of these, the main user interface window and the Menu window, are where you will make the principal layout decisions. The Inspector window, like similar windows in other applications, allows you to view and modify the settings for the different user interface elements. The Library window holds user interface components ready for you to drag into your user interface window. You'll come back to the final window, the Document window, in the second part of this chapter. For now you just need to know that the objects in this window are crucial to the way in which your user interface elements are wired up together to make a working application.

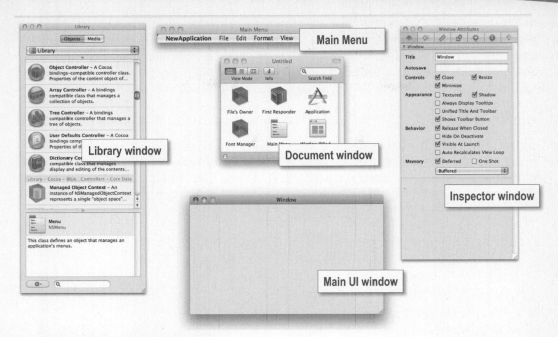

Figure 3–2. *Main Interface Builder windows*

Let's create a few typical user interfaces and, along the way, learn more about how the various Interface Builder components work together.

Adding Some Controls to Your User Interface

The first interface you will build will simply contain a text field that will take a string of text, a button, and a label. The finished user interface will look like Figure 3–3. In the second half of this chapter, we will use an interface like this to create a Hello World application.

Figure 3–3. *Final appearance of the Hello World application*

For now, look in the Library window and make sure that the Objects tab is selected. Open up the tree structure under Cocoa➤Views & Cells➤Inputs & Values and find the two entries for Label and Text Field. Drag one of each over to your main user interface window. Now look under Cocoa➤Views & Cells➤Buttons. Drag a Push Button into the window. Your window should look like Figure 3–4.

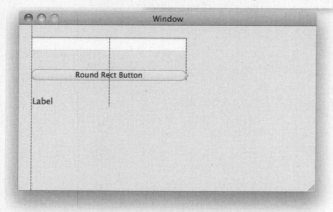

Figure 3–4. *Main interface window after adding controls*

Positioning and Aligning Controls and Windows

Notice the dotted lines in Figure 3–4. Interface Builder has some nice features for aligning and setting the properties of visual elements. You'll notice that guides appear for a moment as you change the size and position of the label, button, and text fields. These are called *automatic guides*. They provide a good way for you to optimally position controls in the user interface.

Interface Builder will also show dynamically updated guides that show you pixel distances between various points in the window—just hold down the Option key while you have a control selected to see its position relative to the window and other controls.

Finally, you can also add your own custom guides. Use the Layout➤Add Vertical Guide (or Horizontal Guide) menu (or use ⌘-Shift-|). These remain visible while you are designing your user interface but don't display when running the program. If you want to remove a custom guide, just drag it off the window. It will disappear in the customary Apple puff of smoke.

While on the subject of aligning and positioning, let's take a look at the Size tab in the Inspector (Figure 3–5). Exactly what you see here depends on the object(s) you currently have selected. In Figure 3–5, the main user interface window is the selected object (to select the window, click in the title bar). Here I have set the size to 290×120 pixels. The Label, Text Field, and Button controls have all been set to 250 pixels wide.

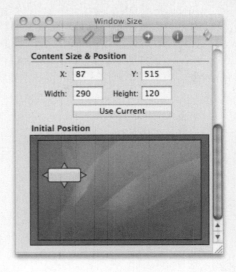

Figure 3–5. *Sizing controls and windows*

The X and Y values in the Inspector set the window position when the application starts up, not the position at design time. You can set this either by typing in the numbers for the pixel locations—note that the origin is the bottom left of the screen, so a larger Y value means higher up and a larger X value means farther to the right—or you can drag the position of the little window in the Initial Position diagram. In this diagram, the little triangles around the window image are called *window anchors*. You can use these to set the absolute distance to any edge of the screen. Click one of these anchors and it springs out to the nearest edge of the "screen," locking your window startup position to that absolute value. Otherwise, the position of your window at startup is calculated as a proportion of the screen size and is decided by the resolution of the user's display.

The one thing you haven't set in the user interface yet is the alignment of the controls—that is, the alignment of text within the control. I'm going to leave it to you to figure out how to center the text in each of these controls (take a look at the Attributes tab of the Inspector).

You are done with this user interface for now, so close the user interface window without saving it. As you will see later, when you create a user interface for real, you will do it slightly differently, so it's not even as though you can reuse this one.

PREVIEWING THE USER INTERFACE

The appearance of your user interface in Interface Builder is a very good approximation of how it will look in the running program; but, of course, the controls won't behave in the way they should (buttons aren't clickable, you can't scroll views or edit text, and so on). The good news is that you can get a quick look at your user interface within Interface Builder simply by choosing File➤Simulate Interface (or use ⌘R).

You can quit the simulator with ⌘Q or by using the Cocoa Simulator Quit menu.

Autosizing Controls

Now let's look at one of the areas that causes a lot of confusion: the autosizing of controls. To get started, you need to delete all of the current controls from the user interface and drag off any custom guides, giving a clean canvas to work on.

The user interface you'll create now is a more complex collection of controls, and you will want these to resize smoothly as you resize the window. First, here is how the finished user interface will look in the simulator at two sizes (see Figure 3–6).

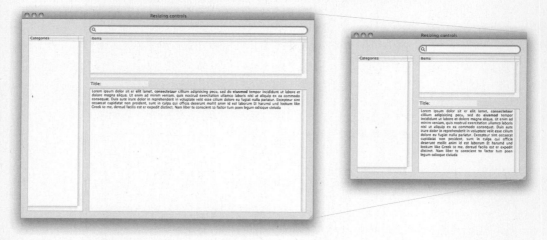

Figure 3–6. *Resizing controls*

Notice how in the larger window the elements have changed their sizes and positions so that they continue to fit nicely into the space.

To reproduce this, start by creating a new Cocoa Application interface (File➤New… in Interface Builder). Drag a Table View out of the Library window into your user interface window. Make the window size 550 pixels wide by 450 pixels high and give it a title by clicking on the title bar and choosing the Size and Window Attributes tabs. Put the Table View on the left, and make it 164 pixels wide and 375 pixels high. Use the automatic guides to get the position and height right (allowing a bigger space at the top). Don't feel bound to use these values—this is just an indication to reproduce the illustrations here. Drag another Table View over and position it to the right of the first; it should be about 328 pixels wide and 128 pixels high. You need to set each of these Table Views to have just one column with a title. Selecting exactly the thing you want is initially a little tricky with Interface Builder, so let's dive into the detail to try to nail this straight away.

First of all, click the window title bar to ensure nothing else is selected. Now click within the Table View. The cursor turns into a hand when you are in the right place, and you will see a selection rectangle around the Table View. At this point, you have not actually selected the table, but rather the Scroll View that contains the Table View (a Scroll View is a container object that allows its contents to, well, scroll). You can confirm the object currently selected by looking at the title bar of the Inspector window—it will read "Scroll View Attributes." The attributes available in the Inspector are those of the Scroll View rather than the table.

Click again in the same place and the selection changes, to a round-cornered rectangle around the table. The Inspector window title bar now reads "Table View Attributes," and now the attributes are those for the table. Change the number of columns in the Inspector window to 1 (use the stepper or type in the number). See Figure 3–7.

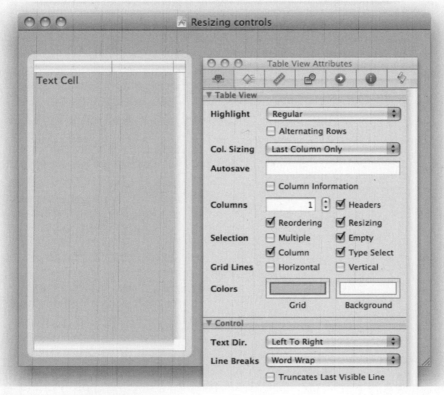

Figure 3–7. *Table View attributes*

Now click again in the Table View; the selection changes again to a rounded rectangle around the column, and the Inspector title bar now reads "Table Column Attributes." Set the Title property to "Categories:". You can also select an individual Table Cell or the Table Header, to set its properties.

This simple yet elegant mechanism enables you quickly to drill down through the object hierarchy to select and set properties at the appropriate level. Make sure you have configured each of the Table Views to have a single column and a title (the example has the title "Items" for the second Table View).

Back in the user interface, look in the Inputs and Value section of the Library and drag out a Search Field (put it at the top) and a Label. Use the guides to match up the width of the Search Field to the Table View below it and to position the Label. For the Label, set its Title attribute to "Title:" (or whatever you prefer), click the "Draws background" checkbox, and then click the Background color well to set a color.

SELECTING COLOR WELLS

Color wells in Mac OS X programs have a subtle property that users don't always immediately notice, which can cause some confusion. That is, the color well has a border that indicates when it is active. You will see on the Attributes panel in Figure 3–16 that there are color wells for the background and foreground, but only one Color Settings panel. How do you know which color well is the one whose color you are changing? It's the one with the dark border. This may be obvious to you, dear reader, but many Mac users don't notice it even though it is a widely used feature of Mac OS X.

You can toggle the active state of a color well by clicking the border. This is useful when you want to play with the Color Settings panel without the change appearing in your control.

The final component to add to your user interface is a Text View (under Inputs & Values). Size it and position it to fit in the remaining space. Your user interface should look something like the left side of Figure 3–8.

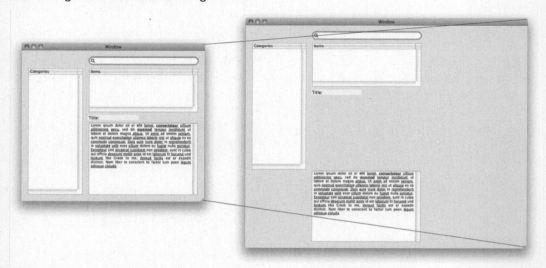

Figure 3–8. *The user interface is complete, but what happens when you resize it?*

Now run the simulator (File➤Simulate Interface or ⌘R) and try changing the window size (see right side of Figure 3–8). Horrible, isn't it? The problem is that Interface Builder has no way of knowing how you want the individual components to behave when the containing window changes size. The results are rarely what you want, so you need to explicitly set the Autosizing behavior that you expect. You do this in the Size tab of the Inspector window. First, a general description of how the Autosizing controls work, then you can work through each one.

Select the first Table View (actually, its Scroll View container) again. Make sure the Size tab of the Inspector window is visible. The Autosize settings will look like those in Figure 3–9.

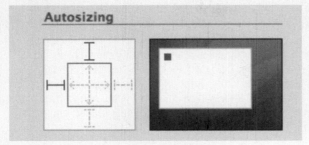

Figure 3–9. *Overview of autosizing controls*

In the Autosizing diagram on the left side of Figure 3–9, the outer box represents the object's container—in this case, the window—and the inner box represents the object itself. Note that although I keep referring to resizing the Table View, in fact the thing you are resizing is its container, which is a Scroll View. It's not a problem, since the two keep in sync. For simplicity, I will talk about the control that we're interested in, not the Scroll View that contains it. The red "I" bars show how the object is anchored to its container, and the red arrows within the object show how the object's size will change. Making a red "I" bar solid (by clicking on it) means you want to anchor the object in that direction. The left and top edges of the Table View are anchored to the top and left edges of the window, and will stay the same distance from them when the window is resized. Making either the horizontal or vertical arrows within the object solid means you want the object to resize in that direction. You can see that the Table View will not resize at all. I found this rather counter-intuitive when I first encountered it, but a little experimentation cemented the rules in my mind.

The animation on the right side of Figure 3–9 gives an indication of how the object will behave as the result of your settings.

Let's get this Table View to resize correctly now. First of all, the anchoring at the top and left is OK, but you also want it anchored to the bottom. Second, the Table View needs to stretch vertically but not horizontally. Click the bottom "I" bar and the vertical arrow (it should look like the settings in Figure 3–10). It might seem at first glance that just choosing the sizing arrow is enough to make the Table View stretch vertically; however, it doesn't work quite correctly, because as you make the window taller the resizing doesn't keep the bottom gap constant. Anchoring the bottom edge too makes sure it stays in place.

Run the simulator (⌘R) to confirm that the Table View is behaving as expected.

Now go ahead and set the remaining user interface components up. Refer to Table 3–1 and Figure 3–10 to see how each one should be configured.

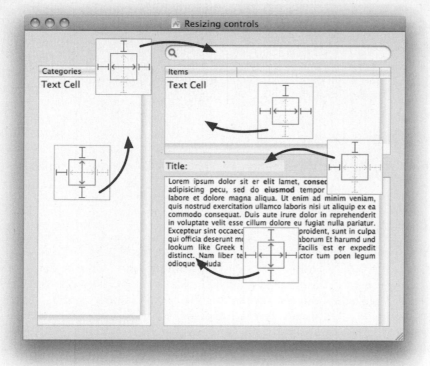

Figure 3–10. *Autosizing properties for the user interface components*

Table 3–1. *Autosizing properties for the user interface components*

Component	Anchor properties	Sizing properties
Table View 1	Top, left, bottom	Vertical
Table View 2	Top, right, left	Horizontal
Search View	Top, right, left	Horizontal
Label	Top, left	None
Text View	Top, right, bottom, left	Horizontal, vertical

There is one more problem you need to resolve. Although the user interface components now behave impeccably when you make the window bigger than its initial value, making it smaller leads to some ugliness. The controls try to make a good job of what you've asked them to do, but of course you get to a point where things just don't fit.

The simplest way to resolve this is to set a minimum size for the window. Click on the window title bar to select it, then choose the Size tab in the Inspector. Check the "Has minimum size" checkbox and enter the width and height (550 and 450, respectively) or click the "Use Current" button to pick up the window size settings.

Run the simulator again. Now your controls will resize when you expand the window, but the window will never get smaller than the size set here as the minimum, so you can avoid any resizing unpleasantness. You can also set maximum size values in this Inspector if you want to constrain your window in this way.

The Library in More Depth

The Library window holds the template components that you will use in your application. Let's take a quick tour.

Library Window Layout

The Library window shows a list of components with a detailed description of the currently selected component (see Figure 3–11).

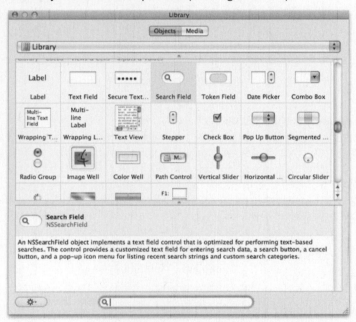

Figure 3–11. *The Library window showing the Icons and Labels option*

Customizing the Layout

You can choose the amount of information displayed in the Item pane: Icons, Icons and Labels, or Icons and Descriptions. (Right-click in this pane or choose the Action menu at the bottom of the Library window.) The Library popup at the top of the window shows an outline list of components; you can make this view persistent by dragging down the little splitter bar below the popup. Drag it back up to turn it back into a popup list.

You can filter the display by typing into the filter text field at the bottom of the Library window: type **rounded** and you will see only "Rounded Rect Button" and "Rounded Textured Button." Finally, you can create Smart Groups. These work in the same way as Smart Folders in other Mac applications and allow you to specify criteria such as recently used components.

Connecting the Pieces

In the first part of this chapter, you saw how to create and customize the user interface components of your application. For these components to be anything more than just eye candy, you will need to make these components the visual machinery that drives your application. They need to interact with you as the user and with each other. For anything beyond the most simple application, you will be writing code (probably large amounts of it), and somehow that code needs to communicate with these components. This will be our focus for the remainder of this chapter.

The Documents Window

Let's look at the Document window now. You can see different views of this window in Figures 3–2 and 3–12.

The Document window contains objects that represent the different objects in your application. Some represent the visible objects that you have been working with already in this chapter. You can also show the Document window in Outline view mode. Figure 3–12 shows this view with the application's window object open to show the Categories Table Column. You can then set attributes in the Inspector for this selection, which gives you an alternate way to configure the objects in your user interface. This can be useful in complex hierarchies of contained objects, allowing you to select precisely the object you want.

Other objects in the Document window are less obvious. File's Owner, First Responder, and Application are invisible objects, because they don't have a visible user interface component. These are called *proxy objects* because they represent or connect objects outside of the NIB file (created purely in code in Xcode Workspace, for example) to objects in the NIB.

The current document (or NIB file) is quite an unusual NIB, since you created it in a vacuum—that is, without reference to any Xcode project. Normally a NIB file is instantiated as part of the creation of an Xcode project rather than standalone as you have created it here. You will see an indicator in the status bar showing the project that owns this NIB, and you can see that for the current Document window there is no project. In fact, this NIB file has served its purpose, so close this file; you may save it for future reference in XML format (XIB) or binary format (NIB). From this point onward you will be creating your NIB files by the more conventional route.

Figure 3–12. *The Document window in outline view, showing Inspector Attributes*

You're going to create a couple of real applications now to illustrate exactly how the objects in the NIB connect to each other and to your code.

The Inevitable Hello World Program

Let's get straight to it: Close Interface Builder completely and start Xcode. Choose the Create a new Xcode project from the "Welcome to Xcode" window (or use the File➤New Project... menu).

Choose the Cocoa Application template, click the Choose... button, and name your project **Hello World**. Now, in the resulting Xcode Workspace window, you will see there is an entry in the Detail pane titled MainMenu.xib.

Double-click on this entry, and Interface Builder's familiar environment will load. If things are looking a little cluttered, use the Finder to hide the extraneous screen furniture (Interface Builder➤Hide Others or ⌘⌥H). Notice that the Document window has the name MainMenu.xib in the title, and it also has the project name HelloWorld.xcodeproj in its status bar.

Now let's set up the user interface. Drag a label and a button into your user interface window. Make the button 250 pixels wide (I know this is not going to win any design awards, by the way) and give it the title "Click me!". Make the window 290 pixels wide and 120 pixels high and the button should fit nicely in the horizontal space. Use the guides to get it just right. Put the label below, and again use the guides to get the size right. Put a message in the label if you want—I have put "Message will appear here" in the example in Figure 3–13—and center it using the appropriate alignment button. Give the window the title "Hello World!". Figure 3–13 shows how your interface should look now.

Figure 3–13. *The basic Hello World user interface*

Your user interface is complete for now. You'll be coming back shortly to finish the crucial part of the interface. Save the NIB file and change over to your Xcode Workspace window.

It's time to introduce one of the underlying themes of Cocoa software development, the Model-View-Controller (MVC) pattern. You will learn more about this in Chapter 6, but in overview, MVC is an approach to software development that separates out the components of the application into those dealing with display of a user interface (the view), those dealing with storage and management of data (the model), and the engine that manages the communications between all of these components (the controller). This is often called *separation of concerns*. Properly done, it ensures that the application is modular and that the work of interface design can be separated from data modeling and coding work. If you have done any Ruby on Rails development, you will already be comfortable with this way of working.

Cocoa applications employ MVC throughout. Xcode Developer Tools go a long way to make this way of working easy, and you will struggle to write applications in Xcode without using this pattern. Actually, one part of your application design, the view, is already done. Since this is a really simple application, the model is extremely simple (it's just the text "Hello, World"). To wire them up, you need a controller.

Make sure you are in your Xcode project. Create a new file (Using File➤New File... or ⌘N), choose the Cocoa Objective-C class template, and name it HelloController.m (make sure the checkbox titled "Also create HelloController.h" is checked). Then choose "Finish." You now have two new files in your workspace: HelloController.h and HelloController.m. These are the counterpart files for your controller.

NOTE: Strictly speaking, for an application as simple as this, you don't actually need to create a new controller. You can use the Hello_WorldAppDelegate object that Xcode has already created for you as your controller. Nevertheless, I'm showing you here how to create your own, because this is something you will frequently need to do.

This is not a book on Objective-C, but since most Cocoa software is written using Objective-C, I will need to cover the necessary code for you to create this application. I would recommend that you look at one of the great books on Objective-C and Cocoa in order to get the best grounding in the language.

Let's think about what this application has to do. There is a button, and when it is clicked that button has to tell the application in some way that it has to write a string of text ("Hello, World!") into the label. Cocoa accomplishes all this by having connections between the button and the controller, and between the label and the controller. The controller, sitting in the center, needs to know about more or less everything that is going on, and this is accomplished by message-passing between the objects. The flow of information in the application looks like Figure 3–14. Pressing the button sends a message to the controller initiating the sayHello: method. This method instructs the Text Field control to set its text—a property called stringValue in Cocoa—to a new value ("Hello, World!").

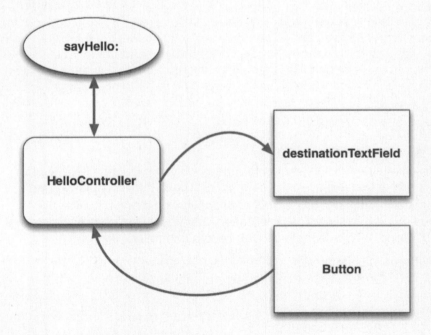

Figure 3–14. *Information flow in Hello World*

The skeleton for this code is already in place. Here is `HelloController.h` (the header comments are omitted).

```
#import <Cocoa/Cocoa.h>

@interface HelloController : NSObject {
}
@end
```

You need to create an *outlet* as the place where the message is sent (the label) and an *action* (`sayHello`) to tell the controller how to send that message. Here are the declarations you need to add (see the bold text in Listing 3–1):

Listing 3–1. *Changes to HelloController.h*

```
#import <Cocoa/Cocoa.h>

@interface HelloController : NSObject {
  IBOutlet NSTextField *destinationTextField;
}
- (IBAction)sayHello:(id)sender;
@end
```

This code is saying that the controller has an outlet called `destinationTextField` and an action called `sayHello`. Now for the implementation: Turn to `HelloController.m`—remember, you can use the little gray counterpart button at the top right of the Editor pane—and make it look like this (add the code in bold text in Listing 3–2).

Listing 3–2. *Changes to HelloController.m*

```
#import "HelloController.h"
@implementation HelloController
-(IBAction)sayHello:(id)sender {
  [destinationTextField setStringValue:@"Hello, World!"];
}
@end
```

Now, a really important step here is to save both of the files you have modified. Apart from being a good practice to save as you go, if you don't save the files the next part won't work. And the next part is to make the connections between the user interface objects (the view) the model (a piece of text) and the controller (your HelloController class).

Go back to Interface Builder. You need to create an object to represent the HelloController. Find NSObject in the Library window and drag it into the Document window.

The next few steps are absolutely key to getting your application wired up correctly.

First, tell Interface Builder that this new object is, in fact, a HelloController. Make sure that the new object is selected in the Document window, and choose the Object Identity tab in the Inspector (it has a small "i" icon). Choose the Class dropdown menu and set it to HelloController (Figure 3–15).

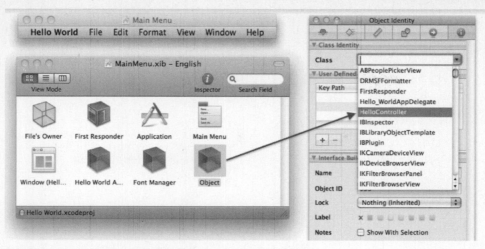

Figure 3–15. *Setting the controller object type in Interface Builder*

Now Interface Builder knows that your new object is an instance of the HelloController class that you described in Xcode; it has even helpfully renamed the object to "HelloController."

> **NOTE:** If you don't see HelloController as an item in the class list, this probably means that you haven't saved your HelloController.h file.

Next, you need to connect the outlet to the controller. Remember from earlier that the controller has a destinationTextField. That is the label in the main user interface window. To connect the two, Control-click or right-click on the HelloController in the Document window. A small head-up display (HUD) panel will appear. Mouse down on the empty circle to the right of the destinationTextField outlet, and drag a line over to the label. Release the mouse button when the label control highlights. You have just told the HelloController that it has an outlet pointing to the label on the main window.

You can confirm the connection by selecting the HelloController in the Document window, and checking its outlets settings (either by right-clicking again and seeing the list in the HUD, or by looking in the Connections tab of the Inspector (Figure 3–16 shows both ways of checking).

Figure 3–16. *Checking that the connection is correct*

So that is where the Controller is sending a message. But what message, and what causes the message to be sent? Clicking the button tells the Controller to send the message by invoking the action method that you created in Xcode (sayHello:). So you need to connect the button to the Controller. Right-click on the button to bring up its HUD, mouse down on the circle next to "selector" under "Sent Actions," then drag a line to the HelloController (remember we are sending a message from the button to the Controller). When the HUD appears, select "sayHello:".

You can check that the connection has worked in the same way as before, in the HUD for the button or the Connections tab of the Inspector.

Save the NIB file and quit Interface Builder. Return to the Xcode Workspace; your application is complete. All that remains is to Build and Run (click the big green button in the toolbar). Assuming all went well, you will see a series of build messages in the status bar and then the running Hello World program (Figure 3–17).

Figure 3–17. *The Hello World program, running at last*

Click on the Click Me! button; you should see the message change to "Hello, World!". Once you know it works, quit from the running program to return to the Xcode Workspace.

If your program did not compile, or didn't produce the expected results, read the error message(s) carefully, and then go back and check everything. Easy for me to say, I know; however, the chances are that a minor syntax error lies behind the failed program. The Objective-C syntax is unforgiving, but it produces informative errors. Double-check that the connections are in place and look the same as in the figures above.

Incremental Development—Adding Features to Your Hello World Program

Well that was a simple example, and you may be thinking that it was quite a performance just to produce a simple message. The important thing to remember is that this process of defining the components, the messages and the connections between the components is the same for most of the applications you will write using the Xcode tools, and once you get into the swing of things it all happens very quickly. It is also easy to build on what you have already got: the beauty of object-oriented software development, and MVC approach in particular, is the ability to incrementally improve and add to your software.

Let's do that now. Suppose you wanted, rather than just popping up "Hello, World!" every time, to create a message and then click the button to display that message in the label. It turns out to be quite straightforward. Here are the things you need to do:

1. There needs to be another outlet (the controller is going to need to communicate with a textField where you type the message—let's call it sourceTextField).

2. The sayHello: method needs tweaking so it picks up the contents of the sourceTextField rather than just "Hello, World!".

3. There needs to be a textField in the user interface window.

4. The new sourceTextField outlet needs to connect to the textField in the interface.

Start by opening HelloController.h. You need to add a new outlet (the bold text in Listing 3–3 below):

Listing 3–3. *Adding another outlet to HelloController.h*

```
#import <Cocoa/Cocoa.h>

@interface HelloController : NSObject {
  IBOutlet NSTextField *destinationTextField;
  IBOutlet NSTextField *sourceTextField;
}
- (IBAction)sayHello:(id)sender;
@end
```

Next, open up HelloController.m. You need to modify the sayHello: method to look like this (see Listing 3–4; the line to change is in bold).

Listing 3–4. *Modifying the sayHello: method in HelloController.m*

```
#import "HelloController.h"
@implementation HelloController
-(IBAction)sayHello:(id)sender {
  //[destinationTextField setStringValue:@"Hello, World!"];
  [destinationTextField setStringValue:[sourceTextField stringValue]];
}
@end
```

The original line is also included but commented out so that you can compare them directly. This code is saying "Set the stringValue property in the destination text field to the text that you get from asking the source text field for its stringValue property."

Those are the only code changes you need. Save the .h and .m files and open Interface Builder (double-click MainMenu.xib). Add a Text Field from the Library, rightclick on the HelloController to bring up the HUD, and connect the new sourceTextField outlet to the new Text Field (see Figure 3–18).

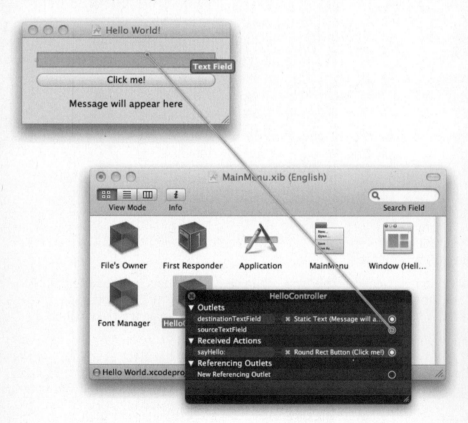

Figure 3–18. *Connecting the new* sourceTextField *outlet to the new Text Field*

If you don't see a sourceTextField outlet in the HUD, you didn't save your HelloController.h file!

You may be slightly confused by what you just did. You have a Text Field that supplies data to the Controller, and yet the connection you just made was the other way around—from the Controller to the Text Field. Why didn't the connection go from Text Field to Controller as it did when you wired up the button? The answer is that the button needed to communicate an action (the user clicking on it) to the Controller, whereas the Text Field is just passively providing its data when the Controller asks for it. The Controller really is in charge of the communications.

Save the NIB, quit Interface Builder, and return to Xcode. Build and Run, and this time you should be able to add a message using the Text Field, click the button, and see the message appear in the label (see Figure 3–19).

Figure 3–19. *The enhanced Hello World application running*

Creating a Document-Based Application

We're going to finish up this chapter by creating a slightly different type of Cocoa application. This will be a simple word-processing program (think of it as TextEdit Lite), though as you will see, it will still have some sophisticated features that will cost little in terms of development effort.

Start a new Cocoa application. This time, when you select the application template, check the box labeled "Create document-based application". In the next pane, give it a suitable name—I called this project "Text Pal"—and save it in a suitable location.

So what is a document-based application, and what are the consequences for you as a developer? From an end-user perspective, Mac applications tend to be either one-pot applications like iPhoto (that is, essentially all of the action takes place in one window), or applications like Pages or Numbers, where you spend most of your time in one or more document windows. In document-based applications, a user may have many document windows open at once and may need to swap the focus between them. The other key difference is that document-based applications need to be able to read and write documents from storage. Other applications may also read and write data, but they tend to take care of that process for you and not allow you much latitude about where that happens.

As a developer, you are presented with some slight additional complexity. Your primary design is going to be centered on the layout of a document rather than a central user interface, and your coding is going to need to take into account the processes of reading and writing documents. Sounds daunting, but as you have doubtless already guessed, Xcode takes care of a lot of this for you. In fact, try compiling and running the project right now (just click on Build and Run). You will see that you have an application running with a document—it temporarily says "Your document contents here" for now. You can already create a new document, swap between documents, bring up the fonts panel, and so on. You even have an "About…" box. Quit the application.

It's worth reiterating that this book is not about Objective-C, but I'll touch on the significant areas of the code as the project goes along.

Let's start with a quick look at the Xcode Workspace. This presents a slightly more extensive set of items than you have seen so far. The main point to note is that there are entries in the Detail panel for the Document.m, .h, and .xib files. These are where you will spend most of your time in this project. Start by double-clicking MyDocument.xib.

Over in Interface Builder, find the main window. You can see the Text Field that supplied the "Your document contents here" message. You won't need that, so just delete it. In its place, drag and drop a Text View. Use the automatic guides to size the Text View to fill most of the window. Now use the Autosizing settings panel in the Inspector to ensure that the Text View resizes to fill the window (enable all four of the I-bars and both the horizontal and vertical arrows). Use the Cocoa Simulator to check that the Text View keeps in step when you resize the window.

There's one more thing you need to do here, and that is some configuration of the Text View. Sadly, there is a slight usability gotcha here in the most recent version of the Xcode Tools. In earlier versions, the Text View control displayed some sample "Lorem Ipsum" text when you dropped it onto a window, and you could click on that text as a nice way of knowing that you had selected the Text View rather than its containing Scroll View. In the current version of the Xcode Tools, you just get a blank control, so it's not quite as straightforward to know when you have selected the Text View rather than the Scroll View. The simplest thing is just to click once in the control to get the Scroll View, then click again within the top of control to get the Text View. Figure 3–20 shows how this should look. You will also see another solution in the same figure. Look at the Document window. If you put it into list mode then you can use the outline feature to get to the Text View.

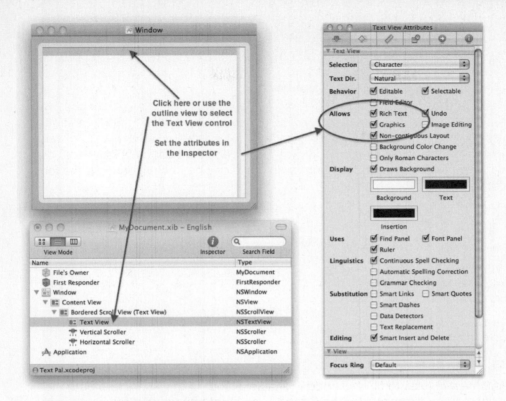

Figure 3–20. *Setting Text View properties and the outline view of the Document window*

Now that you have the Text View properly selected, look at the attributes panel of the Inspector (Figure 3–20). Make sure that Rich Text is selected, and then check the "Graphics" checkbox below it, too. Checking this option allows you to put images within your documents as you will see shortly.

That's all you need to do in Interface Builder. Save the NIB and return to Xcode.

Implementing File Saving and Reading

Back in the Workspace, try running the program. You will see that you already have a capable mini word processor. You can type, copy, and paste. You can bring up the Fonts and Colors panels and set the content accordingly. You can show the Ruler and Set tabs. You can even drag in images.

OK, now close the program. You can see that your application even knows to tell you that you have unsaved work (Figure 3–21). So, the sensible thing is to save, right?

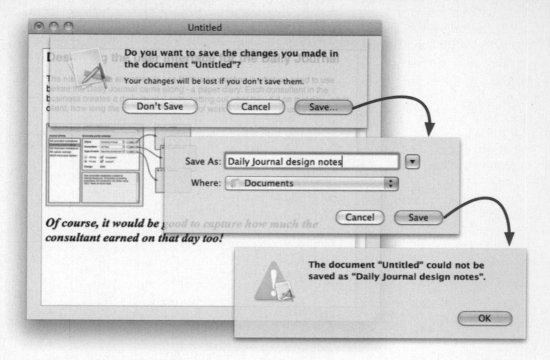

Figure 3–21. *Your application doesn't know how to save documents.*

So what is the problem? Although your application is already very capable, it still lacks a couple of features. Among these is the ability to save and read your documents. Xcode recognizes that you might want to have control over the mechanism and format of the data that you read and write, and so this part is left to the programmer to determine. Let's do that now.

Find the header file MyDocument.h and make it look like Listing 3–5 (you'll be adding the code in bold).

Listing 3–5. *Creating the new outlet and instance variable*

```
#import <Cocoa/Cocoa.h>

@interface MyDocument : NSDocument
{
    IBOutlet NSTextView *textView;
    NSAttributedString *mString;
}

@property (retain) NSTextView *textView;
@property (retain) NSAttributedString *string;

@end
```

So what does this code actually do? Like any header file, you are using this to declare outlets, variables, and methods that you will later implement in the counterpart .m file.

The features that you are introducing here require you to manage a string (actually a NSAttributedString, reflecting the potentially rich nature of the content). You need to get and set that string, and the place where the string is placed is the Text View, which is why you are creating an outlet for it.

To identify the Text View to the controller, you need to create a new outlet for the Text View, and you will also need an instance variable to hold the data that will go in it. The @property statements replace the method signatures for the accessor and mutator methods in Objective-C 2.0—simply use this statement in the header file and the synthesize command in the implementation file, and you can forget about getter and setter methods.

The next stage is to implement the various methods in MyDocument.m.

The method stubs are there already—you are just going to flesh them out. Find the method called windowControllerDidLoadNib. As the name suggests, this method is run when the user interface is loaded, and its purpose is to populate the Text View. Add the code shown in bold in Listing 3–6.

Listing 3–6. *Adding content to the Text View when the NIB loads*

```
- (void)windowControllerDidLoadNib:(NSWindowController *) aController
{
    [super windowControllerDidLoadNib:aController];
    if (self.string != nil) {
    [[textView textStorage] setAttributedString:self.string];
    }
}
```

This means set the value of the textStorage property of the Text View to be the value of the attributed string property of the current object (the window—as you will see shortly, the window is a delegate of the Text View).

Now you need to add the actual code for reading and writing. First let's look at writing the data. The stub method you will be editing is dataOfType (see Listing 3–7). Add the code in bold to make your method look like this:

Listing 3–7. *Editing dataOfType*

```
- (NSData *)dataOfType:(NSString *)typeName error:(NSError **)outError {
    NSData *data;
    self.string = textView.textStorage;
    data = [NSArchiver archivedDataWithRootObject:self.string];
    return data;
}
```

Note that this listing has removed the comments and unused boilerplate from the stub code. Make the appropriate changes to the method for reading archived data (Listing 3–8):

Listing 3–8. *Editing readFromData:*

```
- (BOOL)readFromData:(NSData *)data ofType:(NSString *)typeName error:(NSError **)outError {
    NSAttributedString *tempString = [NSUnarchiver unarchiveObjectWithData: data];
```

```
        self.string = tempString;
        return YES;
}
```

This method simply unarchives the relevant content—that is, reads it from the file on disk—and puts it into the window's data model.

Finally you need to add synthesize commands at the top of the code for the two outlets created in the header file. Using @synthesize saves you having to explicitly write the accessor and mutator methods (as well as making your code clearer and easier to read).

Listing 3–9 shows the resulting MyDocument.m in its entirety.

Listing 3–9. *MyDocument.m*

```
#import "MyDocument.h"

@implementation MyDocument

@synthesize textView;
@synthesize string;

- (id)init {
    self = [super init];
    if (self) {
    }
    return self;
}

- (NSString *)windowNibName {
    return @"MyDocument";
}

- (void)windowControllerDidLoadNib:(NSWindowController *) aController {
    [super windowControllerDidLoadNib:aController];
    if (self.string != nil) {
    [[textView textStorage] setAttributedString:self.string];
    }
}

- (NSData *)dataOfType:(NSString *)typeName error:(NSError **)outError {
    NSData *data;
    self.string = textView.textStorage;
    data = [NSArchiver archivedDataWithRootObject:self.string];
    return data;
}

- (BOOL)readFromData:(NSData *)data ofType:(NSString *)typeName error:(NSError
**)outError {
    NSAttributedString *tempString = [NSUnarchiver unarchiveObjectWithData: data];
    self.string = tempString;
    return YES;
}

@end
```

You're not quite done yet. You know that you created a new outlet in MyDocument.h—now you need to build the connections for this in Interface Builder. Make sure that you have saved MyDocument.h and MyDocument.m, and then double-click on MyDocument.xib. There are two complementary connections you need to make here. First, right-click on File's Owner and drag a connection out to the Text View (make sure you hit this and not the Scroll View). When you drop the connection, choose textView from the HUD dropdown list. Now right-click on the Text View and drag a connection out to File's Owner. When you drop it, choose delegate. Save the NIB, return to Xcode, and Build and Run.

You should now be able to create new documents, add text and drag in images, and then save them. You should also be able to reopen saved documents.

A Little Polish

To finish things up, let's add a few refinements. Your shiny new application doesn't save files with any extension, doesn't have a useful About… box, and doesn't have an application icon. How about addressing these shortcomings?

Let's take a look at the icon and extension first. In Xcode, find the file Text_Pal-Info.plist. You can either edit this file in the Editor pane or double-click it to bring it up in a separate window. This plist allows you to set options such as icons, file extensions, and formats.

If you want to add an icon file to your application, you need a .icns file. You will be learning how to create these from scratch later in the book, so for now let's just grab one from an existing application. A good one to use is the Edit.icns file that is supplied as part of the example TextEdit project (look in /Developer/Examples/TextEdit/). Drag this file into the Xcode Workspace and drop it in the Resources folder. When the dialog pops up, check the option to copy the item into the folder and click Add.

Now configure the plist to know about the icon. Look in the plist for the Icon file entry. In the adjacent box, type **Edit.icns** (there is no picker control for some reason, so make sure you type this correctly). Try Build and Run, and you will see the application icon in the Dock (see Figure 3–22).

Figure 3–22. *Your custom application icon in the Dock*

Now for an extension. Let's make Text Pal save files with a .txtp extension. In the plist, open the Document types item. Within this, set the Item 0 / CFBundleTypeExtensions/Item 0 value to "txtp", the Icon File Name value to "Edit.icns" (to specify the icon for documents as distinct from the application icon—it just happens that we are using the same icon here), and the Document Type Name to "TextPal Document" (Figure 3–23).

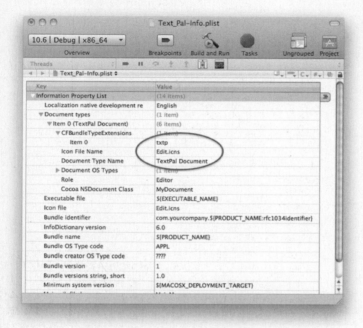

Figure 3–23. *Setting options in the plist*

To create the About… box, find the entry in the Detail panel for Credits.rtf. This is a simple rich text format file. You can edit this in the Editor panel, or even open it in TextEdit if you want more control over layout, fonts, and so on. Try adding your own text and styles to this document. Save it when you have finished.

Your application is complete. Build and Run for a final workout. Wow! Just look at what you have created: a simple word processor that can read and write sophisticated documents with images, styled text, rulers, tabs, and a variety of text alignments. The program has an About box, application and document icons, and your own custom file extensions. It has access to the standard Fonts and Colors settings panels and even to built-in Mac OS X features such as the spellchecker and the Help system (Figure 3–24).

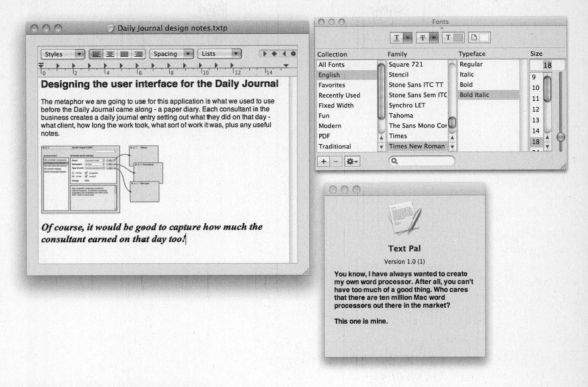

Figure 3–24. *Look at what you have created!*

Summary

This chapter has exposed you to some ideas about software development that may be new to you: outlets, actions, the MVC pattern, and so on. You should now have a clear idea of how to assemble the basic components that go to make up a Cocoa application in Mac OS X. You've managed to create a sophisticated, working Mac application with a few simple yet powerful tools.

Of course, Macs are not the only devices that you might want to write applications for. The iPhone is generating a huge amount of interest amongst developers. How about spending some time checking out the tools that Xcode provides for this intriguing new platform? That's coming up in Chapter 4.

Chapter **4**

Core iPhone Tools

The most exciting platform in computing today—wow, that's quite a claim. Chances are that if you are writing software on the Mac today, you are thinking about writing for the iPhone. The iPhone and its sibling, the iPod Touch, have created a huge amount of interest amongst both end users and developers. Currently (as of late 2009) there are over 100,000 applications available for this platform on the App Store. It's not just the existing devices that cause a stir, either. Apple, as always, plays its cards close to its chest, but you can be sure it has big plans for its mobile computing platform. Yes, definitely the most exciting place to be writing software right now.

The great news is that your investment in learning Xcode and Objective-C can be mostly translated directly to iPhone development. As we'll see, there are some extra tools to learn and some minor differences in the grammar; but overall, if you know how to write software for the Mac with Xcode's tools, you will have little trouble writing software for the iPhone and iPod Touch.

In this chapter, you will be registering for an iPhone developer account, downloading and installing the SDK, and taking the first steps towards—who knows—maybe creating *The Next Big Thing* on the App Store.

First Things First: What You Need to Develop iPhone Software

One of the nicest features of the Xcode tools is that the underlying architecture allows you to plug in additional toolkits in order to target your applications at different devices. The iPhone SDK is a good example of a software development toolkit aimed at a different architecture—the iPhone and iPod Touch. The tools and frameworks needed to develop for this platform slot perfectly into the Xcode tools, giving you a seamless integrated development environment for Mac and iPhone development.

Getting and installing the iPhone SDK is just like getting and installing the Xcode tools themselves. The main difference in the process is that you need to register for iPhone development. Actually, there are two levels in iPhone registration. The first is the simple, free registered iPhone Developer account to get the SDK. You can do this at the `developer.apple.com` site: in effect you will either create a new Apple ID or use your existing ID.

This level of access to the SDK allows you to do more or less everything that we are going to cover in this book. The main things you miss out on with this free level of access are that you can't put your applications onto a real iPhone, and you can't submit them for sale on the App Store. To get those features you need to upgrade your developer registration. This is not free, and the cost depends on whether you register as an individual or a company.

So if you can't upload your application to an actual iPhone, you might be wondering how you get to develop and test your shiny new application idea. The answer is the iPhone emulator. The iPhone SDK includes a faithful emulation of the iPhone—not just the user interface, but the detailed functionality (sadly, without being able to make phone calls!). In practice, the iPhone emulator gives you access to almost everything that you can do on a real iPhone or iPod Touch apart from the networking features.

> **NOTE:** This book is primarily focused on giving you a good grounding in the use of the Xcode Developer Tools and isn't intended to teach you how to write great iPhone software. As such, there are some aspects of Objective-C and application design that we will not be covering here. However there are some great books out there that will do just that, such as the excellent *Beginning iPhone Development* from Apress.

Getting and Installing the SDK

Let's get to it. Go to the developer site, register as an iPhone Developer if you haven't already done so (`http://developer.apple.com/iphone/program/start/register/`), and then go to the downloads page to get the iPhone SDK (`http://developer.apple.com/technology/xcode.html`). By the time you read this, Apple may have released a combined Xcode installation for both Mac OS X and iPhone, in which case you will need to download and install this. It will overwrite your Mac OS X Xcode installation but should not affect your preferences.

Once you've downloaded the kit, you install the iPhone Xcode tools in the usual way. The main difference that you will see once the iPhone SDK is in place is that you will have some new options in the Xcode New Project window (see Figure 4–1). As well as the Mac OS X options, you now have an entry in the list for the iPhone OS.

Figure 4–1. *iPhone application options in the Xcode New Project window*

Writing a Simple iPhone Application

To illustrate the similarities—and some basic differences—between Mac and iPhone development, you are going to recreate one of the programs you wrote in the last chapter, the modified Hello World application. So as not to confuse the applications, you should give this a different name; how about "Show Message". Here is how it is going to look when it is complete (see Figure 4–2).

Start by creating the project. Choose the iPhone OS section, then View-based application. Call it "Show Message". Once in the Xcode workspace, let's start with a little orientation. This is the same old Xcode Project Workspace window you have seen so far, but there are a couple of differences that you can spot pretty quickly. See Figure 4–3.

Figure 4–2. *The completed Show Message application*

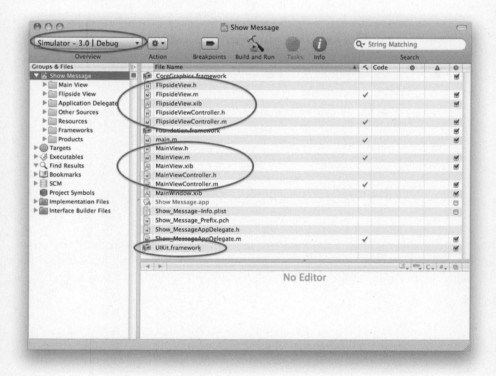

Figure 4–3. *The Project Workspace window for our iPhone application*

In the toolbar you will see that this application is going to be compiled against the iPhone Simulator as a target. Also, we are using the UIKit Framework in place of the normal AppKit Framework. Finally, you will see that you have Controllers and NIB files for the Main View and the Flipside View. This is going to be an iPhone application that has an info button to flip it over. Many iPhone applications use this visually appealing metaphor to show a configuration or About view. Let's see how much it already does. Click on **Build and Go**.

Although you haven't added any code yet, the emulator shows you a working application, including the functionality to flip the application over to see the information screen. To quit the emulator, just choose **Quit** from the **iPhone Simulator** menu or press ⌘Q.

So, onto the code. It makes sense to start with what you had working before, right? So let's have a quick reprise of the code in that earlier application (see Listings 4–1 and 4–2).

Listing 4–1. *HelloController.h*

```
#import <Cocoa/Cocoa.h>

@interface HelloController : NSObject {
    IBOutlet NSTextField *destinationTextField;
    IBOutlet NSTextField *sourceTextField;
}

- (IBAction)sayHello:(id)sender;

@end
```

Listing 4–2. *HelloController.m*

```
#import "HelloController.h"

@implementation HelloController

- (IBAction)sayHello:(id)sender {
  [destinationTextField setStringValue:[sourceTextField stringValue]];
}

@end
```

The code in bold is what you added to the stubs provided by Xcode. So, start by cutting and pasting that code into the corresponding files in your new iPhone application. Make the MainViewController.h file look like Listing 4–3 (you need to add the code in bold):

Listing 4–3. *MainViewController.h*

```
#import "FlipsideViewController.h"
@interface MainViewController : UIViewController <FlipsideViewControllerDelegate> {
    IBOutlet NSTextField *destinationTextField;
    IBOutlet NSTextField *sourceTextField;
}

- (IBAction)showInfo;
- (IBAction)sayHello:(id)sender;
```

@end

I'm going to confess at this point that there is a big deliberate mistake in what you have just done. Can you spot it? (Hint: Objects in the iPhone user interface may not have exactly the same names as similar objects in the Mac OS X interface.)

Also, make a mental note here that when you get to Interface Builder you are going to need to create outlets for `destinationTextField` and `sourceTextField` and the `sayHello:` action. Before we get to that, let's look at the code for `MainViewController.m`. You'll see that there is a lot of stub code there, commented out but ready for you to elaborate should you need to. There are also a few methods there for handling the flip functionality. For this application you won't need to change anything that's there, but just copy the implementation of `sayHello:` and paste it into this class file. Add the code that's in bold in Listing 4–4; I put it immediately after the closing braces of the `initWithNibName` method.

Listing 4–4. *MainViewController.m*

```
[…]
- (IBAction)sayHello:(id)sender {
    [destinationTextField setStringValue:[sourceTextField stringValue]];
}
[…]
```

Now the code's in place. Start up Interface Builder by double-clicking on the `MainView.xib` entry in the detail panel (*not* `MainWindow.xib`—this is just a placeholder NIB file). You will see the Interface Builder user interface more or less as normal (see Figure 4–4).

Figure 4–4. *The Show Message application in Interface Builder*

The interface is familiar—basically the same Interface Builder as the one you'd load if you were building a Mac OS X application. However there are some immediate differences: The window is a fixed size (the size of the iPhone window, 320 × 460 pixels), the parameters available in each of the Inspector tabs are slightly different to suit the needs of an iPhone application, and the controllers in the Library window have a golden background color instead of blue on green. Actually, the main differences you will notice are in the Library window. The tools available are tailored to the iPhone: Web View, Map View, Picker View, and so on. You will be making more use of these later on in the book.

Now, add some controls in the Main View window. We're looking for two TextFields... but here is an interesting difference. The Label control is not an instance of an NSTextField, but rather a UILabel. Similarly, the Rounded Rect Button that sits next to it is a UIButton and the Text Field that will be used to input text is a UITextField. Clearly you are going to need to do some tweaking in the code to accommodate these, since the code refers to NSTextFields. That was the deliberate mistake I asked you to make a little way back: simply put, you can't just cut and paste even for simple examples, since user interface objects may not have the same names or behaviors.

Flip back to Xcode and fix those now. Open MainViewController.h and edit the code to match the bold text in Listing 4–5.

Listing 4–5. *Making the Changes to MainViewController.h*

```
#import "FlipsideViewController.h"
@interface MainViewController : UIViewController <FlipsideViewControllerDelegate> {
    IBOutlet UILabel *destinationTextField;
    IBOutlet UITextField *sourceTextField;
}

- (IBAction)showInfo;
- (IBAction)sayHello:(id)sender;

@end
```

Basically you are changing the two NSTextField references into respectively UILabel and UITextField references. Double-check to ensure you have them the right way around—it didn't matter for Mac OS X since the objects are both NSTextFields, but it matters now!

Back in Interface Builder, drag UILabel, UIButton, and UITextField controls into the Main View window, and position them more or less as they are in Figure 4–5.

Figure 4–5. *Adding the UI controls to the Main View window*

Make each control 280 pixels wide and center the text. For the UITextField, make the Placeholder attribute **Write message here** (the placeholder is text that is shown in a grayed-out form in a Text Field as a hint to the user). Make the window background pale gray (set the **Brightness** value in the Gray Scale Colors panel to 90%).

You may be wondering why all of the controls are in the top half of the window. Run the emulator (⌘R) to see why (Figure 4–6): click in the Text Field and you will see the virtual keyboard come up. Your user interface design should take account of the fact that the keyboard may need to be accommodated on the screen. We'll be looking further at this keyboard shortly.

Quit from the emulator (⌘Q).

Figure 4–6. *Testing the user interface in the emulator*

Next you need to wire up the application. Remember in Chapter 3 when you connected the button to the controller, and the controller to the source and destination Text Fields? That's what needs to happen now. But where is the controller? There is no obvious dedicated controller in the **Document** window.

The answer in this case is File's Owner. File's Owner is a special object that represents the object (in this case `MainViewController`) that owns or loads the user interface. You can confirm this by selecting File's Owner and looking at the Identity panel in the Inspector window. You will see that it is an instance of a `MainViewController`. So this is the controller we want to make our connections to.

This may seem odd, since in a conventional Mac OS X application File's Owner is an instance of `NSApplication`, but in this simple type of iPhone application File's Owner is an instance of `MainViewController` (you can confirm this by selecting File's Owner and looking at the **Identity** panel in the **Inspector** window—you will see that it is an instance of a `MainViewController`). That's where we want to make our connections.

Control-drag from the `UIButton` to File's Owner. When you drop the line on File's Owner, choose the `sayHello:` action (see Figure 4–7).

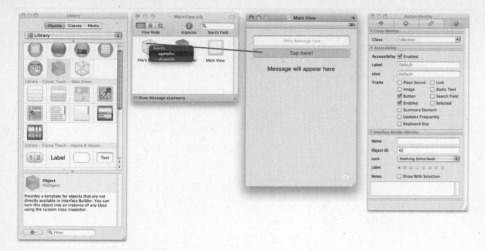

Figure 4–7. *Wiring up the user interface*

Similarly, Control-drag from File's Owner to the UITextField and choose sourceTextField as the outlet, then from File's Owner to the UILabel choosing destinationTextField as the outlet. Save and close Interface Builder.

Excellent. It looks as though the application is ready to roll. **Build and Run**.

Hmm. The application compiles and runs; however, when you click the text, type, and click the button, nothing happens. What has gone wrong here? Quit from the emulator and let's start checking.

In Xcode choose the **Build Results** tab. Ah, there are two warnings (see Figure 4–8):

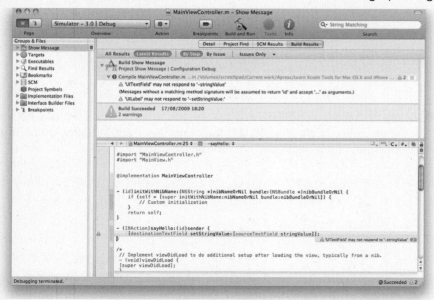

Figure 4–8. *Warnings from the Show Message application run*

The two warning messages are about getting and setting the `stringValue` property. That's where we need to start looking—perhaps there are syntax differences between the `AppKit` and `UIKit` class methods. A good tip here is to use Xcode's code completion features. If `setStringValue` is not correct, what should we be using here? To use this here, position the cursor immediately before `setStringValue` and hit Return to put the rest of the text on the next line (we'll get rid of the text that we just shunted out of the way shortly). Now type **set** (it's a fair bet that the command we're looking for begins with "set") and then hit the Escape key. This pops up a code completion list. Xcode shows all relevant commands for the class (you will see that it is clever enough to know that the method is for a `UILabel` class). See Figure 4–9.

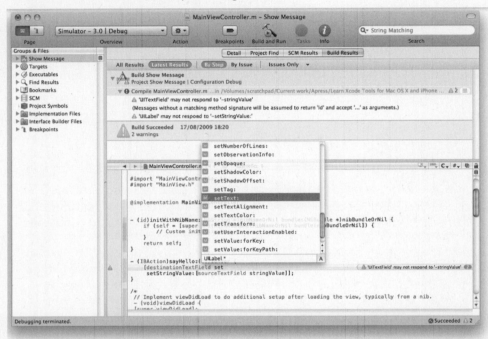

Figure 4–9. *Code completion options*

Scroll through the options in this list and you will see that—sure enough—there is no `setStringValue`. However, there is a `setText`. This looks right, so double-click on it. This updates the code to look like Figure 4–10.

```
- (IBAction)sayHello:(id)sender {
    [destinationTextField setText:(NSString *)                    ⚠ 'UITextField' may not respond to '-stringValue' ⊘2
        setStringValue:[sourceTextField stringValue]];
}
```

Figure 4–10. *Using Xcode's method signature cues in the editor*

Xcode also puts in the next part of the method signature for you as a cue, so just press the Tab key and you can continue typing. The `NSString` that needs to go here is the string value of the `UITextField`, so it will be something like `[sourceTextField getText]`. (Long-time Java programmers will probably try this first.) However, if you start typing

sourceTextField get and then hit the Escape key, you will see that it pops up the message "No completions found." That's obviously not what we need. Delete back over the "get" and hit Escape again; this time there's a long list to track, but you will see that the most likely candidate for completion is simply "text". That must be it (and of course it is, in fact, Objective-C's syntax for handling accessors and mutators).

This gives us the right syntax, so all that remains is to close the line correctly and delete the code debris from the next line; the method should now look like Listing 4–6.

Listing 4–6. *The Method with the (Hopefully) Correct Syntax*

```
- (IBAction)sayHello:(id)sender {
[destinationTextField setText:[sourceTextField text]];
}
```

USING DOT NOTATION

There is an alternative to the standard notation for methods like this. In place of

```
[destinationTextField setText:[sourceTextField text]];
```

you could equally correctly use dot notation:

```
destinationTextField.text = sourceTextField.text;
```

Programmers who are used to Java or C# may find this more familiar, though die-hard Objective-C developers apparently don't like this approach so much. I will be using dot notation more during the remainder of the book.

The application is complete. Let's give it a spin. Save everything and then **Build and Run**. Up comes the iPhone emulator and the program will start. Try typing some text in the box. Notice that the emulator will do predictive text just like a real iPhone. Also, as shown in Figure 4–11, the keyboard and edit controls work in the expected way.

Well, not quite, actually. It's just as well you left room for the onscreen keyboard, because there doesn't seem to be a way to get rid of it! The behavior an iPhone user would expect to see here is that tapping Return should dismiss the keyboard. Let's fix that now.

If you are in the emulator, quit and go back to Xcode. Open `MainViewController.h`. You are going to create a new method. Within the user interface whatever control is currently receiving messages is called First Responder. When you are typing in text using the keyboard the First Responder is the Text Field where the text appears. What we want to do here is to detect the "Did End On Exit" event that is triggered by the Return key. When that event is detected we want the Text Field to stop being First Responder (called *resigning*). That, in turn, causes the keyboard to be dismissed. Declare a new method called `textFieldFinishedWithKeyboard` (add the bold code in Listing 4–7).

Figure 4–11. *The Show Message application running and editing text*

Listing 4–7. *Declaring the New Method in MainViewController.h*

```
#import "FlipsideViewController.h"

@interface MainViewController : UIViewController <FlipsideViewControllerDelegate> {
    IBOutlet UILabel *destinationTextField;
    IBOutlet UITextField *sourceTextField;
}

- (IBAction)showInfo;
- (IBAction)sayHello:(id)sender;
- (IBAction)textFieldFinishedWithKeyboard:(id)sender;
@end
```

The implementation is simple. In MainViewController.m put the method implementation immediately after the sayHello method (see the bold code in Listing 4–8).

Listing 4–8. Implementing the New Method

```
- (IBAction)sayHello:(id)sender {
    [destinationTextField setText:[sourceTextField text]];
}

- (IBAction)textFieldFinishedWithKeyboard:(id)sender {
    [sender resignFirstResponder];
}
[...]
```

Adding Some Polish

Now, in the emulator, try tapping the **Home** button at the bottom of the onscreen iPhone. You will see the Home page and the icon for our application. Looks a little plain, doesn't it? Can we do something about that? We certainly can!

In the sample code for this chapter, look in the images folder and you will see an image called iPhoneIcon.png (Figure 4–12). If you prefer, just create your own PNG (Portable Network Graphics) file, and make it 57 × 57 pixels.

Figure 4–12. *Icon image for our new application*

Making this into an application icon for our application is fairly straightforward. First, in Xcode, choose **Project➤Add to Project** (or ⌥⌘A) and navigate to where the image is stored. Choose the image and click the Add button. In the sheet that follows, make sure the checkbox labeled **Copy items in to destination group's folder (if needed)** is selected, then choose the **Add** button. That ensures the image is copied and compiled into the application, but you also need to set it as the application icon. To do that, make sure the Project name **Show Message** is selected at the top of the Groups and Files list, then find the file Show_Message-Info.plist in the **Detail** panel. Select this file and you will see the plist contents in the **Editor** panel (Figure 4–13). In the empty cell next to the legend Icon file, type in the filename for your icon.

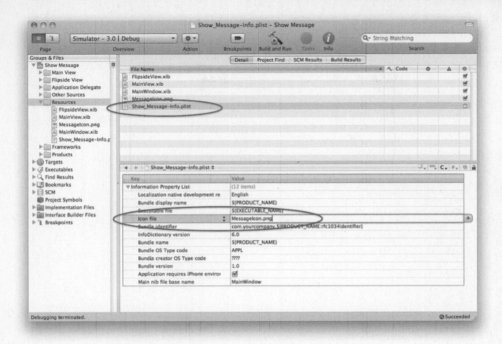

Figure 4–13. *Configuring the icon for the Show Message application*

That's it! **Build and Run** again and hit the **Home** button, and you should see your shiny new application icon (Figure 4–14). Notice that Xcode has made things easier for you by giving the icon the iPhone look and feel treatment: it has rounded the corners and put a nice glassy appearance on the icon.

Figure 4–14. *The new application icon*

> **TIP:** As you create more and more iPhone applications, you will notice that the Home page on the emulator starts to fill up. If you want to clear this page you can delete the contents of the folder `~/Library/Application Support/iPhone Simulator`. Next time you run the Simulator, it will have a clean screen.

Just One More Thing

You're probably way ahead of me, but I missed out one small step in the application: developing the UI for the flip side of the application. Let's do that now.

In Xcode, double-click on `FlipsideView.xib`. The NIB file will open up in Interface Builder. You're an old hand now, so in short, what you need to do here is edit the Title, add a Label to hold a message, and an image control to hold the icon. Make it look like Figure 4–15.

Figure 4–15. *The UI for the flip side of our application view*

When you have completed your FlipsideView user interface, save the NIB and close Interface Builder. This time you really are finished. Go back to Xcode and **Build and Run**. Your completed application allows you to create a message in the Text Field and tap the button to show the message in the Label. If you tap the info button, the application screen will flip over with an elegant animation to show the information message. If you have used the code example from the download site you will see that there is more text on the info screen than what is visible above, demonstrating the built in scrollable behavior of views like these. Tap the **Done** button to flip back.

Summary

So that's it, a brief introduction to the core tools that you will use to develop applications for the iPhone and iPod Touch. You can see that while the tools and techniques are fundamentally the same, there are also differences that can catch you out.

There is a huge amount more to learn about developing for the iPhone. We haven't even touched on the range of controls, rotating views, the accelerometer, integration with other iPhone software, mapping, or anything to do with networking. And to be honest, all of that is more than we are going to be able to cover in this book, but remember that there are some great books out there that focus solely on iPhone development.

Already you will have noticed how modular these basic components are, and how straightforward it is to put them together and begin to make great software. Much of that modularity and ease of use is due to the Framework-based design of Mac OS X and the iPhone OS. Underlying all of Cocoa are the Frameworks—comprehensive libraries of code that drive not only the software you develop but Mac OS X itself. In Chapter 5, you will take a look at the Cocoa Frameworks and begin to explore some of the power that lies within them.

Frameworks in Xcode

If you followed the examples in Chapter 4, you have already used Apple's frameworks. In fact, you use Apple's frameworks every time you use your Mac, since most of the software you use—including most of the software driving the user experience in Mac OS X—is built on them.

This chapter will familiarize you with the different frameworks that make up Cocoa. Along the way, you will create your own custom web browser, a simple membership subscription data application, and even a screensaver. You will see how much of a timesaver the frameworks can be in your Mac OS X development work.

A Short Tour of the Frameworks

First and foremost, what exactly are the frameworks, and why should you be interested in them at all? In a nutshell, the frameworks are a group of libraries of predefined tools and code that save you having to build common application features for yourself. In the old days, if you wanted to build a web browser, you faced the huge task of designing your own networking code, starting with understanding the HTTP protocol, not to mention defining the appearance and behavior of all of the objects in the user interface. Using Cocoa frameworks, you now simply add the WebKit framework to your project and have instant access to those features.

It may seem as though this is letting you off the hook—where's the fun in software development if you just take everything off the shelf? The beauty of using frameworks is that if you really want to implement your own spin on the http protocol or your user UI, you can—you don't *have* to use WebKit. But by using the frameworks, you can focus your creative energies on what is different and special about your killer application rather than investing those energies in solving problems that other clever people have already solved.

What Are the Frameworks?

The frameworks are an integral part of Cocoa. Cocoa is the name Apple has given to the overall object-oriented environment in which you develop Mac OS X software. In a sense, Cocoa is the world you are living in while creating Mac and iPhone applications. The Xcode Tools are what you use to build your houses, factories, and roads. The Cocoa environment is very flexible: you are not restricted to development in one specific programming language and, in fact, you are not even restricted to Xcode as your development environment. If you are so inclined, you can write code in other editors and even compile and run programs from the command line. However, this book focuses on Objective-C code and Xcode. Here are the main components of Cocoa as most developers encounter them:

- Xcode Tools

- The Core Frameworks (Foundation and Application Kit)

- Additional Frameworks: WebKit, Core Data and Core Animation, and many others

The frameworks are essentially highly optimized libraries of code that provide you with a straightforward, intuitive, and consistent interface to most of the underlying power and services within Mac OS X. In fact these libraries are precisely those used within most Mac OS X programs, meaning that the mechanisms you will use to, say, implement and populate a listbox, a web browser view, or a command button are exactly the same as those used in Mail, Safari, or iTunes.

The Foundation framework is the fundamental Cocoa framework, used in all Cocoa applications. It includes, among other things, the fundamental or root class from which all Cocoa objects are descended: NSObject. In effect, all Cocoa objects inherit the features of NSObjects, though they may also have other features specific to their own class. Object orientation is a huge topic and beyond the scope of this book. Still, the chances are that you will already have been exposed to the vocabulary of objects, classes, inheritance, methods, and properties. If not, there are many books and internet resources that will explain object-orientation.

Location of the Frameworks

This is probably only of academic interest to you, but you may like to know where the frameworks are kept on your Mac and how they fit into your Mac environment.

The main Apple-supplied frameworks are in /System/Library/Frameworks. Look in this folder and you will see folders for Foundation.framework, AppKit.framework, CoreData.framework, and many others.

Let's take a quick look at NSObject. Bear in mind that you won't see the source code for NSObject, or for that matter the compiled framework, but simply the header file. Find and open Foundation.framework, then open the alias Headers. You will see all of the classes within the Foundation framework, and, if you want to know the properties and methods of one of these, open it up in a text editor (don't be tempted to try to change it, of course).

This is not the best way to find the properties and methods of a Cocoa class, naturally. There is excellent documentation (which you will be exploring in Chapter 8). The point of this exercise is simply to familiarize yourself with the frameworks and dispel some of the mystery that may surround them.

Other Frameworks

Apart from those supplied by Apple, your Mac may well have other frameworks that contain libraries of code specific to third party products. You can find these in /Library/Frameworks. For example, my computer has additional frameworks for MacRuby, OpenBase, and several other products.

In the course of your development work you may want to bundle together any code libraries that you have built and need to reuse into your own frameworks. This is perfectly feasible, but is way beyond the scope of this book.

Finally, there are frameworks specifically associated with Xcode Developer Tools, in /Developer/Library/PrivateFrameworks and the public developer frameworks in /Developer/Library/Frameworks.

Where to Look for More Information

Few developers ever need more than basic knowledge of the background of frameworks. The really useful information is how to use them in applications. However, you may want to understand in greater depth how the frameworks are designed. Your best bet is to head over to the documentation. The Cocoa Fundamentals Guide (http://developer.apple.com/documentation/Cocoa/Conceptual/CocoaFundamentals) is a great source of really detailed information about the Cocoa frameworks.

Using Frameworks in Applications

One way to use Cocoa frameworks in your applications is by choosing the appropriate Cocoa template when you create a project. However, you can also choose to bring a particular framework into your project to take advantage of its features.

For the rest of this chapter, you are going to be creating a variety of applications that will use Cocoa frameworks to create capable, feature-rich software with a minimum of coding. Along the way you will try different ways to load and use Cocoa frameworks.

The WebKit Framework—Create Your Own Web Browser

WebKit is the framework that underlies Safari, Google Chrome, and various other web client applications. It is an open source framework providing a highly capable web browser engine. The implementation in Cocoa allows you to readily embed a web browser view into your applications.

You are going to create a WebKit-based web browser from scratch. The really striking feature of this project is that you will not need to write a single line of code.

Create a new Xcode project and choose the Cocoa application template; don't select the Document-based application, Core Data, or Spotlight Importer options. Call your project "Browser Pal". When the project workspace window comes up, take a look at the **Frameworks** group (in the **Groups & Files** list). You can see the frameworks available to this project: AppKit, Cocoa, CoreData, and Foundation (see Figure 5–1).

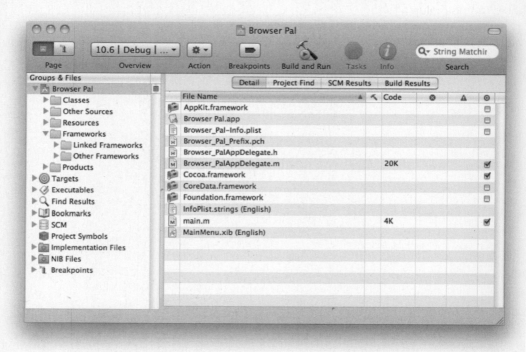

Figure 5–1. *Browser Pal project workspace showing the default frameworks*

You need to add the WebKit framework as a first step. Open up the yellow **Frameworks** folder icon, right-click the **Other Frameworks** folder and, from the contextual menu, choose **Add Existing Frameworks....**

Use the Framework picker to choose WebKit.framework. There are a lot of available items in this picker, so you can use the popup menu at the top to filter just the frameworks. When you have selected WebKit.framework, click on **Add** and you will see the workspace with the new framework in place.

Now it's time to move to Interface Builder. Double-click on `MainMenu.xib` and you will see the main user interface window.

Start by resizing the window to 640 × 320 pixels (remember—choose the window by clicking its title bar, and then choose the **Size** tab in the Inspector) and set its **Minimum Size** value to be 640 × 320, too. Give the window a title—say, "Browser Pal".

This web browser is going to be pretty fully featured: it will have back, forward, stop, and reload buttons; a place to add the URL you want to load; and even buttons to make the text larger or smaller. So to start, let's add those features.

Drag a gradient button onto the window. I chose a gradient button because I wanted something that looked a little like Safari's toolbar buttons. Delete the title in the **Attributes** tab in the Inspector, then use the **Size** tab to set the button's height to 23 pixels (it should be that value already) and the width to 32 pixels. Now hold down the option key and drag the button to the right to make a copy. Do this five more times, so you end up with a row of seven buttons (see Figure 5–2). Notice how the automatic guides help you to keep things in line.

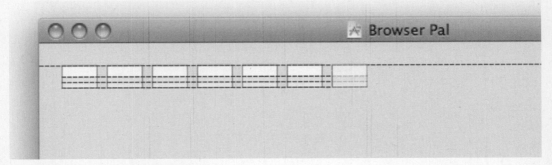

Figure 5–2. *Copying the toolbar buttons*

Now you are going to put some images on those buttons. Select the leftmost button and then choose the **Attributes** tab in the Inspector. You will see a drop-down list with the label Image. In this list, find and choose NSRefreshTemplate. This will add a familiar refresh image to the button.

In a moment, you will add the following images to the remaining buttons, in order: NSStopProgressTemplate, NSGoLeftTemplate, NSGoRightTemplate, and NSFontPanel (the last one is the same for each of the last three buttons). Note that you can save yourself a lot of typing by typing in the textbox next to the drop-down button; it's an auto-complete field. Before you do any typing, though, take a quick look at the **Library** window for another typing-free alternative. When you looked at this in the last chapter, you may have noticed a **Media** tab next to the **Objects** tab. Select it now. You will see that the images that you are about to use are listed here. In fact, as is typical with Xcode, there are at least two ways to do most things, and if you prefer you can just drag the appropriate image from the **Library** window and drop it straight onto the button.

The last three buttons are going to get some special treatment: the first will make the browser text smaller, the second restores the text to a standard size and the third makes it bigger. To differentiate them, add a hyphen (-) as the title of the first button and make it left justified (in the **Attributes** tab). Add a plus sign (+) as the title for the third and leave the second as it is. Finally, drag these three buttons over to the right of the window. I'm not proud of the quality of design, but it's only intended to illustrate after all!

Add a Text Field and make it almost the width of the window. Finally, let's add the WebView. In the **Objects** tab of the **Library** window, scroll down about halfway until you see **Web Kit**. Choose that and you will see an entry with a Safari-like icon—that's a Web View control.

Drag a Web View over and drop it on the main user interface window. Size it to take up most of the remaining space. All of the components are now on the user interface (see Figure 5–3).

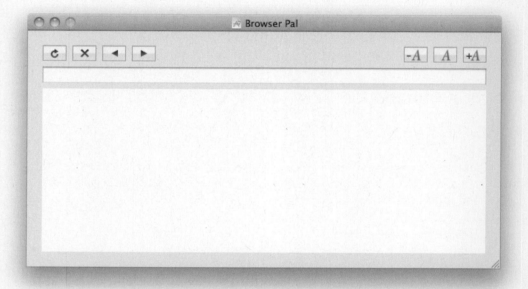

Figure 5–3. *All components added to the user interface*

All that is needed now to complete the user interface is to add the Autosizing properties. Note that where you are going to set a common property for several objects, such as the Anchor and Sizing properties in Table 5–1 below, you can select them all and set the property in the Inspector in one go.

While you have the **Size** tab up in the Inspector it's probably a good idea to set a minimum size for the window to avoid any user interface ugliness. Click in the window title bar to select the window, and then in the tab select the **Minimum Size** checkbox and click on the **Use Current** button. Your user interface is complete. Run the simulator (⌘R) and try resizing the window to check that it autosizes correctly.

Table 5–1. *Autosizing Properties for the User Interface Objects*

Component	Anchor Properties	Sizing Properties
Reload button	Top, left	None
Stop button	Top, left	None
Back button	Top, left	None
Forward button	Top, left	None
Smaller text button	Top, right	None
Standard text button	Top, right	None
Larger text button	Top, right	None
Text Field	Top, right, left	Horizontal
Web View	Top, right, bottom, left	Horizontal, vertical

Finally, you need to wire up the controls. This part is the easiest! First, connect the Text Field. This is going to be where you type a URL, so it makes sense that this should send a message to the Web View. Control-click on the Text Field and drag a line over to the Web View. When you drop the line choose the action takeStringURLFrom:.

Now repeat the process for the buttons. In each case, control-drag a line from the button to the Web View and, when you drop it, choose an action (see Table 5–2 for a full list) to send to the Web View.

Table 5–2. *Connecting the Buttons to the Web View*

Component	Sent Action
Reload button	reload:
Stop button	stopLoading:
Back button	goBack:
Forward button	goForward:
Smaller text button	makeTextSmaller:
Standard text button	makeTextStandardSize:
Larger text button	makeTextLarger:
Text Field	takeStringURLFrom:

Save the NIB. Your application is complete. Go back to the Xcode project workspace and run your program. It should look like Figure 5–4 (showing the Apple UK home page).

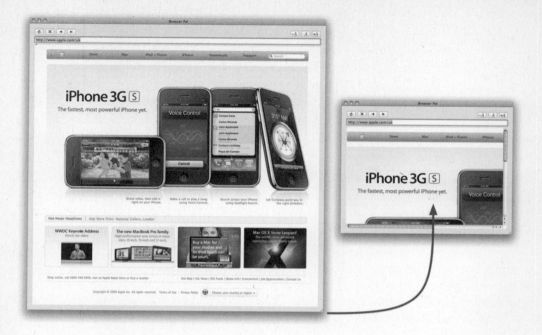

Figure 5–4. *Running the web browser application*

Check that you can use the text size buttons to make text larger, smaller or standard. Try loading a few pages and check that the back, forward, and stop buttons work. Check that you can resize the window (as shown in Figure 5–4).

Let's just briefly review what you have done here. Without writing a line of code—simply by using a sophisticated framework, creating and connecting up controls—you have created a fully functional web browser. OK, it's not Safari, and you don't have bookmarks, printing, saving, or a host of other features. (Well, not yet perhaps.) The head start you have with the WebKit framework means that you never have to worry about how to create the core of a web browser, which is probably the hardest part of the job.

The Core Data Framework—Building a Simple Database Application

For your second example, you are going to use the Core Data framework. This is Apple's framework for modeling, creating, and managing database applications. You are going to create another application without code (don't worry—you will be writing some Objective-C before the end of this chapter, and you will be doing a lot of coding with Core Data in the coming chapters).

For this example you are going to be creating a database program to manage subscription information for a Mac User Group.

For database applications, more than any other type of program, planning is important if you don't want to waste a lot of time on rewriting. So the first job here is to design the data model—that is, the collection of entities and attributes that is going to hold your data. Get this right and everything else tends to follow happily along. A quick sketch with pencil and paper should do it.

I ended up with a single entity for our subscribers, and one for their computers. Now to make this into a data model within Xcode...

Start up Xcode and choose a new project. This will be a Cocoa application, but this time select the **Use Core Data for storage** checkbox. Call it "MUGsub".

Once in the **Xcode Project Workspace** window you will see that there is an additional item in the **Detail** pane, called `MUGsub_DataModel.xcdatamodel`. Double-click on this to open the data model editor in a new window (if your display resolution is high enough, you can just choose the datamodel item and edit the model in the editor pane).

The top part of the model editor shows entities (these equate to tables in traditional database-speak), properties (this is where you will add attributes for entities and relationships between the entities), and a detail inspector (for whatever is currently selected to the left). The bottom part (with the graph paper background) will show the model represented graphically.

Thinking about the requirements here, it's likely that you will have two entities— subscribers and computers—that map onto the objects you want to track. In Xcode language, tables are entities, fields are attributes, and the relationships are, well, relationships. Click on the **Add** button beneath the **Entity** pane and create an entity called "subscriber" (use the Inspector to the right to edit the name). Do the same thing again to add an entity called "computer". Your editor should look like Figure 5–5. Note that in the lower part of the editor you have objects representing the two entities.

Now you are going to add the attributes for the subscriber entity. In the **Property** pane, use the **Add** button to create an attribute. Call it "firstname". This is going to be a `String`, so choose **String** from the drop-down menu in the Inspector. You will notice as you add the attributes that the entity in the graphical representation updates to reflect the values.

Work through the information in Table 5–3 to populate all of the attribute information for the subscriber and computer entities.

These are the entities with their attributes. There's something missing though: the relationship between these entities. It's probably fair to say that more than one subscriber will have a particular model of computer (all Macs, naturally) so there is a One-To-Many relationship (one computer model to many subscribers). To achieve this you need to add two relationships.

First, select the **subscriber** entity. In the middle panel, click the **Add** button and choose to add a relationship. Call this relationship "maincomputer". Set the **computer** entity as the **Destination**. Leave the **Inverse** popup for now, and leave the **To-Many** box unchecked.

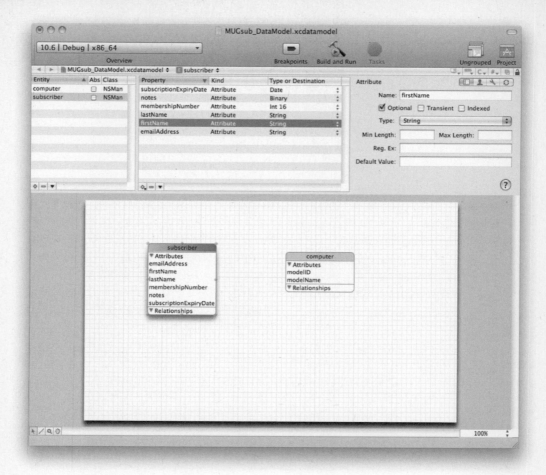

Figure 5–5. *Adding entities*

For the other relationship, choose the **computer** entity, click on the **Add** button in the
middle panel and add a relationship called "owners" (notice the plural—this is a
convention for a To-Many relationship). Choose **subscriber** as the **Destination** entity and
check the **To-Many** checkbox. You should see two arrows linking the entities. Now click
on the **Inverse** popup and choose **maincomputer** as the inverse relationship. Now the
arrows will collapse into one, with a single head pointing to the **computer** entity and a
double head pointing to "subscriber".

Once you are done your model should look like Figure 5–6. If it doesn't, don't worry—it's
easy to miss something when you are doing this. Go carefully over Table 5–3.

Table 5–3. *The Subscriber Entity, Attributes, and Data Types*

Entity	Attribute	Data Type
subscriber	firstName	String
subscriber	lastName	String
subscriber	membershipNumber	Integer16
subscriber	emailAddress	String
subscriber	subscriptionExpiryDate	Date
subscriber	notes	Binary data
computer	modelName	String
computer	modelID	String

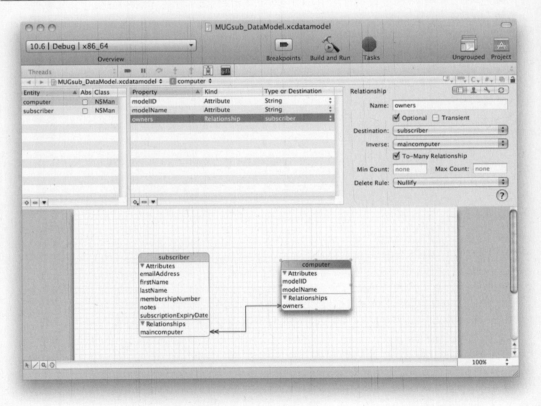

Figure 5–6. *The completed datamodel for the MUGsub application*

The notes field is set as binary data so that you can use that field for rich text later on if we choose. Also, note that you cannot have spaces in entity or attribute names.

Your datamodel is complete. Save and close the datamodel editor window. Now, you have the model for your application established—the first part of the MVC triumvirate. Next, the view and controller. Back in the project workspace, double-click the MainMenu.xib entry to open up the NIB file. Open up the main user interface window if it is not already open and give it a title—say, "MUG Subscribers Database".

There is one bit of forward planning that is worth doing here. You could choose to put each entity in its own window, but for a fairly simple system like this it seems like overkill. Instead, let's put a tabbed panel control into the window and use tabs for our entities. So, drag a Tab View object out of the Library. Click on the first tab button and give it the title "Subscribers". Do likewise for the second button, calling it "Computers". Now you can get on with populating the user interface with the data controls.

Since you are using the Core Data framework, the otherwise complex business of connecting up the view and controller to the model has some nice shortcuts. Choose the **Library** window and find **Core Data** under the **Objects & Controllers** section (by the way, you can use a Spotlight-style search to quickly filter out the library item you are after: try typing **Core** into the search box at the bottom). Drag the Core Data Entity controller into the user interface window.

This brings up the **New Core Data Entity Interface Assistant**. In this window, choose the only project and data model on offer. In a really complex development environment you may have several data models to choose from, but not for this example. In the next column, choose the subscriber entity, then click the **Next** button. In this window, you can choose how you want the data from that entity to be displayed. Choose **Master/Detail View** and select all three checkboxes. By selecting these options, you will see a main table view representing your entity, and as you choose each row in the table you will see the details for that record elsewhere in the window. The **Add/Remove** checkbox provides you with the buttons necessary to maintain database records.

Choose the **Next** button again and you will be able to choose which attributes to display from this entity (see Figure 5–7—if your model has relationships, then you will be able to select those here, too).

The available properties are all checked by default; leave them that way and choose **Finish**.

You should now see your user interface populated with a range of controls In truth, the user interface is not very attractive at this stage: the ordering of controls is not logical; the control for your notes field is, for some reason, an Image View; and the whole layout is a little cramped. However, you can sort that out fairly easily. The important thing to note is that Interface Builder has created a complete user interface for your Core Data application, *including making all of the necessary connections.* Most of what you need to do to make this a complete working application is now done. Let's go ahead and check what is here and what needs to be sorted out.

Figure 5–7. *The Core Data Assistant*

Before investigating the user interface in depth, take a look at the **Document** window. You should see two new array controllers have appeared, called Subscribers Array Controller and Computers Array Controller. As you will see soon, these are already wired up to your user interface—that is the Data Assistant's handiwork. You may be wondering why you have two array controllers, by the way. This is because you need to manage not just the attributes for the subscriber entity, but also the relationship with the **computer** entity. Each needs a controller.

> **TIP:** I tend to use a naming convention for objects in the **Document** window; for example, I renamed the two array controllers here to `acSubscribers` and `acComputerForSubscriber`—the latter indicating that it is a controller managing a relationship. This helps avoid confusion if you have a number of array controllers to manage (as you will in this project shortly).

First, you will see that all of the controls are grouped together in a box. This is a feature of Interface Builder that you may want to use in other cases. In this case we already have the controls collected in a tab control, so let's remove the box. To do this, deselect everything and then click once on the title of the box (if you have followed the example so far this will say "Subscriber"), then choose the menu item **Layout➤Unembed Objects**. All of the objects are now available to move and resize as you wish in the interface.

You can use the adjacent menu item to embed a selection of objects in the user interface in a variety of containers, such as a box (as is the case here), a tab view, a scroll view, and so on. So in fact you could have simply dropped the Core Data Entity controller onto the bare window and embedded the controls in a tab view afterwards; at least you now know more than one way to achieve the result.

The next thing to address is the table view. The Assistant has added all of the available fields to both the Master (Table View) and Detail Views in the interface. There's no need for both, so let's just remove some of those unneeded table columns (select and delete). While you're at it, tidy up the window generally: size it to about 800 × 600 pixels and move the various controls around to improve the layout. Figure 5–8 shows an improved user interface, though you can definitely improve on this!

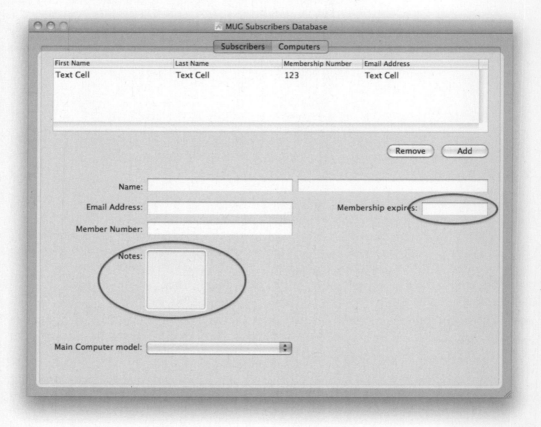

Figure 5–8. *Improving the user interface*

Actually, this exercise exposes some of the shortcomings of the Core Data Assistant. Apart from the interesting ordering of controls, there are a couple of problems with the controls themselves. First, the **Notes** field ought to be a Text View, not an Image Well. Second, the field where you are intending to put the subscription expiry date is a Text Field (albeit one with a Date Formatter), which is not the friendliest way to enter a date. These are indicated in Figure 5–8. These are easy enough to rectify. Just drag out a Text View control and a Date Picker control and drop them in a convenient place in the window. Don't delete the existing controls yet—they have some useful information to impart!

The biggest benefit of the Core Data Assistant is that it doesn't just create user interface objects for you—it also creates and connects these controls to the appropriate controllers using Data Bindings. Let's see how this works. Select the Text Field for the date attribute (the little orange button that appears next to it, by the way, is the formatter—use this to configure the format of the content of the Text Field) and then choose the **Bindings** tab in the Inspector. See Figure 5–9.

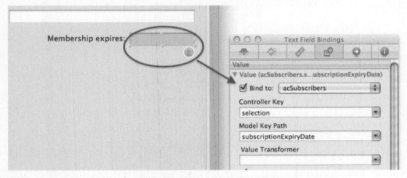

Figure 5–9. *Inspecting the Data Bindings for the expiry date Text Field*

The object on the user interface window is bound to the subscribers controller (this is the controller that the Assistant created for you) and specifically to the `subscriptionExpiryDate` attribute value for the current selection. In other words, whatever subscriber is currently selected will have an expiry date, and the value of that will be passed by the controller to this control. OK—let's add the same binding to our new Date Picker control. Select the Date Picker and inspect its bindings. There aren't any yet, of course, because this is a new control freshly added from the Library. Find the **Value** section and open it up using the disclosure arrow. From the **Bind to:** popup, choose the **Subscribers** array controller, and select the checkbox next to it. From the **Controller Key** popup, choose **selection**, and from the **Model Key Path** popup, choose **subscriptionExpiryDate**. Now you can delete the old Text Field and position the Date Picker as you want it. Notice in Figure 5–10 that I have chosen to display the graphical form of the Date Picker. You can optionally choose the text version with a stepper arrow.

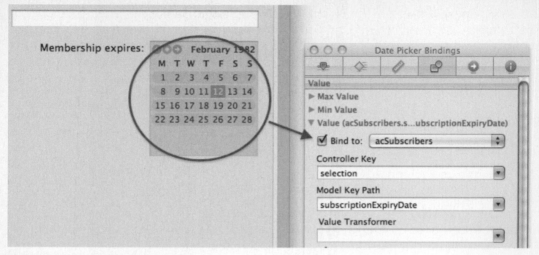

Figure 5–10. *The updated Date control*

You can use the same approach to replace the Image Well with the Text View, so I'm not going to describe it step by step.

The main item that I haven't yet described is the **Main Computer** popup. As the name suggests, this is where you will be able to see or set the main model of computer owned by the current subscriber. Select this popup and inspect the bindings. The popup uses the `maincomputer` relationship of the `acComputerForSubscriber` controller, it is holding a collection of **computer** entities, and it is ready to display the `modelName` attribute for the selected **computer** entity.

Right, that's the **Subscribers** tab dealt with. Now for the **Computers** tab. Repeat the exercise with the Assistant: drag out a Core Data Entity array controller and follow the Assistant through. Choose Master-Detail again and select all of the attributes and the relationship (called *owners*).

Tidy up the user interface again—a smaller job this time as there aren't many attributes to consider.

There is something odd, though. On the **Subscribers** tab you saw an interface control that supports the relationship between the subscriber and computer entities. You might have expected to see something similar here—maybe a Table View to show the list of users for the currently-selected computer model. But there isn't, and if you look at the **Document** window it has created only one controller (which I named "acComputers"). It seems to be one of the shortcomings of the Assistant that the "many" end of the "To-Many" relationship doesn't get automatically created. No matter, it'll be instructive to create it manually.

First you are going to need a new array controller. Drag one into the **Computers** window and call it "acSubscribersForComputer".

You need to provide this with a binding to the Subscribers array controller, and particularly to the relationship called *owners* (since that's what we want ultimately to put in the list). So, select the `acSubscribersForComputer` controller and create a binding in the **Controller Content (Content Set)** section. Bind this controller to the `acComputers` controller, choosing selection as the **Controller Key** and owners as the **Model Key Path** (you will see that this is abbreviated to `acComputers.selection.owners` in the panel).

Now I need somewhere to show the data in the user interface. Drag an NSTableView into the **Computers** window. Give this Table View two columns and bind the columns to the `acSubscribersForComputer` controller, choosing the **Value** section. Give Column 1 the binding `acSubscribersForComputer.arrangedObjects.firstName` and Column 2 the binding `acSubscribersForComputer.arrangedObjects.lastName`.

That is it—the user interface and all of the wiring is complete. Adding objects and bindings in this way can seem a little involved at first, but they are quite logical.

You are ready to try out the application. To run the application, save the NIB file, return to Xcode, and choose **Build and Go**. You should see a running program something like Figure 5–11. You can see on the **Computers** tab the list of computer models and also the people who own the currently selected model.

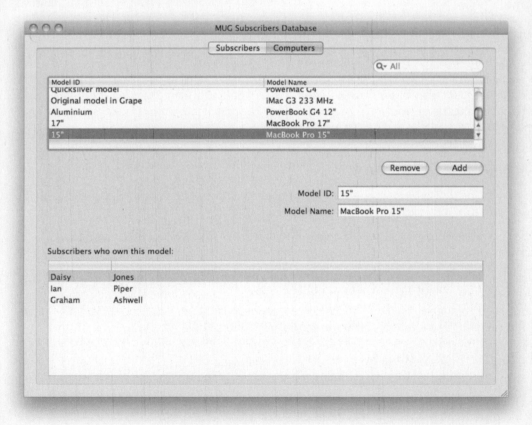

Figure 5–11. *The MUGsub application running, showing the To-Many relationship*

A Potential Gotcha

As you work with a data model in Core Data you may find yourself suddenly confronted with this error message on running the program:

"The model configuration used to open the store is incompatible with the one that was used to create the store."

While alarming, this error message is easily sorted out. By default, Core Data stores its data in an XML file (there are other storage options and you will cover those later). If you have changed the data model, the version stored the first time you ran the program may be different to the current storage structure. Hence this message—your program doesn't understand the structure of the data store.

The solution is simply to find the persistent store (by default this will be ~/Library/Application Support/[your application name]/storedata and just delete the file. Go ahead—it will be regenerated the next time you run the program (of course, you will lose any data in the store, sadly). There is an alternative, which you might like to investigate if the data is too important to lose. Xcode provides migration tools to allow you to migrate data from one version of a data model to another. Search the Developer Documentation for "Core Data Migration" or look here: http://developer.apple.com/mac/library/documentation/Cocoa/Conceptual/CoreDataV ersioning/Introduction/Introduction.html. This is a quite advanced topic and you should aim to be comfortable with Core Data programming before investigating it in-depth.

Choosing a Data Store

You may be wondering where your database is located. Nothing in this example so far has indicated how or where your data is being stored.

In fact, Core Data gives you a degree of choice about this. By default, your data is stored as an XML file in the location ~/Library/Application Support/[your application name]/storedata as mentioned in the previous section, "A Potential Gotcha." However, you also have the option to store it in SQLite or binary formats. Here's how.

Look in the file MUG_AppDelegate.m and find the method called persistentStoreCoordinator. In Listing 5–1 you will see the significant code fragment:

Listing 5–1. *Setting the Storage Options for a Core Data Application*

```
NSURL *url = [NSURL fileURLWithPath: [applicationSupportDirectory
stringByAppendingPathComponent: @"storedata"]];
    persistentStoreCoordinator = [[NSPersistentStoreCoordinator alloc]
initWithManagedObjectModel: mom];
    if (![persistentStoreCoordinator addPersistentStoreWithType:NSXMLStoreType
                                        configuration:nil
                                        URL:url
```

```
                                 options:nil
                                 error:&error]){
      [[NSApplication sharedApplication] presentError:error];
      [persistentStoreCoordinator release], persistentStoreCoordinator = nil;
      return nil;
   }
}
```

The first bold section shows the file name used to store your data. You can actually give this any name you like: a.b, for example. The second bold section is where you choose the storage format. Your choices are NSXMLStoreType (the default, as an XML file), NSSQLiteStoreType (for a SQLite database) or NSBinaryStoreType (for the more traditional binary data format used for Mac OS X data stores before the days of Core Data).

The Core Data framework is a very large and complex component of Cocoa, and you have barely scratched the surface here. You will return to Core Data programming in much more depth in Chapter 9.

The ScreenSaver Framework

Screen savers in Mac OS X, like in other operating systems, are normal applications, but with some additional features that allow them to fit into the screen saver mechanism that is managed within **System Preferences**. In this section, you are going to build a screen saver that makes use of the OpenGL drawing framework.

I make no pretence of being an OpenGL developer, by the way. The example that you will follow here draws on some great resources, notably the chapter on OpenGL programming in Aaron Hillegass's master work *Cocoa Programming for Mac OS X*, 3rd Edition, and also the excellent articles by Brian Christensen on the Cocoa Dev Central website (www.cocoadevcentral.com). The code here should be easy to follow, but you can get more detail on the underlying code in these and other resources.

You are going to create a screen saver that shows the famous OpenGL teapot. When it is complete the screen saver will look like this (see Figure 5–12).

You start in the by now familiar way, although unlike most Cocoa projects you are not going to use Interface Builder in this example. In Xcode, choose a new project. This time choose the **System Plug-in** item in the **User templates** list and select **Screen Saver**.

Give the project the name "TumblingTeapot". You will see the usual Xcode project window, but notice the ScreenSaver.framework item in the detail list.

Take a look at the structure of your class (TumblingTeapot.m). All of the basic routines for your screensaver are already there. In fact, this is already a working screensaver. If you really wanted, you could build this and install it. Of course, all it would do is give you a blank screen, but if you should ever want a simple blank screen saver, this is one way to do it!

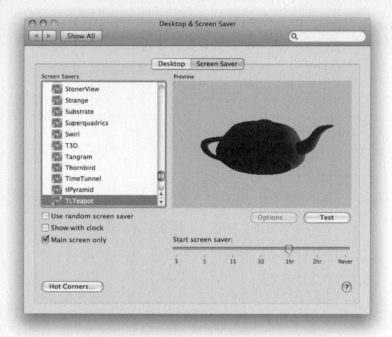

Figure 5–12. *The completed Tumbling Teapot screen saver*

The main methods in this class are in Table 5–4.

Table 5–4. *Methods Provided in the Default Screen Saver Project*

initWithFrame	This is where any initialization needs to happen.
startAnimation	Anything that needs to happen at the beginning of the animation stage can go in here.
stopAnimation	Likewise, anything that happens at the end of the animation goes here.
drawRect	This is the main drawing routine. All of the code that delivers your images, if it is anything more than really trivial, should go here.
animateOneFrame	This controls the animation process for the screen saver. In this example, it is simply setting up a motion and asking the display to redraw.
hasConfigureSheet	If your screen saver has configuration parameters, set the return value here to true.
configureSheet	If you have set hasConfigureSheet to YES then you need to code the loading of the configuration sheet here.

The main work to do here is to add code to the appropriate methods, as well as to create a few extra utility methods.

Before you get going on the coding, you need to bring in two other frameworks: OpenGL.framework and GLUT.framework (the latter is there just to provide access to the teapot drawing functions). To add these frameworks, right-click on the project name in the **Groups and Files** list and choose **Add Existing Frameworks**. Select OpenGL.framework and GLUT.framework (use the Command key to select both at once), then choose the **Add** button. Now the workspace shows the added frameworks.

You need to start by opening up TumblingTeapot.h and adding the variables you will need (see the bold text in Listing 5–2).

Listing 5–2. *TumblingTeapot.h*

```
#import <ScreenSaver/ScreenSaver.h>

@interface TumblingTeapotView : ScreenSaverView {
    NSOpenGLView *glView;
    GLfloat rotation;
    int displayList;
}

- (void)startUpOpenGL;

@end
```

The NSOpenGLView here is where you will construct the image later.

Move to TumblingTeapot.m (by the way, there are two shortcuts for moving between the .h and .m counterparts in the Xcode editor. One is to click the little icon that looks like two overlapping squares at the top right of the editor, and the other is to use the keyboard shortcut ⌘ ⌥ up arrow).

As a first step, add the import statement for glut.h (the bold line—it's easy to forget it later, in all the excitement). See Listing 5–3.

Listing 5–3. *Adding the Import Statement*

```
#import <GLUT/glut.h>
#import "TumblingTeapotView.h"

@implementation TumblingTeapotView
```

You are going to add the NSOpenGLView as a sub-view of the ScreenSaverView. Edit the initWithFrame method to look like this (added lines are in bold in Listing 5–4):

Listing 5–4. *Adding the NSOpenGLView as a Subview of ScreenSaverView*

```
- (id)initWithFrame:(NSRect)frame isPreview:(BOOL)isPreview
{
    self = [super initWithFrame:frame isPreview:isPreview];
    if (self) {
        NSOpenGLPixelFormatAttribute attributes[] = {NSOpenGLPFAAccelerated,
NSOpenGLPFADepthSize, 16, NSOpenGLPFAMinimumPolicy, NSOpenGLPFAClosestPolicy, 0};
        NSOpenGLPixelFormat *format;

        format = [[[NSOpenGLPixelFormat alloc] initWithAttributes:attributes]
autorelease];
```

```
        glView = [[NSOpenGLView alloc] initWithFrame:NSZeroRect pixelFormat:format];
        if (!glView) {
            NSLog(@"Couldn't get OpenGL View going");
            [self autorelease];
            return nil;
        }
        [self addSubview:glView];
        [self startUpOpenGL];
        [self setAnimationTimeInterval:1/30.0];
    }
    return self;
}
```

This method does some special OpenGL initializations, then adds the subview and calls
the startUpOpenGL method. Add the method now, after the initWithFrame method (see
Listing 5–5).

Listing 5–5. *startUpOpenGL*

```
- (void)startUpOpenGL {
    NSLog(@"starting up OpenGL");
    [[glView openGLContext] makeCurrentContext];

    // configure the view
    glShadeModel(GL_SMOOTH);
    glEnable(GL_LIGHTING);
    glEnable(GL_DEPTH_TEST);

    // add ambient lighting
    GLfloat ambient[] = {0.2, 0.2, 0.2, 1.0};
    glLightModelfv(GL_LIGHT_MODEL_AMBIENT, ambient);

    // initialise the light
    GLfloat diffuse[] = {1.0, 1.0, 1.0, 1.0};
    glLightfv(GL_LIGHT0, GL_DIFFUSE, diffuse);
    // turn light on
    glEnable(GL_LIGHT0);

    // set material properties under ambient light
    // These values for the mat array will give a
// dark purple colour to the teapot
    GLfloat mat[] = {0.9, 0.1, 0.7, 1.0};
    glMaterialfv(GL_FRONT, GL_AMBIENT, mat);
    // set material properties under diffuse light
    glMaterialfv(GL_FRONT, GL_DIFFUSE, mat);
rotation = 0.0f;

}
```

The next method sets the frame size. This method is called when the view is initialized
and whenever the view is resized and we don't need explicitly to call it (see Listing 5–6).

Listing 5–6. *setFrameSize*

```
-(void)setFrameSize:(NSSize)newSize {
    [super setFrameSize:newSize];
    [glView setFrameSize:newSize];
    [[glView openGLContext] makeCurrentContext];
```

```
glViewport(0, 0, (GLsizei)newSize.width, (GLsizei)newSize.height);
glMatrixMode(GL_PROJECTION);
glLoadIdentity();
glMatrixMode(GL_MODELVIEW);
glLoadIdentity();
[[glView openGLContext] update];
}
```

Next comes the drawRect method, where the really hard work is happening. Once again, this method is called when the view needs to redraw and does not need to be explicitly called (see Listing 5–7).

Listing 5–7. drawRect

```
- (void)drawRect:(NSRect)rect
{
    [super drawRect:rect];
    [[glView openGLContext] makeCurrentContext];
    // clear the background - this sets a pale blue-ish background
    glClearColor(0.75, 0.75, 0.95, 0.0);
    glClear(GL_COLOR_BUFFER_BIT | GL_DEPTH_BUFFER_BIT);
    // set the viewpoint
    glMatrixMode(GL_MODELVIEW);
    glLoadIdentity();
    // the arguments to glRotatef determine the axes of rotation
    // (in this case, x and y)
glRotatef( rotation, 1.0f, 1.0f, 0.0f );
    // put the light in place
    GLfloat lightPosition [] = {1.6, 1, 3, 0.0};
    glLightfv(GL_LIGHT0, GL_POSITION, lightPosition);
    if (!displayList) {
        displayList = glGenLists(1);
        glNewList(displayList, GL_COMPILE_AND_EXECUTE);
        // do the drawing - this draws a teapot at the center of the viewport
        glTranslatef(0, 0, 0);
        glutSolidTeapot(0.5);
        glEndList();
    } else {
        glCallList(displayList);
    }
    glFinish();

}
```

First the graphics context is established. This is in effect the environment in which the drawing happens. Then the method clears the view and sets the background to a pale blue color. It then sets up a variety of OpenGL properties governing the placement and lighting for the diagram. Finally it draws the teapot. Note that if you go exploring in glut.h you will find method signatures for a whole range of shapes, including spheres, toruses, cubes, and so on. You might like to try adding drawing steps for other shapes either in addition or as alternatives to the teapot.

Now add the code for the animation. This is much shorter—it simply sets the incremental rotation for the object and refreshes the display. If this were a simple example, all of the drawing code might be in animateOneFrame, and in that case you wouldn't need to add the setNeedsDisplay command (see Listing 5–8).

Listing 5–8. *animateOneFrame*

```
- (void)animateOneFrame
{
    rotation += 0.2f;
    [self setNeedsDisplay:YES];
}
```

You are also going to need a `dealloc` method to ensure you free up the memory you have allocated, shown in Listing 5–9:

Listing 5–9. Freeing Up the Unneeded Memory

```
- (void)dealloc {
    [glView removeFromSuperview];
    [glView release];
    [super dealloc];
}
```

If you have galloped ahead and built and installed the screen saver, you will probably have noticed that it doesn't work. I'm afraid I have deliberately left it until now to mention that there is a peculiarity (let's not mince words—to a relative layman like me, it's a bug) in the way that `drawRect` works. It has to do with opaque views. In effect your screen saver is working, it's just working in an opaque view, and hence you can't see anything.

This needs fixing, obviously. Here is what you do.

First, create a new Objective-C class file. Call it "TLOpenGLView" (create the `.h` and `.m` files when asked). Now, make the `TLOpenGLView.h` file look like this (only the bold line in Listing 5–10 needs changing):

Listing 5–10. *Fixing the View Opacity in the TLOpenGLView Header File*

```
#import <Cocoa/Cocoa.h>


@interface TLOpenGLView : NSOpenGLView {

}

@end
```

In the corresponding `.m` file, you need to tell the application that the view is not opaque after all (see Listing 5–11):

Listing 5–11. *Fixing the View Opacity in the TLOpenGLView Implementation File*

```
#import "TLOpenGLView.h"


@implementation TLOpenGLView

- (BOOL)isOpaque {

    return NO;
}

@end
```

Next, you need to visit the TumblingTeapot.h file (see Listing 5–12):

Listing 5–12. *Implementing the Changes in TumblingTeapot.h*

```
#import <ScreenSaver/ScreenSaver.h>
#import "TLOpenGLView.h"

@interface TumblingTeapotView : ScreenSaverView
{
    TLOpenGLView *glView;
    GLfloat rotation;
    int displayList;
}

- (void)startUpOpenGL;


@end
```

And finally you need to make a single change in TumblingTeapot.m, in the initWithFrame method, shown in Listing 5–13:

Listing 5–13. *The Final Change in TumblingTeapot.m*

```
- (id)initWithFrame:(NSRect)frame isPreview:(BOOL)isPreview

{
    self = [super initWithFrame:frame isPreview:isPreview];
    if (self) {
        NSOpenGLPixelFormatAttribute attributes[] = {NSOpenGLPFAAccelerated,
NSOpenGLPFADepthSize, 16, NSOpenGLPFAMinimumPolicy, NSOpenGLPFAClosestPolicy, 0};
        NSOpenGLPixelFormat *format;

        format = [[[NSOpenGLPixelFormat alloc] initWithAttributes:attributes]
autorelease];
        glView = [[TLOpenGLView alloc] initWithFrame:NSZeroRect pixelFormat:format];
        if (!glView) {
            NSLog(@"Couldn't get Open GL View going");
            [self autorelease];
            return nil;
        }
        [self addSubview:glView];
        [self startUpOpenGL];
        [self setAnimationTimeInterval:1/30.0];
    }
    return self;
}
```

Listings 5–14 to 5–17 show the completed TLOpenGLView.h, TLOpenGLView.m, TumblingTeapot.h, and TumblingTeapot.m files.

Listing 5–14. *TLOpenGLView.h*

```
#import <Cocoa/Cocoa.h>

@interface TLOpenGLView : NSOpenGLView {

}
```

```
@end
```

Listing 5–15. *TLOpenGLView.m*

```objc
#import "TLOpenGLView.h"

@implementation TLOpenGLView

- (BOOL)isOpaque {

    return NO;
}

@end
```

Listing 5–16. *TumblingTeapot.h*

```objc
#import <ScreenSaver/ScreenSaver.h>
#import "TLOpenGLView.h"

@interface TumblingTeapotView : ScreenSaverView
{
    TLOpenGLView *glView;
    GLfloat rotation;
    int displayList;
}

- (void)startUpOpenGL;

@end
```

Listing 5–17. *TumblingTeapot.m*

```objc
#import "TumblingTeapotView.h"
#import <GLUT/glut.h>

@implementation TumblingTeapotView

- (id)initWithFrame:(NSRect)frame isPreview:(BOOL)isPreview
{
    self = [super initWithFrame:frame isPreview:isPreview];
    if (self) {
        NSOpenGLPixelFormatAttribute attributes[] = {NSOpenGLPFAAccelerated,
NSOpenGLPFADepthSize, 16, NSOpenGLPFAMinimumPolicy, NSOpenGLPFAClosestPolicy, 0};
        NSOpenGLPixelFormat *format;

        format = [[[NSOpenGLPixelFormat alloc] initWithAttributes:attributes]
autorelease];
        glView = [[TLOpenGLView alloc] initWithFrame:NSZeroRect pixelFormat:format];
        if (!glView) {
            NSLog(@"Couldn't get OpenGL View going");
            [self autorelease];
            return nil;
        }
        [self addSubview:glView];
        [self startUpOpenGL];
        [self setAnimationTimeInterval:1/30.0];
    }
    return self;
}
```

```objc
- (void)dealloc {
    [glView removeFromSuperview];
    [glView release];
    [super dealloc];
}

- (void)startUpOpenGL {
    NSLog(@"starting up OpenGL");
    [[glView openGLContext] makeCurrentContext];

    // configure the view
    glShadeModel(GL_SMOOTH);
    glEnable(GL_LIGHTING);
    glEnable(GL_DEPTH_TEST);

    // add ambient lighting
    GLfloat ambient[] = {0.2, 0.2, 0.2, 1.0};
    glLightModelfv(GL_LIGHT_MODEL_AMBIENT, ambient);

    // initialise the light
    GLfloat diffuse[] = {1.0, 1.0, 1.0, 1.0};
    glLightfv(GL_LIGHT0, GL_DIFFUSE, diffuse);
    // turn light on
    glEnable(GL_LIGHT0);

    // set material properties under ambient light
    // These values for the mat array will give a
    // dark purple colour to the teapot
    GLfloat mat[] = {0.9, 0.1, 0.7, 1.0};
    glMaterialfv(GL_FRONT, GL_AMBIENT, mat);
    // set material properties under diffuse light
    glMaterialfv(GL_FRONT, GL_DIFFUSE, mat);
    rotation = 0.0f;
}

-(void)setFrameSize:(NSSize)newSize {
    [super setFrameSize:newSize];
    [glView setFrameSize:newSize];
    [[glView openGLContext] makeCurrentContext];
    glViewport(0, 0, (GLsizei)newSize.width, (GLsizei)newSize.height);
    glMatrixMode(GL_PROJECTION);
    glLoadIdentity();
    glMatrixMode(GL_MODELVIEW);
    glLoadIdentity();
    [[glView openGLContext] update];
}


- (void)startAnimation
{
    [super startAnimation];
}

- (void)stopAnimation
{
    [super stopAnimation];
```

```
}

- (void)drawRect:(NSRect)rect
{
    [super drawRect:rect];
    [[glView openGLContext] makeCurrentContext];
    // clear the background
    glClearColor(0.75, 0.75, 0.95, 0.0);
    glClear(GL_COLOR_BUFFER_BIT | GL_DEPTH_BUFFER_BIT);
    // set the viewpoint
    glMatrixMode(GL_MODELVIEW);
    glLoadIdentity();
    glRotatef( rotation, 1.0f, 1.0f, 0.0f );
    // put the light in place
    GLfloat lightPosition [] = {1.6, 1, 3, 0.0};
    glLightfv(GL_LIGHT0, GL_POSITION, lightPosition);

    if (!displayList) {
        displayList = glGenLists(1);
        glNewList(displayList, GL_COMPILE_AND_EXECUTE);
        // do the drawing
        glTranslatef(0, 0, 0);
        glutSolidTeapot(0.5);
        glEndList();
    } else {
        glCallList(displayList);
    }
    glFinish();

}


- (void)animateOneFrame
{
    rotation += 0.2f;
[self setNeedsDisplay:YES];}

- (BOOL)hasConfigureSheet
{
    return NO;
}

- (NSWindow*)configureSheet
{
    return nil;
}
```

@end

Right, it's time to run the finished screensaver. You can't actually run or simulate screen savers within Xcode, so there is nothing for it but to install it. First, build the application (use ⌘B, or choose the **Build Build** menu item. All being well you should see the message "Build succeeded" in the Xcode workspace status bar. Having built it, you need to go and find the built application. In the Finder, locate your project folder, and in that open the build and then Debug folders. You should see your newly created TumblingTeapot.saver file.

Double-click this file and you will see a message asking whether you want to install the screen saver just for you or for all users. Choose one of the options (it doesn't really matter which—it's probably easier to install it just for you since you then don't need to authenticate as an admin user) and click Install.

Summary

You've achieved a lot in this chapter. By now you should be very comfortable working with Interface Builder, and understanding how actions, connections, and bindings work. You have grappled with some of the most important Cocoa frameworks and have written some neat applications into the bargain.

In Chapter 6, you are going to take a closer look at Model View Controller, the design principle that underlies most of the development work you will do in Cocoa. You will see a couple of examples that I hope will cement this architectural pattern for you (remember, this is one of those major barriers to understanding that you need to overcome to get a good working relationship with Cocoa). If you have ever seen this phrase, or its acronym "MVC," batted around and felt that you weren't quite sure what it meant, this next chapter is for you.

Chapter 6

Model-View-Controller in Xcode

The Model-View-Controller pattern (or MVC as it is more commonly known) is at the heart of modern object-oriented software development.

MVC can cause a lot of confusion in the mind of the new developer, but the principles governing its use are fairly easy to understand. More importantly for you as a Cocoa developer, MVC is absolutely fundamental to using Xcode and Cocoa for Mac OS X development. That is why it is now time to take a short detour away from tools to nail this particular technology. In this chapter you are going to cover the fundamentals underlying MVC, and in particular the way in which it applies to Cocoa development using Xcode tools. You will take a look under the hood of a variety of projects to explore their MVC credentials.

If you are already comfortable with the MVC architectural pattern, you may want to skip this chapter, though you may still find it useful to see how the principles are applied in Cocoa.

Understanding MVC

The Model-View-Controller pattern is one of a number of architectural and design patterns that emerged from the object-oriented design community. In fact, its origins can be traced back to Smalltalk, though it was first properly described by Trygve Reenskaug (for a potted history, see http://heim.ifi.uio.no/~trygver/themes/mvc/mvc-index.html).

The simple idea behind MVC is *separation of concerns*. This means that the components of a software system are separated (the word often used here is *decomposed)* into three categories:

- Those that are concerned with managing structure and storage of data (the Model)

- Those that are concerned with providing a user interface and interaction (the View)

- Those that govern the flow of control in the application and the traffic of information between the View and the Model (the Controller)

The Controller is the lynchpin in this design: instances of the Model only communicate with the user interface via the Controller, for example.

Using MVC in your software design reduces the coupling between your objects (the degree to which one component in your design depends on another). Ideally, you want each component to behave as independently as possible. Doing this means it's easier to reuse and replace your components. For example, you could switch your data store from SQLite to MySQL without having to recode the mechanisms that use the data. Or you might want to display or use the information produced by your system using a web browser instead of a desktop program.

To see what this means when you design software in Cocoa, let's take a closer look at each part of MVC, with a couple of examples.

ARCHITECTURAL AND DESIGN PATTERNS

This is not a book about programming languages or techniques, so there is not a great deal of room to talk about patterns in depth. The best definition of patterns I have come across is that they are templates that offer best-practice approaches to architecting systems and designing code to solve common, recurring software problems.

There are some excellent resources on patterns, no further than a Google away, and of course the original "Gang of Four" book (*Design Patterns: Elements of Reusable Object-Oriented Software* by Gamma, Helm, Johnson, and Vlissides) is the classic work.

Several writers have observed that in the evolution of software development languages good architectural and design patterns simply become part of the language. You can see how many of the original design patterns have been implemented within the Cocoa frameworks in this review on the Apple Developer site: `http://developer.apple.com/documentation/Cocoa/Conceptual/CocoaFundamentals/Coc oaDesignPatterns/CocoaDesignPatterns.html`.

The Simplest Example

Even the simplest applications will have a Model, View, and Controller. Let's take a look at the simplest application you have built so far in this book, the simple Hello World program from Chapter 3.

If you followed along with this example, open up the project now (if you didn't create this project yourself, you can download the completed project from the book's page on `http://www.apress.com`).

Open the project and load the NIB file (`MainMenu.xib`). You'll remember that you created the user interface elements—a Text Field control to hold the text entered by the user, a

Label control to hold the text produced by the program and a Button control to initiate the transformation. This collection of components, including the window itself, make up the View. You also then created some connections that determined the routes for carrying messages. These connections all involve the HelloController object. If you right-click (or Control-click) on HelloController in the **Document** window you will see its connections.

This is the Controller. You can see that the Button invokes an action method called sayHello:, and it does that by sending a message to HelloController (in effect, saying "run the sayHello method"). HelloController in turn sends messages to the Text Field (amounting to "tell me what you have") and (once it has the data back from the Text Field) to the Label (amounting to "display this"). The flow of messages is shown in Figure 6–1. So given that both the messages go from HelloController to these objects, how is the program to know which way around things have to happen? Well, go back to the Xcode project window and check out the sayHello method in HelloController.m (see Listing 6–1).

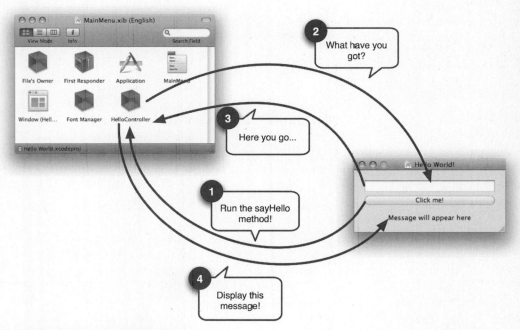

Figure 6–1. *Message flow in Hello World*

Listing 6–1. *The sayHello: Method*

```
@implementation HelloController

- (IBAction)sayHello:(id)sender {
    [destinationTextField setStringValue:[sourceTextField stringValue]];
}
@end
```

The code in bold specifies what needs to happen. Set the content of the Label control (destinationTextField) to the content of the Text Field (sourceTextField).

So where in all of this is the Model? Well, this is a very simple example and the Model in this case is the Text Field into which the user types the message. Nevertheless the fundamentals are the same for most Cocoa programs you will write. The controller takes the data provided by the Model and carries out whatever processing is necessary to interact with the View.

In practice, as you will see in more complex examples, you will have a Controller corresponding to each View component that you need to manage, and an underlying Model.

A More Complex Example

One of the best-known example projects in Cocoa is the Currency Converter project. Let's try a variation on that example and build a temperature converter. This will allow you to enter a temperature value in the Fahrenheit or Centigrade boxes, and the converted value will appear in the other box. The completed project will look like Figure 6–2.

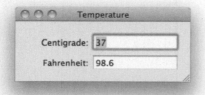

Figure 6–2. *The Temperature Converter program running*

You're a seasoned veteran now, so there's no need to describe this in step-by-step detail. So, create a new Cocoa project (make sure the **Core Data** and **Document-based application** options are not checked) and call it TemperatureConverter. Create a new Objective-C class (and the corresponding header file) and call it Converter. At this stage, your project workspace looks like Figure 6–3:

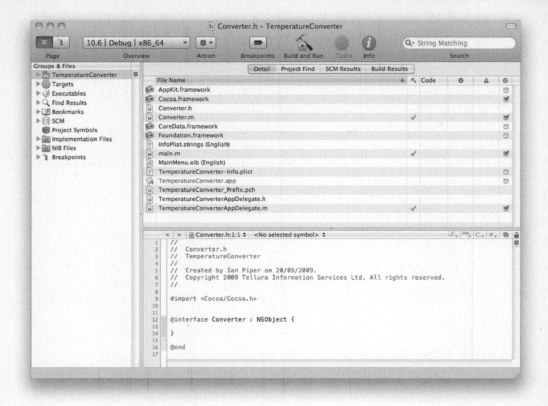

Figure 6–3 . *TemperatureConverter project workspace*

Before building and wiring up the user interface, you are going to add the code. Let's think about the Model first. You have probably already guessed that this is the reason you created the Converter class—this is where your Model is going to live.

The Model for the TemperatureConverter program has to contain a variable for the original temperature, a method or methods for conversion and the Converter class. The conversion process takes an original temperature and returns a converted temperature.

Let's start by declaring the variable.

The Model needs to understand the data and the data manipulation logic. You are going to need methods to do the data conversion and properties to hold the data. Figure 6–4 shows how the messages flow in the application (for simplicity, this figure shows the conversion from Centigrade to Fahrenheit).

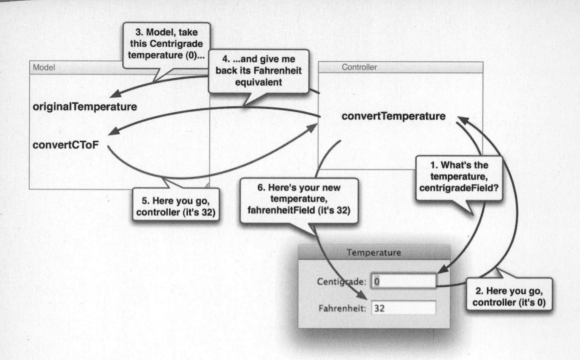

Figure 6–4. *MVC and message flow in the TemperatureConverter application*

A consequence of this design is that the data and the logic for the conversion are stored in the Model. If you wanted to change to a different algorithm for the conversion, or to introduce a different conversion (say, to and from degrees Kelvin), that work would happen almost entirely within the Model. The Controller takes the values from the View (the user interface) and feeds those values into the Model. The resulting value from the conversion is then placed back in the View to update the converted temperature value.

Open Converter.h and make it look like Listing 6–2.

Listing 6–2. *Converter.h*

```
#import <Cocoa/Cocoa.h>

@interface Converter : NSObject {
float originalTemp;
}

@property(readwrite) float originalTemp;

- (float)convertCToF;
- (float)convertFToC;

@end
```

Now open Converter.m and add code to make it look like Listing 6–3.

Listing 6–3. *Converter.m*

```
#import "Converter.h"

@implementation Converter

@synthesize originalTemp;

- (float)convertCToF {
    return ((self.originalTemp * 1.8) + 32.0);
}
- (float)convertFToC {
    return ((self.originalTemp - 32.0) / 1.8);
}
@end
```

This is the Model for the application. The Model will receive an original temperature value, either in centigrade or Fahrenheit, and then the appropriate method will be called (by the Controller, as you will see shortly). After transforming it the Model returns the new temperature value.

Now let's move to the Controller. Open TemperatureConverterAppDelegate.h and add code to it as shown in Listing 6–4.

Listing 6–4. *TemperatureConverterAppDelegate.h*

```
#import <Cocoa/Cocoa.h>
#import "Converter.h"

@interface TemperatureConverterAppDelegate : NSObject <NSApplicationDelegate> {

    IBOutlet NSTextField *centigradeField;
    IBOutlet NSTextField *fahrenheitField;
    Converter *temperatureConverter;
}

- (IBAction)convertTemperature:(id)sender;

@end
```

Note that the Controller imports Converter.h—this makes the Controller aware of the Model. The other declarations in this file are for the outlets that you will be building shortly in Interface Builder, and the method that is invoked by changes in the user interface. Now open the implementation file TemperatureConverterAppDelegate.m and update it to look like Listing 6–5.

Listing 6–5. *TemperatureConverterAppDelegate.m*

```
#import "TemperatureConverterAppDelegate.h"

@implementation TemperatureConverterAppDelegate

@synthesize window;

- (void)awakeFromNib {
    fahrenheitField.floatValue = 32.0;
    centigradeField.floatValue = 0.0;
    tempConverter = Converter.new;
```

```
}

- (IBAction)convertTemperature:(id)sender {
    float temperatureF = fahrenheitField.floatValue;
    float temperatureC = centigradeField.floatValue;
    if(sender == fahrenheitField) {
        tempConverter.originalTemp = temperatureF;
        temperatureC = tempConverter.convertFToC;
        centigradeField.floatValue = temperatureC;
    } else if (sender == centigradeField) {
        tempConverter.originalTemp = temperatureC;
        temperatureF = tempConverter.convertCToF;
        fahrenheitField.floatValue = temperatureF;
    }
}
}

@end
```

The awakeFromNib method simply initializes some objects with starting values. The convertTemperature method takes the value from one Text Field, depending on which is the sender, sets the original temperature value and calls the appropriate method in the Model object, takes back the converted value and places it in the other Text Field.

Notice that the Controller is not aware of exactly how the conversion takes place—that is the concern of the Model.

USING GARBAGE COLLECTION

Experienced Cocoa developers will note (perhaps with horror) that there is no alloc and no dealloc in TemperatureConverterAppDelegate.m. Normally, this is a recipe for disaster—conventional Cocoa memory management practice dictates that you actively manage memory allocation. In practice, this means that you allocate memory for objects and then later, when the objects are no longer needed, you release the memory. If you don't do this, the result is memory leakage and possible crashes.

Objective-C v2.0 introduces garbage collection as an option. This monitors object allocation and automatically releases object memory when an object goes out of scope. The TemperatureConverter project uses garbage collection.

If you want to set up garbage collection for a project, choose the Project▶Edit Project Settings menu.

The Build tab in this window has dozens of options, but you can zero in on the Garbage Collection option using the search field (see Figure 6–7). Change the value for Objective-C Garbage Collection to Required. Also, change the Configuration: popup to All Configurations.

In principle garbage collection (which is a common technology in other application development systems such as Java and C #) offers greater simplicity to the developer. However, it is fair to say that for Objective-C, garbage collection is a new and hot topic of discussion at the time of writing, and for many developers there is no alternative to the conventional alloc-retain-release mechanism.

Now let's turn to the View. Open MainMenu.xib and add two Text Field controls and two Label controls. Your Controller is already there (that's the Temperature Converter App Delegate). Make it look like Figure 6–2. Notice that there is no button—you aren't going to need one in this application.

Note that you don't have to tell Interface Builder about the Model object—this is MVC, and the Controller is the only component in the design that talks to the Model. All you need to do here is wire up the user interface to the Controller.

First, Control-click (or right-click) on the first Text Field control and drag a line to the Temperature Converter App Delegate. In the pop-up menu, choose convertTemperature: as the action. Do the same for the other Text Field—remember, either Text Field should act as the source. Of course, either Text Field should act as the outlet from the Controller too, so let's wire that up now. Control-drag a line from the Controller to one of the Text Field controls, and from the popup choose the appropriate outlet. Do this for the other Text Field, too.

One other nice touch you can add is to add the capability to tab between the Text Field controls. Control-click one Text Field and from the popup drag from the circle next to nextKeyView to the other Text Field. Do the same thing in the other direction.

The final thing to do is specify which Text Field is the first to be selected at startup. Control-drag from the **Window** icon in the **Document** window to one of the Text Fields (I chose the centigradeField) and from the popup choose InitialFirstResponder.

You're done. Save the NIB, quit Interface Builder and run the application. You should be able to enter a number in either field, and when you tab to the other field (or press Enter) the other field will show the converted temperature.

In closing, let's just review the architecture of the application (see Figure 6–4). The separation of concerns is very clear: the Model contains the logic that accepts, stores, modifies and returns data. The View contains the user interface objects. The Controller sits between them and manages the flow of information.

Summary

You should be starting to have a good picture now of how the Model-View-Controller pattern is used in Cocoa. It really is a core aspect of Cocoa development, and as you embark on new applications it is worth some initial planning to identify your Models, Controllers, and Views.

This was intended only to be a brief foray into underlying technologies, and there will be one or two similar diversions as the book goes on. For now, however, it's time to get back to the tools. In Chapter 7, you will take a detailed look at Xcode's debugging tools.

Debugging Your Xcode Projects

No developer writes perfect code the first time—we're all human. Even when the editor provides Code Sense to help you to get your syntax right, you are going to make the occasional slip. You will also make mistakes in your code design and structure. So when you get bugs in your code, you need good support tools to help you to expunge them. In this short chapter, you will cover Xcode's tools for tracking and debugging your code.

The Debugger and Console Views

Remember back in Chapter 2 when you learned how you can use the **General Preferences** pane to choose from a variety of layouts in the Xcode Workspace. The default layout provides detached views for the different tools, including the two you're going to learn about in this chapter.

The All-In-One layout puts these two tools into a second panel in the main window, and you can get access to this panel using the **Page** toolbar buttons (see Figure 7–1).

Which layout you use is a personal preference—you have access to the same features whichever you use—but I tend to use the All-In-One layout because I prefer to keep everything in one window.

It's worth noting one other feature in the toolbar: the **Active Configuration** drop-down list. You can use this to select the active build configuration. By default, new projects are in Debug mode, which simply means that the products are built with debugging symbols available. You will come back to this much later in the book, when you create a release version of an application. For now, ensure that you leave the **Active Configuration** as **Debug**.

What is a debugger, anyway? In a nutshell, the Xcode debugger is a collection of tools that allow you to monitor your application as it runs, providing you with information about the current state of the program line by line. Effective use of the debugger will give you insights into how your code is performing and, most importantly, pointers to where it may be going wrong.

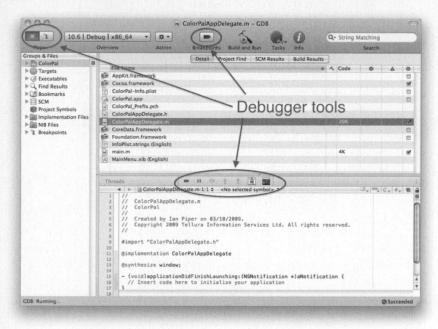

Figure 7–1. *Debugger tools in the All-In-One layout*

Creating a Project to Debug

Before you can use the debugger, you need something to debug. Let's create a small application and use the debugging tools (with, naturally, a leavening of common sense) to sort out any problems that crop up. The application you are going to work with in this chapter is a simple utility that allows you to set red, green, blue, and alpha values and see the resulting RGBA color. The final program will look like Figure 7–2. Create a new Cocoa project (you don't need to use the Document-based or Core Data options) and call it "ColorPal".

Your program is going to read and set values for the red, green, blue, and alpha (transparency) components of a color. When you get to Interface Builder, you are going to use Sliders and Text Fields as the controls to manipulate the user interface. The program is also going to use those values to update a control in the window, and you will use a Color Well control for this. Before visiting Interface Builder, though, let's write some code. You are going to need to set a Controller to manage the messages between the various objects in the system. You could create a dedicated Controller (remember, choose the **Project➤New File** menu and select an Objective-C class) but as this is such a simple application let's just use the default `ColorPalAppDelegate` object as your Controller. So that's where our code, to declare and implement the various components, needs to go. Choose `ColorPalAppDelegate.h` and add the bold code in Listing 7–1.

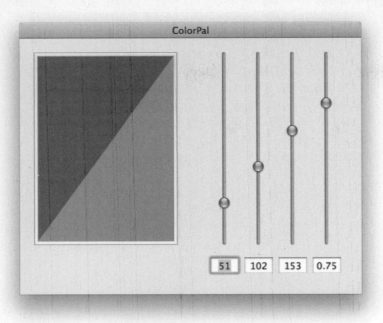

Figure 7–2. *The finished ColorPal project*

Listing 7–1. *ColorPalAppDelegate.h*

```
#import <Cocoa/Cocoa.h>
@interface ColorPalAppDelegate : NSObject <NSApplicationDelegate> {
NSWindow *window;
    int redIntValue;
    int greenIntValue;
    int blueIntValue;
    int alphaIntValue;
    IBOutlet NSColorWell *colorWell;
}

@property (assign) IBOutlet NSWindow *window;
@property(readwrite, assign) int redIntValue;
@property(readwrite, assign) int greenIntValue;
@property(readwrite, assign) int blueIntValue;
@property(readwrite, assign) int alphaIntValue;

- (IBAction)setNewColor:(id)sender;
- (void)updateColorWell;

@end
```

Here you are declaring properties to manage the red, green, blue, and alpha values, a method to create a color and another to update the Color Well. If you are used to earlier versions of Objective-C, the @property declaration may be new. This is Objective-C v2.0 syntax and provides an effective shortcut for variables that would normally have getter and setter methods. By using @property declarations here and the @synthesize command in the implementation file (see Listing 7–2) you save yourself a lot of coding.

Now move to ColorPalAppDelegate.m and make it look like Listing 7–2 (add the code in bold—the rest is just boilerplate code provided by Xcode as part of the AppDelegate object).

Listing 7–2. *ColorPalAppDelegate.m*

```
#import "ColorPalAppDelegate.h"

@implementation ColorPalAppDelegate
@synthesize window;

- (void)applicationDidFinishLaunching:(NSNotification *)aNotification {
    // Insert code here to initialize your application
}

@synthesize redValue;
@synthesize greenIntValue;
@synthesize blueIntValue;
@synthesize alphaIntValue;

- (void)awakeFromNib {
    [self setValue:[NSNumber numberWithInt:51] forKey:@"redIntValue"];
    [self setValue:[NSNumber numberWithInt:102] forKey:@"greenIntValue"];
    [self setValue:[NSNumber numberWithInt:153] forKey:@"blueIntValue"];
    [self setValue:[NSNumber numberWithInt:1.0] forKey:@"alphaIntValue"];
    [self updateColorWell];
}

- (IBAction)setNewColor:(id)sender {
    [self updateColorWell];
}

- (void)updateColorWell {
    NSColor *theColor = [NSColor colorWithCalibratedRed:((float)redIntValue/255)
        green:((float)greenIntValue/255)
        blue:((float)blueIntValue/255)
        alpha:(alphaIntValue)];
    [colorWell setColor:theColor];
}


@end
```

This code defines the accessor methods for the color value properties (using @synthesize), then the awakeFromNib method sets up some initial color values. The color in the Color Well (a mid-blue color) is set at the end of this method by calling updateColorWell. The same method is called as the result of the setNewColor: action method, which as you will see shortly happens whenever you change a Slider or number value in the user interface.

The more observant Objective-C coders will have spotted some errors in the code above; they are deliberate.

Check that you have saved both the .h and .m files, then open Interface Builder by double-clicking MainMenu.xib. Since you are using the AppDelegate object as the Controller, there is no need to add one from the Library as you would have had to do if you had created a dedicated Controller in the Xcode Project Workspace. So let's continue on and build the user interface. First, make the window 480 pixels wide and 360 pixels high (**Size Inspector** tab). Uncheck the **Close**, **Resize**, and **Minimize** controls in the **Attributes Inspector** tab—this is going to be a simple nonresizable window. Select the **Library** window and drag out a Color Well, a Vertical Slider, and a Text Field.

For the Vertical Slider, set the Height value to 260 pixels, the Minimum Value to 0, the Maximum Value to 255 and the Current value to 128. Set the state to Continuous. Set the Text Field's Alignment to Centered, its width to 40 and leave the Height as 22. Now copy the Vertical Slider and Text Field controls three times (opt-drag is an easy way to do this). The fourth Slider should have a Maximum Value of 1.0 and a Current Value of 0.5. The user interface should look something like Figure 7–3.

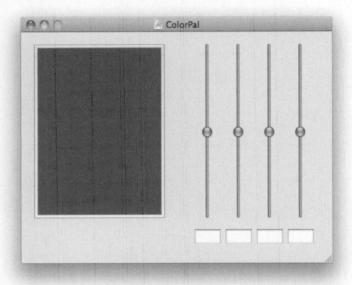

Figure 7–3. *The completed ColorPal user interface*

To set the connections, Control-drag from each of the Vertical Sliders and each of the Text Fields in turn in the user interface to the Color Pal App Delegate Controller in the Document window. Choose setNewColor: from the popup in each case (in other words, make eight connections). Now Control-drag from the Color Pal App Delegate Controller to the Color Well, and choose colorWell as the outlet.

That completes the work of building the user interface (again, observant or experienced developers will have spotted some omissions, but they are also deliberate). Save the NIB and close Interface Builder, returning to Xcode.

Running and Debugging the Project

OK, now **Build and Run**. There is an immediate problem and the build fails—see Figure 7–4.

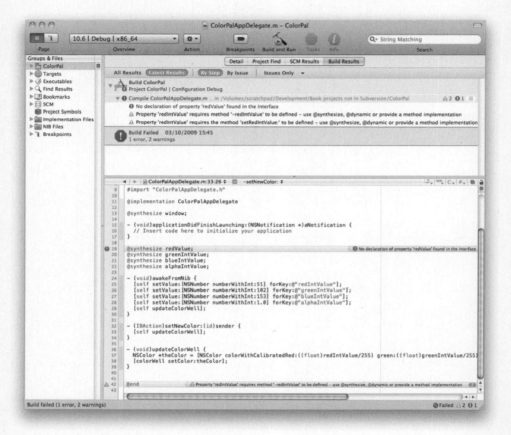

Figure 7–4. *Syntax error highlighted in the Build Results tab*

Syntax Errors

This is an easy syntax error to spot (and as I know to my cost, an easy one to make). To see more detail for this error, you can choose the **Build Results** tab in the Detail pane as shown in Figure 7–4.

The messages here spell out the mistake: `redValue` was not defined in the interface (.h) file, and there is no accessor method for the property `redIntValue`. Of course, the `@synthesize` call should be `redIntValue`, not `redValue`. Correct that error and **Build and Run** again. This time the build succeeds and the program runs.

It's quickly apparent that there are still some big problems. For one thing, although the pale blue color in the Color Well initially looks right, the Sliders haven't moved to the positions you might have expected and the Text Fields are blank. Also, nothing happens when you change any of the Sliders or the Text Fields.

What's happened here? Quit the program and let's look at the code.

The first thing that happens in the program is in the awakeFromNib method (Listing 7–3).

Listing 7–3. *The awakeFromNib Method*

```
- (void)awakeFromNib {
    [self setValue:[NSNumber numberWithInt:51] forKey:@"redIntValue"];
    [self setValue:[NSNumber numberWithInt:102] forKey:@"greenIntValue"];
    [self setValue:[NSNumber numberWithInt:153] forKey:@"blueIntValue"];
    [self setValue:[NSNumber numberWithInt:1.0] forKey:@"alphaIntValue"];
    [self updateColorWell];
}
```

This sets initial values for the red, green, blue and alpha components of the color, and then calls updateColorWell (Listing 7–4):

Listing 7–4. *The updateColorWell method*

```
- (void)updateColorWell {
    NSColor *theColor = [NSColor
            colorWithCalibratedRed:((float)redIntValue/255)
            green:((float)greenIntValue/255)
            blue:((float)blueIntValue/255)
            alpha:(alphaIntValue)];
    [colorWell setColor:theColor];
}
```

The updateColorWell method instantiates an NSColor object with the starting values defined in awakeFromNib, then sets the color of the Color Well to that NSColor.

Curious. We know that this must be working, because the Color Well is showing the right color on startup. It's time for some debugging.

Debugging with Breakpoints

First you need to set a breakpoint. A breakpoint is just an instruction in the code that says "stop when you get here." When the breakpoint is reached, the execution of the program pauses and you have an opportunity to inspect the current state of the application, including the current values of any properties. Once the breakpoint is reached and your program is paused, the debugger allows you a variety of ways to control how the program then continues. You'll get to this shortly.

The first place to try putting a breakpoint is probably at the line [self updateColorWell] in awakeFromNib. Adding a breakpoint is easy—just click in the gray gutter to the left of the code editor. A blue arrow appears at the line you have selected (see Figure 7–5).

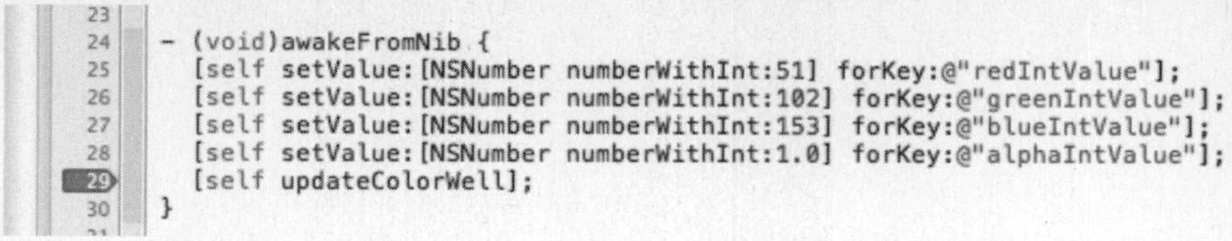

```
23
24    - (void)awakeFromNib {
25        [self setValue:[NSNumber numberWithInt:51] forKey:@"redIntValue"];
26        [self setValue:[NSNumber numberWithInt:102] forKey:@"greenIntValue"];
27        [self setValue:[NSNumber numberWithInt:153] forKey:@"blueIntValue"];
28        [self setValue:[NSNumber numberWithInt:1.0] forKey:@"alphaIntValue"];
29        [self updateColorWell];
30    }
31
```

Figure 7–5. *Adding a breakpoint*

You can remove a breakpoint by right-clicking on the blue breakpoint arrow and choosing **Remove Breakpoint** or by dragging it off the gutter. You can deactivate a breakpoint by clicking the blue Breakpoint button, or all of the breakpoints by clicking the gray **Breakpoints** button in the main Xcode toolbar. Now choose **Build and Debug** (notice that while breakpoints are active the **Build and Run** button changes to **Build and Debug**). You will see the program begin but then stop. Your breakpoint line is highlighted and the breakpoint has a red arrow overlaid on it (Figure 7–6):

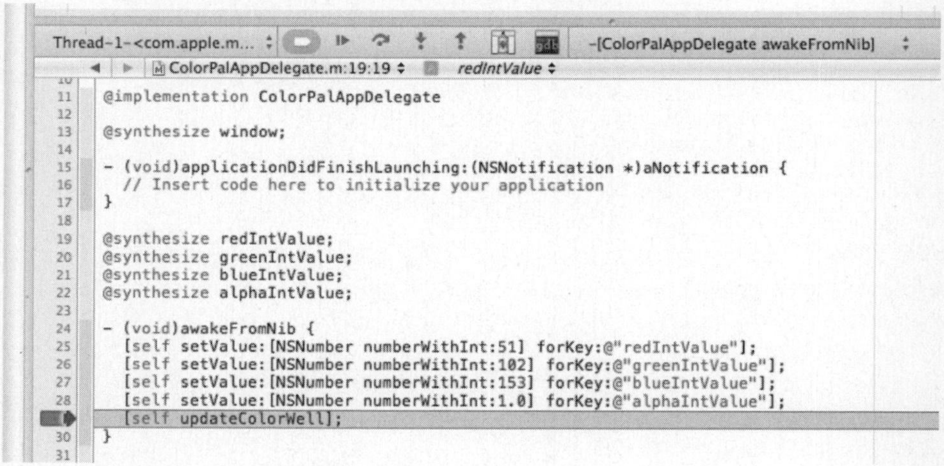

```
Thread-1-<com.apple.m...  ⬤ ▶ ↻ ↓ ↑ 🔲 📇    -[ColorPalAppDelegate awakeFromNib]  ⬍
◀ ▶  ColorPalAppDelegate.m:19:19 ⬍   redIntValue ⬍
11    @implementation ColorPalAppDelegate
12
13    @synthesize window;
14
15    - (void)applicationDidFinishLaunching:(NSNotification *)aNotification {
16        // Insert code here to initialize your application
17    }
18
19    @synthesize redIntValue;
20    @synthesize greenIntValue;
21    @synthesize blueIntValue;
22    @synthesize alphaIntValue;
23
24    - (void)awakeFromNib {
25        [self setValue:[NSNumber numberWithInt:51] forKey:@"redIntValue"];
26        [self setValue:[NSNumber numberWithInt:102] forKey:@"greenIntValue"];
27        [self setValue:[NSNumber numberWithInt:153] forKey:@"blueIntValue"];
28        [self setValue:[NSNumber numberWithInt:1.0] forKey:@"alphaIntValue"];
29        [self updateColorWell];
30    }
31
```

Figure 7–6. *ColorPal stopping execution at a breakpoint*

You will also notice that the ribbon menu above the code editor has changed to show debugging functions. You can use this to control the flow of execution of the program by stepping over (that is, ignoring) a method, stepping into or out of a method, or just continuing execution. You can also open the **Console** or **Debugger** window (or both if you are using the All-In-One layout). Let's open the **Debugger** window and take a closer look at what's happening.

Click the **Debugger** button in the ribbon menu or in the **Page** toolbar menu. The window you see now is quite daunting at first glance. There is a lot going on! See Figure 7–7.

Figure 7–7. *The Debugger and Console views*

The toolbar shows the same debugging controls that you had in the normal **Project** view. In the center of the window is a code editor panel. This enables you to edit your code and continue execution without leaving the **Debug** view. Below this is the **Console** view, and you'll be coming back to this shortly. The first thing to do here is inspect what's going on in the current method. You will see in the top left panel that the selected item in the main thread of the application is awakeFromNib. The panel to the right of this shows the variables that exist at the current point in the program. In effect, this allows you to understand all of the properties currently set. A lot of the data here is way beyond what you will need to worry about initially, but it is good to know that you can drill into your application to whatever depth you need. Make sure awakeFromNib is selected, then find the self argument and open it up with the disclosure arrow (see Figure 7–8).

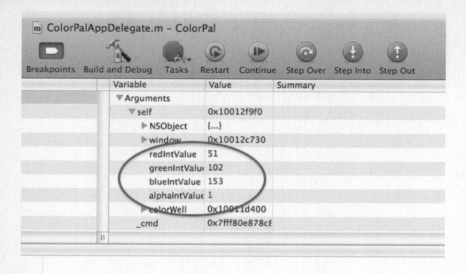

Figure 7–8. *Inspecting variable values at a breakpoint*

Stop the program using the big red button. How about putting the breakpoint in the setNewColor action, since that is what seems not to be working? Try it: drag the breakpoint arrow from its current location to the line [self updateColorWell]; in setNewColor. Now the execution will pause every time the updateColorWell method is called, which should be whenever the values change. **Run and Debug** again. The program will run and load the user interface. Since nothing is happening that would trigger the updateColorWell method, the program is running normally. Try changing the color value (say, the value in the Text Field for the red component) and then tab to the next field. See Figure 7–9. The breakpoint will be reached again, pausing the program.

Sadly, that isn't very helpful. You can see that the various color values have been set as expected. So perhaps that wasn't the best place to put the breakpoint. Probably the hardest part about using breakpoints is figuring out where to put them: there is no substitute for practice here. In this case having a breakpoint in awakeFromNib didn't help, since that part of the code was already working OK.

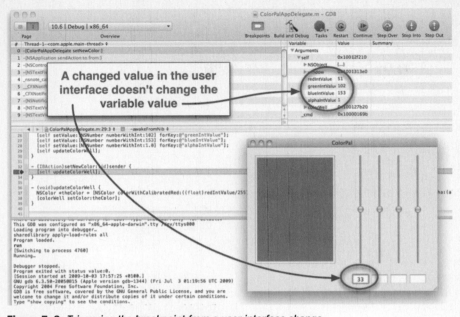

Figure 7-9. *Triggering the breakpoint from a user interface change*

Interesting—changing the red component from its original value of 51 to 33 has not changed the value of redIntValue as recorded in the debugger.

OK—this gets us a bit closer. Clearly the connection between the user interface controls and the updateColorWell method is not working. If the application is working as far as awakeFromNib, but not when the controls change, then clearly updateColorWell has values to work with when it is called from awakeFromNib but not when it is called from setNewColor.

Perhaps the problem is back in Interface Builder: perhaps you haven't made all of the right connections? Let's take a look. Quit from the debugging session and go back to Interface Builder. Recall that you have made connections that will send messages from the Slider and Text Field controls to the Controller and then on to the Color Well. However, there is nothing yet to tell the Controller to update the Slider or the Text Fields. That would explain why their values don't change. OK, you need to bind those controls to the Controller. Choose the first Slider control (this will be the red Slider), and in the **Inspector Bindings** tab bind the value property of the Slider control to the **App Delegate Controller** with the **Model Key Path** redIntValue (see Figure 7–10).

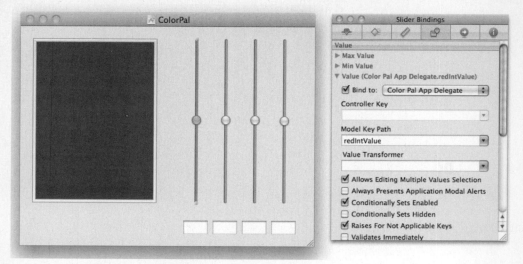

Figure 7–10. *Creating the control bindings in Interface Builder*

Now do the same for the Text Field that will hold the redIntValue, and repeat for the green, blue, and alpha Sliders and Text Fields.

Now save the NIB and go back to Xcode. **Build and Debug**. Try changing some values and see the effect in the debugger (Figure 7–11).

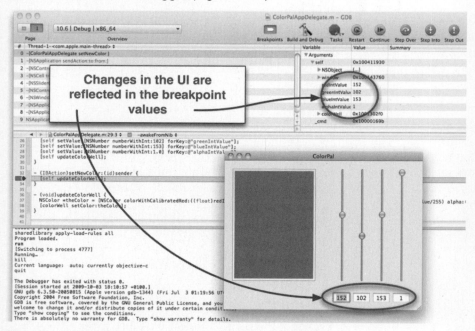

Figure 7–11. *The breakpoint now shows the updated values correctly.*

That's much more like it. Changing the red, green, or blue values now shows correct values in the debugger window. The Color Well shows the correct color and the Sliders and Text Fields have the correct values. However, the behavior of the application is erratic. Try changing the alpha Slider. You'd expect to see a smooth change in the alpha (transparency) value here; instead, it is either a full color or black and white. Also, the alphaIntValue is either 1 or 0. What is the problem now? You can maybe work out what's wrong from this observation, but let's look at other tools to get to the bottom of this.

Using NSLog to Track Changing Properties

As well as looking up values of variables in the debugger, you can also add NSLog statements in your code. You can then use these effectively to watch the values of variables as the code executes. Let's try that now. Remove the breakpoint that you set earlier. Now, in the method updateColorWell, add the line of code in bold in Listing 7–5.

Listing 7–5. *Adding a NSLog Statement*

```
- (void)updateColorWell {
    NSLog(@"Updating the Color Well with Red value: %d Green value: %d Blue value: %d
Alpha value %d", redIntValue, greenIntValue, blueIntValue, alphaIntValue);
    NSColor *theColor = [NSColor colorWithCalibratedRed:((float)redIntValue/255
green:((float)greenIntValue/255) blue:((float)blueIntValue/255) alpha:(alphaIntValue)];
    [colorWell setColor:theColor];
}
```

Now make sure you have the **Debugger view is selected with the Console enabled,** and choose **Build and Debug.** Try changing the color Sliders and the alpha Slider. Notice that although the color component values change smoothly as you move the Sliders, the alpha value is either 1 (when the Slider is at the top) or 0 (any other time). You are closer to the source of the bug.

Checking Syntax in the Documentation

Perhaps the key is in how you are setting the color—is the syntax right? A nice feature of the Xcode documentation is that you can look up a particular method simply by holding down the ⌥ (Opt or Alt) key and double-clicking on the method name.

> **TIP:** ⌥double-click brings up the QuickHelp window, a compact popup with summary information. You can also display the full documentation window using ⌘⌥double-click.

Try this now with the method name colorWithCalibratedRed:.

OK—this gives the answer. The method colorWithCalibratedRed: requires four floats as its arguments. It sets the red, green, blue, and alpha values as floats between 0 and 1 (which is why you need to divide the RGB integer values by 255 and then cast them to floats). Look what is happening in the ColorPal code (Listing 7–6):

Listing 7–6. *The updateColorWell Method*

```
(void)updateColorWell {
NSLog(@"Updating the Color Well with Red value: %d Green value: %d Blue value: %d Alpha
value %d", redIntValue, greenIntValue, blueIntValue, alphaIntValue);
    NSColor *theColor = [NSColor colorWithCalibratedRed:((float)redIntValue/255)
green:((float)greenIntValue/255) blue:((float)blueIntValue/255)
alpha:(alphaIntValue)];
    [colorWell setColor:theColor];
}
```

The line in bold shows where the problem lies—or at least, where **a** problem lies. While the red, green, and blue int values are being cast to floats, the alpha int value is not. As a result, the method is returning an incorrect value most of the time. So all along, the code has been incorrectly setting the alpha component value for the color—it was pure luck that most of the time it was returning a value of 1, which shows a fully opaque color. You need to visit a few places to sort this out:

- In ColorController.h, you need to declare a float called alphaFloatValue and change any occurrences of alphaIntValue to alphaFloatValue.

- In ColorController.m you need to change any occurrences of alphaIntValue to alphaFloatValue.

- In ColorController.m the NSLog statement needs to use %f to correctly format the alphaValue rather than %d.

- In Interface Builder, the Slider and Text Field for the alpha value needs to bind to alphaFloatValue, not alphaIntValue.

When you have finished, the code should look like Listings 7–7 and 7–8. The changes you need to make are highlighted in bold.

Listing 7–7. *The Corrected ColorController.h Code*

```
#import <Cocoa/Cocoa.h>

@interface ColorController : NSObject {
    int redIntValue;
    int greenIntValue;
    int blueIntValue;
    float alphaFloatValue;
    IBOutlet NSColorWell *colorWell;
}

@property(readwrite, assign) int redIntValue;
@property(readwrite, assign) int greenIntValue;
@property(readwrite, assign) int blueIntValue;
@property(readwrite, assign) float alphaFloatValue;
- (IBAction)setNewColor:(id)sender;
- (void)updateColorWell;

@end
```

Listing 7–8. *The Corrected ColorController.m Code*

```
#import "ColorController.h"
@implementation ColorController
@synthesize redIntValue;
@synthesize greenIntValue;
@synthesize blueIntValue;
@synthesize alphaFloatValue;

- (void)awakeFromNib {
    [self setValue:[NSNumber numberWithInt:51] forKey:@"redIntValue"];
    [self setValue:[NSNumber numberWithInt:102] forKey:@"greenIntValue"];
    [self setValue:[NSNumber numberWithInt:153] forKey:@"blueIntValue"];
    [self setValue:[NSNumber numberWithFloat:1.0] forKey:@"alphaFloatValue"];
    [self updateColorWell];

}

- (IBAction)setNewColor:(id)sender {
    [self updateColorWell];
}

- (void)updateColorWell {
    NSLog(@"Updating the Color Well with Red value: %d Green value: %d Blue value: %d
Alpha value %f", redIntValue, greenIntValue, blueIntValue, alphaFloatValue);
    NSColor *theColor = [NSColor colorWithCalibratedRed:((float)redIntValue/255)
green:((float)greenIntValue/255) blue:((float)blueIntValue/255)
alpha:(alphaFloatValue)];
    [colorWell setColor:theColor];
}

@end
```

Don't forget that visit to Interface Builder to change the binding of your Slider and Text Field controls, or you will surely see an exception thrown when you run the program.

If you now **Build and Run** the program will behave correctly: the color well changes smoothly as the Slider or Text Field values change.

Exploring the Debugger

As you have probably come to expect given the flexibility of Xcode's Developer Tools, there are several ways to use debugger features in Xcode. Overall you have four approaches to debugging:

- The Code Editor
- The **Debugger** window
- The Mini Debugger
- The **Console** view

You have some flexibility in choosing which debugging approach Xcode uses. In Xcode's **Debugging Preferences**, the drop-down list labeled **On Start** allows you to select how Xcode starts up debugging. By default, this is set to **Do Nothing**. If you don't want to prescribe a debugging approach, leave it at that setting and simply choose the approach that suits your current need. Let's look at each approach in turn.

Debugging Features in the Code Editor

The Code Editor is where you are likely to encounter Debugger features for the first time. If you have set a breakpoint in your code then you will see the **Debugger** ribbon menu at the top of the code window when the program is running. The ribbon menu looks like Figure 7–12.

Figure 7–12. *The Debugger ribbon menu in the code editor*

The menu is context-sensitive—that is, it is only visible when you are debugging. When a debugging session completes the normal **Code Editor** ribbon menu is restored. The **Debugger** ribbon menu gives you quick access to the principal debugging features. The buttons allow you to

- Activate and deactivate breakpoints
- Pause and continue execution
- Step over a method
- Step into a method
- Step out of the current method
- Show the debugger window
- Show the console window
- See exception and other messages, such as the current method name

There is not a great deal more to say about this view: the tools are fundamentally the same debugger tools provided in the main and Mini Debugger views. Bear in mind as you read the next section that you can accomplish most of the debugging workflow by using the Code Editor as an alternative to the main **Debugger** window.

The Main Debugger Window

You have already seen something of the main **Debugger** window. This is displayed either as a detached window (with the Default layout) or in a separate page in the **Project Workspace** window (with the All-In-One layout). Let's look at an example of its use with one of the projects you worked on in an earlier chapter—the TemperatureConverter project.

Locate that project and open it up. You're not going to make any changes to the project, just use the **Debugger** window to inspect some variables.

Add breakpoints to the code in TemperatureConverterAppDelegate.m (the Controller file) and Converter.m (the model file) at the points indicated in Figures 7–13.

```
28        if(sender == fahrenheitField) {
29            temperatureC=[tempConverter convertFToC:temperatureF];
30            [centigradeField setFloatValue:temperatureC];
31        } else if (sender == centigradeField) {
32            temperatureF = [tempConverter convertCToF:temperatureC];
33            [fahrenheitField setFloatValue:temperatureF];
34        }
```

```
12    @implementation Converter
13
14    -(float)convertCToF:(float)tempC {
15        return ((tempC * 1.8) + 32.0);
16    }
17
18    - (float)convertFToC:(float)tempF {
19        return ((tempF - 32.0) / 1.8);
20    }
```

Figure 7–13. *Breakpoints in* TemperatureConverterAppDelegate.m *(top) and* Converter.m *(bottom)*

These are the main points at which temperature values are calculated and passed between the model and Controller. So let's see what happens when the program runs. Choose **Build and Debug** and switch to the **Debugger** window.

You will see that there is nothing noteworthy in the **Debugger** window. That is because the program hasn't yet reached a breakpoint. Type in the number **25** in the **Centigrade** field, then press the Tab key. You will see that the program hits its first breakpoint (which is in the Converter.m convertCToF method, as you might expect). In the top-right hand panel, you can see the current value for temperatureC (25) and you can also inspect that value by hovering over the variable name in the code—you will see a popup over the variable name showing its current value.

Now click the **Continue** button (the green button in the main toolbar). The program moves ahead to the next breakpoint, in the convertTemperature method in the AppDelegate.m file. This is the point at which the newly calculated Fahrenheit temperature value is written back to the Text Field. Checking the variable values in the top-right debugger panel you can see the temperatureC variable is 25 and the temperatureF variable has the value 77 (which seems about right). Hover over the temperatureF variable reference in the code at the breakpoint and sure enough it pops up as 77 (see Figure 7–14).

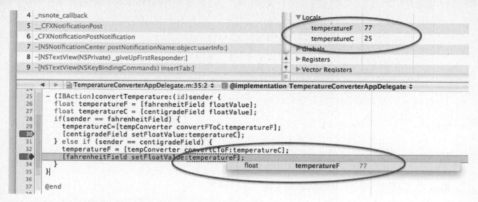

Figure 7–14. *Inspecting the updated Fahrenheit value*

Notice though that in the program window the Fahrenheit temperature value still says 32. This is because the breakpoint occurs before the code on this line has executed. Click **Continue** again and the program window updates to the new Fahrenheit value.

Suppose you typed an illegal value into one of the fields? Type the word **ten** into the **Fahrenheit** field and hit Tab. The breakpoint variable inspection tells you that the value recorded for temperatureF is 0. So when you click on **Continue** the calculation simply works out the Centigrade equivalent of 0 degrees Fahrenheit and you see the value 32 in the user interface.

At least the program didn't crash, though actually an honest-to-goodness crash is often a better guide to the source of the problem than unexpected incorrect results! Clearly, you would want to put some validation into this program if you were writing it as a real application.

It may be clear that the main **Debugger** window is my approach of choice, and I tend to use it to the exclusion of either the code editor or Mini Debugger approaches. That's the great thing about Xcode, of course: you can work the way *you* want to.

The Mini Debugger

The Mini Debugger provides a small floating HUD-style window that gives access to the main debugging features with the smallest screen footprint.

Open up the TemperatureConverter project if it is not already open. Put the breakpoints in as you had them earlier (refer to Figure 7–13). Now **Build and Debug**. Once the program has started to run, choose the **Run➤Mini Debugger** menu. You will see the small HUD window (see Figure 7–15).

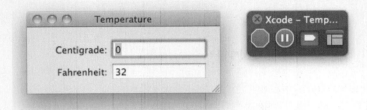

Figure 7-15. *The HUD window for the Mini Debugger*

It may not look like it is doing very much. Enter a new Centigrade temperature value. The result should look like Figure 7–16. The HUD display zooms up to a larger window to show the point of execution.

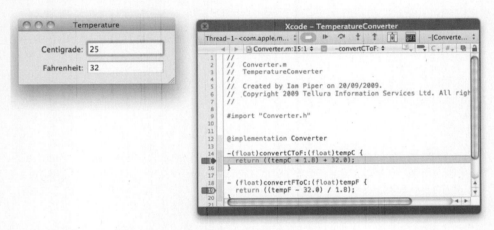

Figure 7-16. *The expanded HUD window in the Mini Debugger*

When you use one of the controls on the ribbon menu to continue past the breakpoint, the window zooms back down to the minimal view. The nice thing about the Mini Debugger view is that it is compact: if you are limited on screen space it can be a useful way to manage your debugging; however, it has some drawbacks. For one thing, code is not editable in the HUD code view. The continual zooming of windows can also be a little confusing. To be honest, I have never used the Mini Debugger and see little advantage over the standard debugger display.

The Console

You have seen most of what the **Console** has to offer already. It is a very useful place to see the output from NSLog messages as you saw earlier. Any errors that would normally go to stderr (a Unix convention providing a standard place to write error messages) would also appear here. If you should happen to be writing command line programs, you can also use the **Console** for handling stdin and stdout traffic. In practice, I use the **Console** a lot for NSLog messages from my code and that is about it.

Summary

This short chapter gave you a good idea of how to use the Xcode Debugger, and something of the benefits and drawbacks of the different approaches to using the Debugger in your projects.

There was a brief introduction in this chapter on looking up documentation from within your code—a very brief introduction to a very important topic, and one that is Xcode's best-kept secret: the developer documentation. That is where you are heading in the next chapter.

Chapter 8

Xcode Documentation

Documentation—ugh. For many developers, it's all about writing great applications; wading through reams of documentation is the last thing on your mind. Xcode's documentation is a strange mixture of comprehensiveness and complexity. The answer you are looking for is almost certainly in there somewhere, but locating it can be a challenge.

In this chapter, you will explore the complexities of Xcode's documentation and learn how to navigate directly to the information you need. You will also learn about other places to find useful documentation. Finally, you will learn how to create effective documentation for your own code.

Overview of Documentation Resources for Xcode

Let's start with the big picture view. There are, broadly speaking, five places where you can get help in your Xcode development (in addition to books such as this one, of course).

- Quick Help
- ADC documentation
- Code samples
- Articles, tutorials, and sample applications on third-party websites
- Community resources like web forums and mailing lists

You will be drawing on each of these resources as you develop your applications, but a brief tour of each follows. Some features described in this chapter—particularly the ADC documentation—require an internet connection and your ADC login.

Quick Help

Quick Help is a new name in Xcode 3.2 (Snow Leopard only) for what *was* called the Research Assistant in earlier Xcode versions. If you ⌥⌘click on a method name or other documented symbol in the Code Editor, a small pop-up window appears with a description of the symbol (you may already know that Control⌥double-click takes you to the full reference documentation rather than the **Quick Help** popup).

Here is an example. In the previous chapter, you created a small application for creating colors using slider controls. Apart from methods that you wrote for yourself, you made use of a Cocoa Framework method called `colorWithCalibratedRed:`. Open that project now and find the method call (use the **Project Find** tab for this—see the note below).

> **NOTE:** If you want to use **Search** to find code, you may be surprised that the Spotlight-style search box in the **Project Workspace** window doesn't find it. In fact, the search box is only used to find items in the **Overview** panel. If you want to search for code in your project, you need to go to the **Project Find** tab. This gives you a comprehensive interface for searching.

You will remember, too, that you looked this method up. Let's do that again and take a closer look. ⌥double-click the method call and the **Quick Help** window appears (see Figure 8-1).

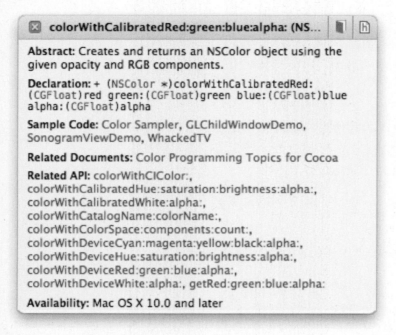

Figure 8-1. *Quick Help window for colorWithCalibratedRed*

This window shows you the abstract and declaration and various other pieces of information about the symbol you have selected. Once it's loaded, keep this mini-window on screen, as you can then inspect other symbols simply by clicking on them. Try scrolling up in the **Code Editor** window and choosing other symbols such as `awakeFromNib`, `numberWithInt`, `NSNumber`, and so on. If Xcode can find documentation for a symbol, it will display here.

The **Quick Help** window provides more than just descriptions for a method. If sample code is available, or useful related documents, you will see those, too.

Click back on `colorWithCalibratedRed:`. The title bar in this window has two small buttons at the top right. The button marked by a small **h** brings up the method declaration in a new code window, while the button with a small book image takes you to the **Class Reference** page for that method in the documentation window (this is one of the points where you need to be connected to the Net). You can see from the method description that all of its arguments are floats and that it expects values between 0 and 1 (which was where the application came to grief, you will recall). You will be looking at the documentation window in more detail shortly, so just close it for the moment. The **Quick Help** window also shows links to relevant sample code. Try **Color Sampler**. Up comes a window featuring the sample code for that application (see Figure 8-2).

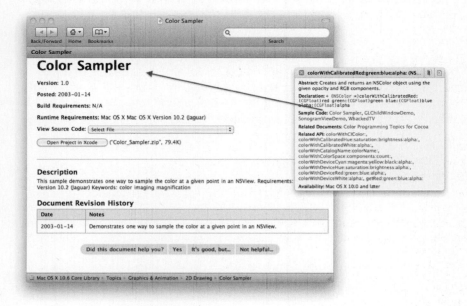

Figure 8-2. *Finding sample code*

From here you can open either the source code in the browser window or the whole project in Xcode. The **Quick Help** window is an extremely useful way to discover how the code you are interested in should be used.

ADC Documentation

Your installation of Xcode Developer Tools will have placed a vast set of useful documentation and code samples on your computer, together with links to an even larger set of documents on the ADC website. Many developers don't make as much use as they might of these resources because, frankly, they are not that obvious or accessible. So here is a high-level guide to how to find and use the documentation that will help you cement your knowledge of Xcode, Cocoa, and Objective-C.

You might think that the best place to look for the documentation would be somewhere like /Developer/Documentation. Sure enough, there is such a folder, but it doesn't look promising; there is a set of folders leading to Perl, Python, and other similar documentation (not much use to us here), and another folder called DocSets. In this folder, you will find a number of docset packages. Like any other Mac package, these are folders, and you can open them using the right-click contextual menu to show their contents. You may like to explore these as this is where your local copy of the Developer Documentation resides. The documentation is a collection of html and image files. The sample code for the documentation set is also stored in this docset.

Your quickest and most effective route into the documentation (apart from using Quick Help) is via the **Help Developer Documentation** menu (or use Shift⌥⌘? as a shortcut). You will see the main **Developer Documentation** window.

Apple's developer documentation can be a little difficult grasp, in my experience, so it's worth taking a moment to orient yourself in this window. There are three main sections under the title **Xcode Quick Start**. Under each section, each of which expands when you click on the **Read More** link, there are links to useful high-level resources. We won't bother going into all of these here because we have covered the ground in earlier chapters; however, some of these resources are well worth reading as they have coverage beyond this book.

Cocoa Fundamentals Guide

This gives a detailed description of the Cocoa Frameworks (which you covered to some extent back in Chapter 5). It also provides links to more advanced topics such as **The Objective-C Programming Language**, **Cocoa Design Patterns**, and **Garbage Collection Programming** (see Figure 8-3).

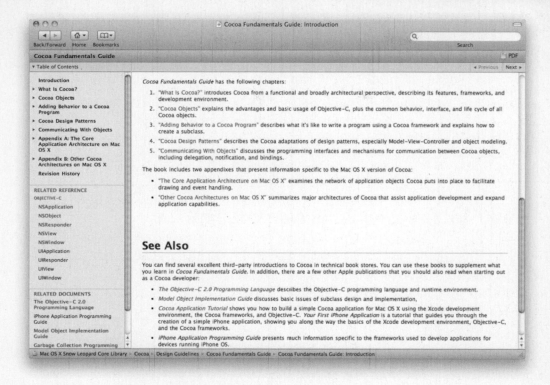

Figure 8-3. *Typical Documentation window, showing the Cocoa Fundamentals Guide*

NOTE: Many of the documents you encounter in the documentation are also available as PDF files. Just click the PDF icon link, either in the title bar (see Figure 8-3) or above the Table of Contents in the top-left corner of the document. These can be very useful if you prefer to work with paper. Also, note that some of the documents are online, so when you are without a network connection, the PDF is the only option (provided that you have already downloaded it, of course!).

Xcode Workflow and Cocoa Application Tutorials

Follow these pages on the ADC website, to get some basic Xcode programming tutorials. While these are useful, if you have followed the examples in earlier chapters you are already way past these in your learning!

Recommended Reading for Xcode Developers

Read this page for a good overview of the reference documentation divided into different aspects of development, including **Design**, **Code**, **Build**, and so on.

One that you might like to follow is **Document-Based Applications Overview**. In addition to straightforward single-window applications, you can also create Document-based applications within Xcode. You met one back in Chapter 3 in fact, when you created the TextPal application. As the name suggests, a Document-based application is centered on the idea that your user will interact with the application primarily by creating and managing documents. It's more complex than that: as well as controlling the flow of execution overall, your program has to work with the extra complications of opening, managing, and storing data to and from documents. Many applications, from TextEdit to Photoshop, exhibit Document-based behavior. Xcode provides the usual high standard of tool support for creating Document-based applications, and this document provides a detailed discussion of the Cocoa document architecture.

Getting Around the ADC Documentation

Navigating the ADC Documentation can be a frustrating and slightly daunting business. There is no *single* central navigation mechanism; the links from the main **Documentation** window can take you off to long excursions around very useful articles, but it is hard to get a feel for the overall information architecture of this information system. In practice, you are likely to end up getting to know the documentation search box very well.

Suppose you wanted to know about building Document-based applications. If you didn't know that you could get to this from the main documentation window (choose the **Getting Started with Xcode** link, then **Recommended Reading for Xcode Developers**, then **Document-Based Applications Overview**), it isn't obvious. The search mechanism in the Xcode Documentation works pretty well, though. Back in the main documentation window, start typing **document-based**. The window immediately changes. Spotlight-style selection buttons appear in the usual location just below the toolbar, and a results list appears in a panel on the left. As you type, the results dynamically refine. By the time you get two characters into the word "based," you have a window like Figure 8-4 and can see a number of relevant hits.

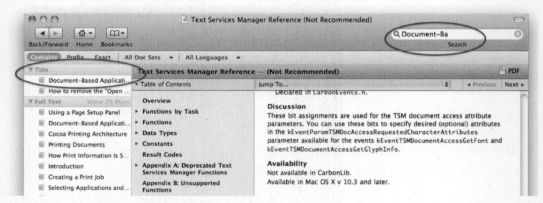

Figure 8-4. *Searching for documents in the Documentation*

The first item in the **Title** section of the results list is our friend **Document-Based Application Overview**. Click on that, and the document appears.

Once you have found a useful document, you might want to bookmark it. Use the **Bookmarks** toolbar button; the drop-down menu shows the current document is shown by default (Figure 8-5). You can add or remove bookmarks with the **Manage Bookmarks** window (in the same drop-down menu).

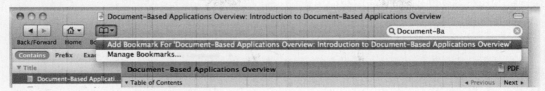

Figure 8-5. *Adding a Documentation bookmark*

NOTE: You can resize the results list by just mousing down over the junction between the list and the **Table of Contents** and dragging. There is no drag handle, so you have to position the mouse *exactly* on the junction. If you drag the junction to the left, the list suddenly disappears, which is a little startling the first time it happens. You can bring it back into view by grabbing the left edge of the window and dragging it in to the right.

There doesn't seem to be an obvious way to remove the Spotlight-style selection buttons once they have appeared.

Like all search-based information discovery, this presupposes that you know what you are looking for. What if you just want to see what is there?

Of course, there is a browser-based approach, though it is not immediately obvious. This comprises the Core and Developer Tools Reference Libraries. In the toolbar, clicking on the **Home** button provides a drop-down menu (see Figure 8-6).

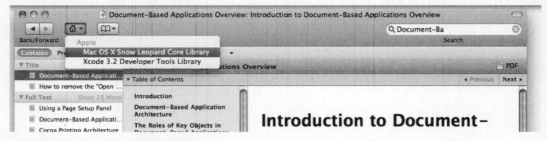

FIGURE 8-6. *Choosing a reference library*

Choose either the **Mac OS X 10.6 Core Library** or **Xcode 3.2 Developer Tools Library** item to go to the corresponding reference library home page.

> **NOTE:** The list of reference libraries that appears in this menu depends on the settings in the **Documentation Preferences**. In this preference panel, you can choose from a range of Documentation docsets to load, and each one will appear in this menu.

Now this is more like it! These reference library entrypoints are the key to effective navigation of the Apple documentation.

First let's take a look at the Mac OS X 10.6 Core Library. This layout shows a number of lists of resources divided into categories (see Figure 8-7).

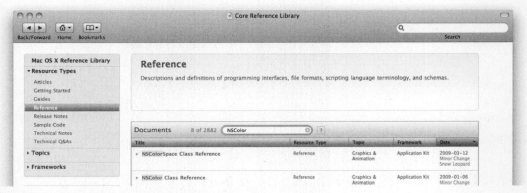

Figure 8-7. *The entrypoint to the Core Reference Library*

As this is really just a custom web browser, you have access to some browser-like features, such as being able to open links in a new window or even a new Safari window (right-click or Control-click on a link), and bookmarks as you have already seen.

As you can see in Figure 8-7, there is a category listing that you can open up to show sub-categories, and for each there is a list of relevant resources. You can sort these resources by each of the categories (these repeat as column headings in the **Documents** list), and you can narrow the list down using the Spotlight-style document list filter. In Figure 8-7 I have chosen the **Resources Reference** category and narrowed my document list down using **NSColor** as a filter.

The Developer Tools Reference Library (use the **Home** drop-down menu again) is similar but simpler. It presents essentially a list of documents—fairly stark, but easy enough to navigate. The list shows the same categories as in the Core Reference Library but there is not category-based navigation.

While there is a large amount of useful information in this reference library, it's a simple structure and there's not much more to say about it. Let's use it, however, to show the detailed documentation that we can get out of it.

From the Developer Reference Library page, type in **data** to filter down the document list. You will see something like Figure 8-8 (your view may be different if newer documents become available in the library).

Developer Tools & Languages Reference Library

Create stunning software with the software development tools and programming-and-scripting language support that are supplied free with Mac OS X. Use these tools and languages to build, debug, and optimize software applications.

Documents	6 of 139	data		?

Title	Resource Type	Topic	Framework	Date
▸ Creating a Managed Object Model with Xcode	Guides	Tools & Languages	Core Data	2009-03-02 Content Update
▸ Xcode Mapping Tool for Core Data	Guides	Tools & Languages	Core Data	2009-03-02 Content Update
▸ Interface Builder Kit Data Types Reference	Reference	Tools & Languages	Interface Builder Kit	2007-04-02 First Version
▸ ManagedObjectDataFormatter	Sample Code	Tools & Languages		2005-06-01 First Version
▸ WcharDataFormatter	Sample Code	Tools & Languages		2006-03-31 First Version
▸ Xcode Tools for Core Data	Guides	Tools & Languages	Core Data	2008-04-15 First Version

Figure 8-8. *Finding relevant documents in the Developer Tools Reference Library*

Following a link takes you to the full documentation page. This will look something like Figure 8-3 and may include links to PDF versions and/or sample code.

Other Resources on the Apple Developer Site

Unless you are using the original version of Xcode that came with your Mac, you will probably have a subscription to the Developer Connection (http://developer.apple.com). The entry-level membership (Online or Student) gives you access to the latest Xcode installation kit, and if you have one of the paid levels of membership (Select or Premier) you will also have access to the latest developer releases of the operating systems (Mac OS X and Mac OS X Server) and other Apple software.

Also on the ADC website are the ADC reference libraries described above.

A nice extra that is available on the ADC site, though not widely advertised, is the Core Data video tutorial (http://developer.apple.com/cocoa/coredatatutorial/index.html). This is a 14-step collection of QuickTime videos that show you how to create a Core Data application from scratch. The tutorial is a model of clarity and highly recommended. At the time of writing, this is the only such video tutorial on the ADC site. The web page is titled "ADC Video Tutorial Series," so let's hope it really is a series.

Third-Party Online Resources

As an Apple developer, you are privileged: the world of Apple software development is well-served with clever and selfless people who have put up tutorials, how-tos, sample applications, plug-ins, and even whole websites devoted to sharing knowledge of Xcode tools and Objective-C development. They can be invaluable in getting you through programming problems.

The internet being the dynamic entity that it is, this is obviously a snapshot as of mid-2009. Websites come and go, but chances are good that these will be around when you come to look at them:

- Cocoadevcentral (http://www.cocoadevcentral.com/).

- The Mac Developer Network (http://www.mac-developer-network.com/)

- Cocoabuilder (http://www.cocoabuilder.com/archive/bydate)

- Instinctive code (http://instinctivecode.com/)

- CocoaDev (http://www.cocoadev.com/)

- Cocoa Samurai (http://cocoasamurai.blogspot.com/)

- Cocoa with Love (http://cocoawithlove.com/)

- Cocoa Is My Girlfriend (http://www.cimgf.com/)

- Stepwise (http://www.stepwise.com/)

Other Sources of Information

If documentation doesn't help (and often it doesn't), all is not lost. There are large communities of Apple developers who are active on mailing lists and web forums, and they can be excellent sources of valuable information.

Keeping a High Signal-to-Noise Ratio

A word of cautionary advice for newcomers to the Apple mailing lists. In the case of the cocoa-dev and similar Apple hosted lists, and unusually for internet mailing lists, there is a very high *signal-to-noise ratio*—that is, a high proportion of what you read there is useful and on-topic. That is good for you as a consumer of the information, but it is achieved at a cost. That cost is an expectation that you have carried out due diligence first—that you have read the documentation, used Google, and in general have done reasonable background research into your problem. That way you don't waste people's time and clutter up the list with another round on a well-known problem. You also need to make sure that your question is relevant—the terms of reference for these mailing lists are well defined and rigorously enforced.

If you follow the guidelines, you will find that the responses you get from the denizens of these communities are helpful and focused. If you don't, you can expect a firm hand from the moderators and little patience from the rest of the community. Does all this seem a little harsh, perhaps narrow-minded? Absolutely, and long may it continue so. The people who, on the whole, use these mailing lists understand the importance of keeping the discussion focused and within the parameters for which the list was set up.

There are plenty of badly focused, ill-disciplined, and noisy mailing lists out there for you to choose from if this makes you uncomfortable.

Mailing Lists and Web Forums

Apple hosts over 100 mailing lists aimed at the developer community. With these on offer, you are likely to find something of interest here—the most sensible places to start if you are a Mac developer are the Cocoa-dev and Xcode-dev lists. Like most internet mailing lists, you need to actively subscribe to the list. Once subscribed you are able to post questions, comments and answers to the list and all other subscribers will receive a copy. To see what's offered, go to http://lists.apple.com.

You will probably have used the Apple Discussion Forums at one time or another. Apple have recently introduced a range of Developer Forums hosted at https://devforums.apple.com/community/mac. These are restricted forums aimed at developers who want to create software targeted at new versions of Mac OS X. You will need to have either a Select or Premier Apple Developer Connection subscription to get access to these forums.

RSS Feeds

On many pages in the ADC reference libraries and other help resources, you will see an RSS logo.

Follow the link, where you see it, to go to the Apple Developer RSS Feeds page. For example, right-click on the **Leopard Reference Library** link and choose to load the link in a new browser window. This loads the RSS feed into your chosen browser. Just as with any other RSS feed, you can choose to have this sent to your Apple Mail client or other RSS reader software.

Creating Your Own Developer Documentation

You might be creating software that someone else will maintain, or you might be working as part of a development team. Or you might, like me, be someone who can't remember today how the code you wrote three months ago works. In any of these cases, it's a good idea to document your code.

Obviously you can, and probably do, add comments to your code at significant points. With a little more work you can take those comments and turn them into nicely formatted HTML documentation that will enhance the value and maintainability of your software.

In this last part of the chapter, you will be using a third-party tool to generate documentation. If you have developed in Java or .NET you may have used documentation generators like JavaDoc and NDoc. You will be using a similar approach with a program called Doxygen.

Doxygen is really the only practical option if you want to create this kind of documentation. It seems rather surprising that this isn't core Xcode functionality, and maybe one day it will be.

Downloading and Installing Doxygen

For this example, I downloaded the version 1.6.1 Mac OS X Universal binary of Doxygen from http://www.stack.nl/~dimitri/doxygen/download.html. You can optionally download the source code and compile it yourself from the same site. After mounting the .dmg file, just drag the executable to the desired location. For the sake of tidiness, I put it in /Developer/Applications/Utilities.

Overview of Documentation Creation with Doxygen

Let's first run through the process involved, then you can give it a try with a real example.

The ultimate aim is to produce a docset which, as you saw earlier in the chapter, is a package folder containing html and sometimes other files. You will be producing this docset, but first you need to create the source HTML files. These are generated by Doxygen from your source .h and .m files. To achieve this Doxygen needs to find the appropriate pieces of marked-up comment text in the files.

So let's give it a spin. For this example let's create some documentation for the TemperatureConverter program that you created back in Chapter 6.

Commenting the Code

The first thing you need to do if you are going to create meaningful documentation is to add some comments to your code. We are going to add comments to the Converter class (our model in the program). Open up Converter.h and make it look like Listing 8-1 (as usual, add the code in bold).

Listing 8-1. *Adding Documentation Comments to* Converter.h

```
#import <Cocoa/Cocoa.h>

/**
 Interface for Converter Model class
*/
@interface Converter : NSObject {
    float originalTempC; /**< model storage for the incoming Centigrade temperature
value */
    float originalTempF; /**< model storage for the incoming Centigrade temperature
value */
}

@property (readwrite) float originalTempC;
@property (readwrite) float originalTempF;
```

```
/**
 This method converts a Centigrade temperature value to a Fahrenheit value
 */
- (float)convertCToF;

/**
 This method converts a Fahrenheit temperature value to a Centigrade value
 */
- (float)convertFToC;

@end
```

Now, in the `Converter.m` counterpart file, add the code in bold in Listing 8-2.

Listing 8-2. *Adding Documentation Comments to Converter.m*

```
#import "Converter.h"

/**
 Implementation for Converter Model class
 */
@implementation Converter

@synthesize originalTempC;
@synthesize originalTempF;

/**
 The method takes a float value for the original temperature in Centigrade,
 applies a conversion function on that value and returns the resulting Fahrenheit
 temperature value, also as a float
 */
- (float)convertCToF {
    return ((self.originalTempC * 1.8) + 32.0);
}
/**
 The method takes a float value for the original temperature in Fahrenheit,
 applies a conversion function on that value and returns the resulting Centigrade
 temperature value, also as a float
 */
- (float)convertFToC {
    return ((self.originalTempF - 32.0) / 1.8);
}

}
```

This commenting syntax will be familiar to you if you have used JavaDoc or NDoc, but basically it is a way of flagging the adjacent code so that the documentation tool can recognize and associate the comment to the relevant code. There are other variations on the basic `/** ... comments ... */` form (the Doxygen online documentation has a full list), but the example shown here should give you a good idea.

OK, that's enough commenting to illustrate how things work. Time to create the documentation. You will be doing this in two steps: the first within Doxygen, and the second in the Terminal.

Creating Documentation for TemperatureConverter

Fire up Doxygen. The program opens with the configuration window, which looks like Figure 8-9 (the user interface may be slightly different depending on your version—this is for v1.6.1):

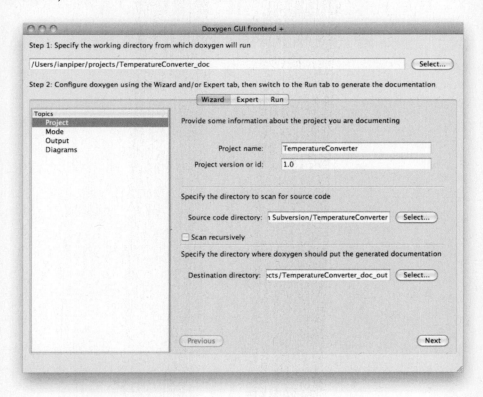

Figure 8-9. *The Doxygen setup wizard*

The setup wizard is quite complex and a little daunting, but fortunately you don't need to add much information just to get going. You will be able to explore the detailed options (and there are many) once you have seen the basic operation.

In this first screen, you need to provide a working directory. This is used as a place for Doxygen to do its work and can be anywhere on your local system. You also need to give it a project name—I used TemperatureConverter—and a version—1.0. Most importantly, you need to tell Doxygen where to find the source code (this is your project's top-level folder) and where to put the output files (this is a temporary home, as you will see shortly, and can also be anywhere on your local system).

Use the **Next** button to get to the **Mode** screen. All you need to set here is **All Entities** in the extraction mode section and **Optimize for C++ output** in the programming language section. Click on **Next** to continue to the **Output** screen. Here you need to ensure that only HTML is selected (deselect **LaTeX**, **Man pages**, **RTF**, and **XML** if they are checked). On the next screen (**Diagrams**), you don't need to change anything.

The next place you need to visit is in the **Expert** tab. Choose this tab and in the **Topics** panel, choose **HTML**. On this screen, you need to select the **GENERATE_DOCSET** option. This tells Doxygen that you will not only want to generate the HTML documentation but you will also want to create a Docset package. See Figure 8-10 to see how this screen looks.

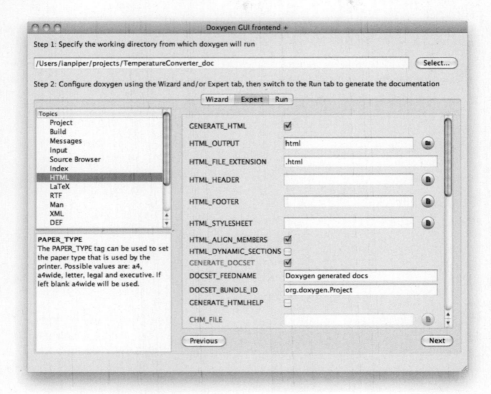

Figure 8-10. *Telling Doxygen to generate a docset package*

Finally, choose the **Run** tab and click on the **Run doxygen** button. All being well, you will see a report window like that in Figure 8-11. Check that there are no errors in the transcript.

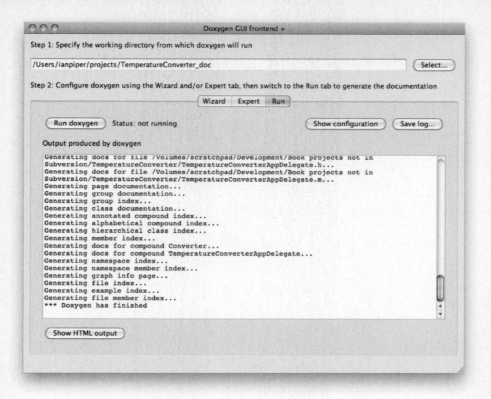

Figure 8-11. *Doxygen Run screen with the output transcript*

You are done with Doxygen now, but it is worth exploring some of the many options I haven't had space to cover here. Save the doxygen file (you will find it easier to recreate your documentation in future when your code or requirements change) and close the program.

Converting the HTML into a Docset

If you go to the Finder and open the folder where you told Doxygen to put its output, you will see a collection of HTML files, images and folders. One of these files is called Makefile. This is a text file that was created by Doxygen as a result of you checking the **GENERATE_DOCSET** option (see Figure 8-10). To complete the documentation generation process you need to run the Terminal shell command make install from this folder. So open up a Terminal window and navigate to the Doxygen output folder.

TIP: It can sometimes be a pain navigating to a folder like this one using Terminal commands. Luckily, there are alternatives. I use an AppleScript utility called OpenTerminalHere to make this kind of thing easier. Drag this script into the toolbar of the Finder and you will then be able to open a Terminal window at the current Finder location. It's the counterpart of the open . Terminal command, which opens a Finder window at the current file system location in the Terminal.

You can download OpenTerminalHere from the excellent website of Marc Liyanage (`http://www.entropy.ch/software/applescript/welcome.html`). There are a lot of very useful utilities here for the Mac developer.

At the Terminal prompt, type **make install** and hit Return. After a short time, you should see a success message like that in Figure 8-12.

```
3: interface_converter.html
4: functions.html
5: main.html
6: annotated.html
7: globals.html
8: _temperature_converter_app_delegate_8m.html
9: _temperature_converter_app_delegate_8h.html
10: _converter_8m.html
11: files.html
12: main_8m.html
Loading symbols from /Users/ianpiper/projects/TemperatureConverter_doc_out/html/
org.doxygen.Project.docset/Contents/Resources/Tokens.xml
*    16 tokens processed (  0.0 sec)
Linking up related token references
Sorting tokens
rm -f org.doxygen.Project.docset/Contents/Resources/Documents/Nodes.xml
rm -f org.doxygen.Project.docset/Contents/Resources/Documents/Info.plist
rm -f org.doxygen.Project.docset/Contents/Resources/Documents/Makefile
rm -f org.doxygen.Project.docset/Contents/Resources/Nodes.xml
rm -f org.doxygen.Project.docset/Contents/Resources/Tokens.xml
mkdir -p ~/Library/Developer/Shared/Documentation/DocSets
cp -R org.doxygen.Project.docset ~/Library/Developer/Shared/Documentation/DocSet
s
frost:html ianpiper$
```

Figure 8-12. *Using make install to generate the docset*

Notice the last line of the report. This tells you where your docset has been saved (if the folder structure doesn't already exist, the script creates it). This is where Xcode will look by default for nonApple documentation. If you navigate to this folder in the Finder (`~/Library/Developer/Shared/Documentation/DocSets/`) you will see a new docset icon (see Figure 8-13). In my case, this had the name org.doxygen.Project.docset. The option for the organization prefix (which you should probably set to your own value) and the name were other parameters that you can set in Doxygen, and I leave this as exercises for the reader!

org.doxygen.Project.docset

Figure 8-13. *The newly created docset package*

So what does this documentation look like? Open up Xcode, go to the **Documentation** main window, and click the **Home** dropdown menu (look back at Figure 8-6 if you need to refresh your memory about where this is). You should see a new entry in the menu list, called **Unknown Publisher** and beneath that an entry for **TemperatureConverter** (see Figure 8-14)

```
Apple
    iPhone OS 3.0 Library
    iPhone OS Library
    Mac OS X 10.6 Core Library
    Mac OS X Leopard Core Library
    Xcode 3.2 Developer Tools Library
Unknown Publisher
    TemperatureConverter
```

Figure 8-14. *Entry in the Home menu for the new documentation*

Choose that menu item and you will see the documentation for your project in the now-familiar format. In Figure 8-15, I have navigated from the documentation home page to the class reference for the Converter class; you can see the comments that you added a few pages ago (see Listings 8-1 and 8-2) have appeared in the **Member Function Documentation** section.

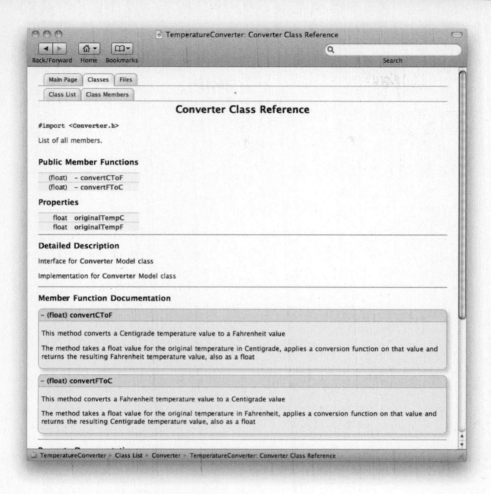

Figure 8-15. *The new documentation installed in Xcode*

Advanced Doxygen Topics

There is not sufficient room here to discuss the more advanced features of Doxygen. There is some good community support through the Doxygen forum (available at the SourceForge website: `http://sourceforge.net/mail/?group_id=5971`). One feature is worth introducing here, however.

Rather than using the Doxygen interface to generate HTML and then `make install` to generate the docset, you can create a configuration script within Doxygen that you can then load into Xcode as a build phase in order to allow you to do the build process within Xcode. This is quite an advanced topic and requires creating a Docset build script. If you would like to try this out take a look at this document in the Apple Developer Documentation: "Using Doxygen to Create Xcode Documentation Sets."

Summary

The Xcode Tools are underpinned by a comprehensive body of relevant and easy-to-use documents and code samples. Once you have a clear picture of how to navigate and use this body of resources it will enhance and accelerate your software development projects.

It's time to get back to building software. You have all the necessary core tools, technologies, and resources under your belt. In the next chapter, you will be putting much of this into practice as you create a real application.

Chapter 9

Developing an Application

So far you have covered the core tools, technologies, and techniques you need to get moving in Cocoa development in Xcode. It's time to put these together and apply them to a real problem. In this chapter you are going to run through the process of developing a complete working application—from the initial planning, through data modeling and interface design, through to the building and enhancement of the program. Even if you are an experienced developer, I recommend that you work through this example—you will be returning to it later in the book as you explore the Xcode tools further.

Defining the Problem

As with any serious undertaking, a little planning goes a long way. It's always tempting to dive in and begin writing code, but initial planning makes a lot of sense. A good way to start is to think about the problem your application is intended to address. It helps you to focus on what your creation is meant to do and, just as important, why anyone might want to use it. I suppose that is why big companies spend a fortune on market research.

Having said that, it is also true to say that some of the best software comes about from the vision of a single developer creating something to suit his own needs rather than those of a customer. For that reason, sometimes a developer just has to go with instinct—there may not be a market demand, but all the same there is an unmet need (even if it's only the developer's unmet need!) The same rules apply, of focusing on the problem that the program is going to solve.

That's the case with the DailyJournal. This program idea came from my own work as a Consultant. I saw no market requirement, but my own need existed, and the project was born from that need.

In my consultancy work I have to keep track of a wide range of clients and their projects. I need to record what project I work on for a particular day so that I know how to charge out my time. I'd also like to be able to get a picture of how my work divides down among my various clients.

Of course there are programs that help you to keep track of your time, and time-billing programs, and Getting Things Done programs. I wanted something subtly different from any of those, and once I had decided on that there was only really one course of action. I had to build it for myself.

Designing the Application

I started by considering the requirement at the most general level: what am I lacking at the moment? Here were my first thoughts:

- I must record the client and the task that I am working on today.

- I must be able to check who I worked for and what I did on any day.

- I should know who owes me for work and how much.

- I should be able to keep track of my clients and their contact information.

- I could do with knowing how much to invoice any client.

- It could be useful to get a profile of my work across clients.

- I don't need to bill my time by the hour—just by the day.

- I don't want an accounting system.

Notice the language I used. Already, by thinking about the different degrees of my unmet needs, I am setting some priorities. You are probably familiar with Agile Development principles and may have come across the MoSCoW Method—these provide a really good way to prioritize the requirements into some sort of priority (this rather tortured acronym stands for Must have, Should have, Could have, Won't have yet). It's worth describing the requirements of your program in these terms and, carefully done, this list should tell you where you should be focusing your efforts in creating the first iteration.

AGILE DEVELOPMENT

The term "Agile Development" is used to describe approaches to software development that focus on speed of delivery, flexibility, and clearly defined priorities. Like any other software-development methodology, it can be a good servant and a poor master, and getting the best out of an Agile approach requires a good understanding of its benefits and problems. However, there are some general principles that help any development project to hum along in a more or less Agile fashion:

- Get the priorities clear.

- Deliver the highest priorities first.

- Get the general right before the specific.

- Don't create a specification (they are pretty well meaningless in practice).

- Work closely throughout with the customer (fairly easy if you are the customer).

- Deliver the product in time-boxed iterations.

- Be flexible and ruthless—if something isn't working, throw it out and try it a different way. If something isn't needed, throw it out altogether.

This is not a book on Agile development, and I am making no claims that this is a complete or systematic description of the Agile way. There are some great sources of useful information on the Web, and, of course, some great books too. It's true that the Agile approach is not universally liked and may not be for you. But it is worth checking out if you have not already come across it in your work—it may just completely change the way you develop software.

Sketching Out the Problem Space

I decided that I was going to build in the "must" and "should" priorities for my first iteration, and worked up a more detailed picture of what I was going to create.

I knew that I wanted to keep track of my work on a day-by-day basis. That more or less decided part of the design: I would need a day-by-day view of my work in the program. I thought about how the Consultants in my business do this at the moment: a paper diary, one page per day. In this diary each Consultant writes out what they did on that day, where they were, and what the charge would be. That system works pretty well, apart from the shortcomings of any paper-based system. What if I modeled the new program on that?

I was ready to sketch out how the program might look, and came up with the rough design in Figure 9–1.

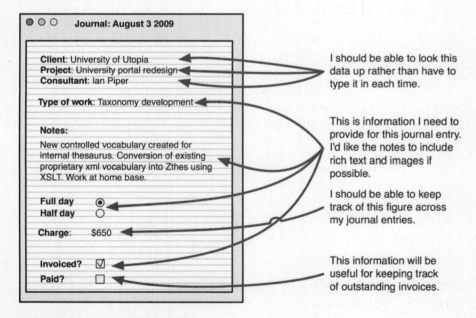

Figure 9–1. *Initial user-interface ideas*

It still looks like the diary page, but I have started to separate out what data I expect to provide for this journal entry, what I would like to be able to look up, and what should be calculated. This was starting to suggest a data model. Before creating the data model in detail I needed to think about the entities I would be managing in general. I needed to keep track of clients, and each client might have several projects, and there could be many journal entries for any project. Also, since there are a number of Consultants who work in the company, I needed to store information about them too. This was starting to suggest a complexity further down the road—is this a multiuser system, with login and user-management features? No . . . this was a good time to put my Agile foot down: this is not a high-priority feature, and, while keeping in mind the possibility (and therefore not consciously designing a system that cannot be multiuser), I decided not to do anything more about it yet, beyond allowing the creation and management of multiple Consultants.

The Data Model

At this stage I could say some things about the data model:

- A Client can appear in many journal entries, but an entry is for only one Client (Clients and journal entries therefore have a one-to-many relationship).

- A taskType can feature in many journal entries, but a journal entry has just one taskType (taskTypes and journal entries therefore are also one-to-many). Actually, a single journal entry could contain more than one taskType, but that would complicate things. If I design my model and implement it correctly, this is something that I could change later. I decided to keep it simple.

- A journal entry is worked on by one Consultant, while a Consultant will have many entries, so Consultants and journal entries have a one-to-many relationship.

- The Consultant can work for any Client. However, the relationship is not significant in the data model until I introduce multi-Consultant features, and those features aren't going in yet, so I don't need to create a relationship.

- A Consultant needs to record the charge for a journal entry.

Here is my refined list of features:

- I can create, edit, and delete journal entries.

- I can create, edit, and delete Clients.

- I can create, edit, and delete task types.

At this point, I could sketch out a data model (see Figure 9–2):

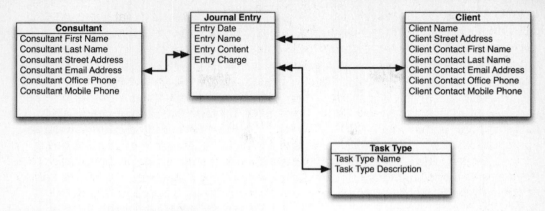

Figure 9–2. *Data model for the DailyJournal application*

That model also suggests something about the user interface, doesn't it? Good application design ensures that you handle your data in the appropriate place. This data model has the journal entry as the centerpiece, and it makes sense to have this data available in the main window. Likewise it seems like a good idea to manage Clients, Consultants, and tasks as secondary and separate windows. Figure 9–3 is an updated sketch for the user interfaces you are going to build. It's still not very detailed—it doesn't have to be.

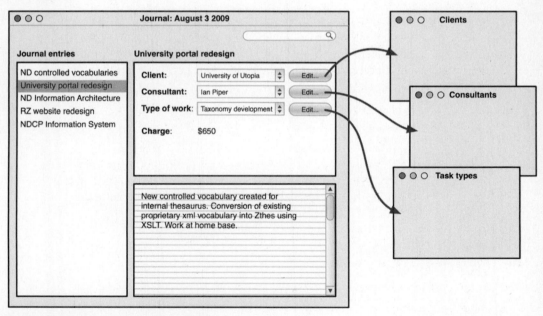

Figure 9–3. *Updated sketch of the UI design*

This is enough to get you started. Remember, if it doesn't work out, you can revisit it: this is Agile development!

Creating the Project

Let's crack on. Create a new Cocoa project and make sure you choose the checkbox **Use Core Data for storage** (leave the option **Document-based application** unchecked). Call the project DailyJournal. Once in the **Workspace**, double-click the **DailyJournal_DataModel.xcdatamodel** entry in the **Detail** panel. This will load the data model user interface in a new window. You will be creating a data model that matches the model in Figure 9–2. You will recall from Chapter 5 that you use the data model window to create entities and assign attributes and relationships to those entities. In this case you are going to create entities for Journal Entries, Consultants, Clients, and TaskTypes. You're an old hand now, so there's no need to go through the detail of how to create the various objects, so Table 9–1 shows them all. When complete, your data model should look like Figure 9–4.

Table 9–1. *Information for creating the data model*

Entity	Property	Kind	Type or Destination
client	clientContactEmailAddress	Attribute	String
client	clientContactFirstName	Attribute	String
client	clientContactLastName	Attribute	String
client	clientContactMobilePhone	Attribute	String
client	clientContactOfficePhone	Attribute	String
client	clientName	Attribute	String
client	clientStreetAddress	Attribute	String
client	entriesForClient	Relationship	journalEntry (To-Many)
consultant	consultantFirstName	Attribute	String
consultant	consultantLastName	Attribute	String
consultant	consultantMobilePhone	Attribute	String
consultant	consultantOfficePhone	Attribute	String
consultant	consultantStreetAddress	Attribute	String
consultant	entriesForConsultant	Relationship	journalEntry (To-Many)
journalEntry	clientForEntry	Relationship	client
journalEntry	consultantForEntry	Relationship	consultant
journalEntry	entryCharge	Attribute	Float
journalEntry	entryContent	Attribute	Binary data
journalEntry	entryDate	Attribute	Date
journalEntry	entryInvoiced	Attribute	Boolean
journalEntry	entryName	Attribute	String
journalEntry	taskTypeForEntry	Relationship	taskType
taskType	entriesForTaskType	Relationship	journalEntry (To-Many)
taskType	taskTypeDescription	Attribute	String
taskType	taskTypeName	Attribute	String

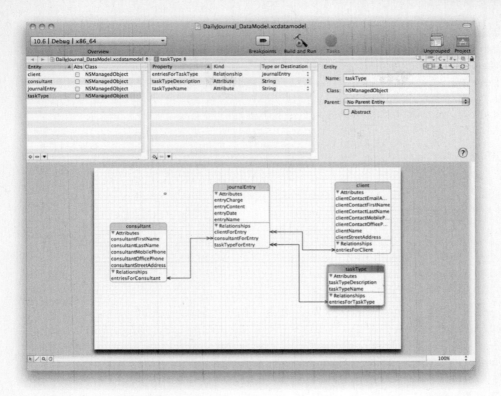

Figure 9–4. *The Data Model in Xcode*

Once you have built the data model, save it and close the window (if it is in a separate window). That's all you need to do in Xcode for now—time to move to Interface Builder to create the user interface components.

Choosing the Data Store Format

When you create a Core Data Cocoa application you have a choice of three different formats for storage: SQLite, XML or binary. This is configured in the DailyJournal_AppDelegate.m file, in the method called persistentStoreCoordinator. In Listing 9–1 you will see the significant code fragment:

Listing 9–1. *Setting the Storage Options for the DailyJournal Application*

```
url = [NSURL fileURLWithPath: [applicationSupportFolder stringByAppendingPathComponent:
    @"storedata"]];
    persistentStoreCoordinator = [[NSPersistentStoreCoordinator alloc]
      initWithManagedObjectModel: [self managedObjectModel]];
    if (![persistentStoreCoordinator addPersistentStoreWithType:NSXMLStoreType
      configuration:nil URL:url options:nil error:&error]){
        [[NSApplication sharedApplication] presentError:error];
    }
```

The first bold section shows the filename used to store your data. You can actually give this any name you like: a.b, for example. The second bold section is where you choose the storage format. Your choices are NSXMLStoreType (the default, as an XML file), NSSQLiteStoreType (for a SQLite database), or NSBinaryStoreType (for the more traditional binary data format used for Mac OS X data stores before the days of Core Data). Generally speaking, the XML format is the best option to use during development, as it is easy to make changes to your data model and also to inspect the data file using external tools such as XML editors.

When you go into production you may want to change over to one of the other storage formats—SQLite is more scalable than XML if your database is likely to grow.

Building the User Interfaces

The main user interface for this application is going to display a list and detail view of journal entries. So there will be a list of the entries—probably by name. For each entry selected, the detail part of the interface will show the other information. We will want a way to add and remove entries, too.

Start by giving the main user interface window a more useful name (it's just called **Window** in the **Document** window)—I usually begin the names of windows with a lowercase w, so I called this one **wJournalEntries**. It is not actually necessary to rename objects in the **Document** window, but you will be creating several windows and controllers during this project, and it is a good practice to give meaningful names to such objects.

The Core Data Entity Interface Assistant

Now open the window and drag a Core Data Entity object into it from the **Library**. This brings up the **New Core Data Entity Interface** assistant. Choose the DailyJournal project, then the DailyJournal_DataModel.xcdatamodel model—these are the only options, but in more complex projects you may have a variety of models to choose from. In the last column choose the journalEntry entity, then click **Next** (see Figure 9–5).

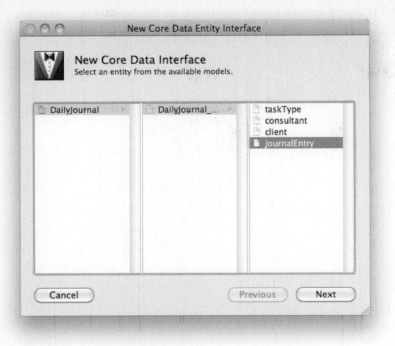

Figure 9–5. *Core Data Entity Interface assistant*

You already know that this is going to show both a list and the detail for each item, so in the next window of the assistant, choose **Master/Detail View** from the drop-down list. Now let's consider the other options. The first, **Search Field**, seems like a good choice. There could eventually be many journal entries and so a Spotlight-style mechanism for filtering will be useful. Check that option. You will want to see the detail for each item selected, so check that box. Finally, you also want to be able to add and remove entries, so check that box too. Click **Next**. In this final step of the assistant you need to specify which property fields from the **journalEntry** entity should be shown in the user interface. In fact, you want all of these one way or another, so leave them all checked (the default). Click on the **Finish** button, and you will see something like Figure 9–6.

Well, that is seriously ugly isn't it? That's the problem with auto-generated interfaces of course—they are intelligent, but really not that intelligent. What you have here is a collection of controls that have the appropriate connections to the controller, but the layout leaves much to be desired. Also, you will see that the process of generating the controls doesn't always get it right. Look at the control that the assistant has generated for the **Entry Content**. It's an Image Well control—since you specified that the attribute needed to contain binary data, the assistant (reasonably, perhaps, but incorrectly) concluded that you wanted an Image View control. You'll need to change that, since you actually want to store text and images here (a Text View seems more appropriate). Given the amount of change that you will need to make here it's arguable that it would have been better to create the controls from scratch. However, the auto-generated interface has its place, so let's work with it and see what we can do with it.

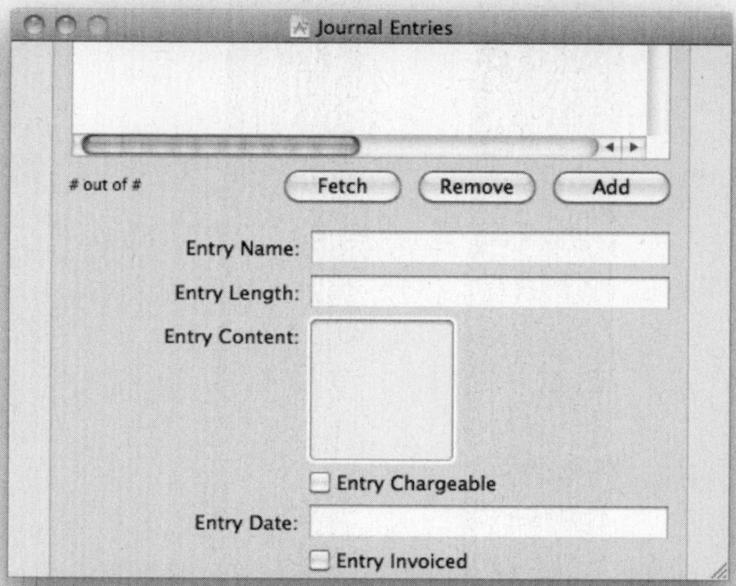

Figure 9–6. *Main user interface with autogenerated Core Data elements*

Developing the User Interface

Before starting on developing the user interface, it is a good idea to visit the **Document** window and check on the various objects that the assistant has created here. You will see that there are four new array controllers: one for the Journal Entry and one for each of the other entities. These are here because of the to-many relationships between the **journalEntry** entity and each of these entities. However, you will find that as you build more and more complex interfaces these controllers can be a little confusing as they are simply named for their entity. So, for example, every array controller that the assistant creates for the **Consultant** entity will be called **Consultant Array Controller**. So it is a good idea to adopt a naming convention that unambiguously names each controller. I tend to use a convention for windows, too. So in this case I gave the window the name **wJournalEntry** and I renamed the **Journal Entry Array Controller** to **ac Journal Entry**. For the other array controllers, I wanted to make the relationship clear in the name. I renamed **Consultant Array Controller** to **ac Consultant for Journal Entry** (since that relationship is what the controller is managing), and so on. See Figure 9–7.

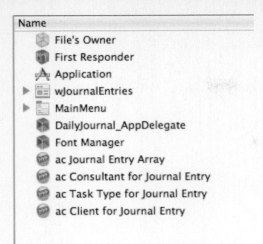

Figure 9-7. *Renaming the objects in the Document window for clarity*

Now back to the user interface window. First, give yourself some breathing space—make this window bigger—say, 800 pixels wide × 600 pixels high.

> **NOTE:** There is a behavior in Interface Builder—some might call it a bijoux bugette—that you need to be aware of. One of the current problems with the UI is that the controls take up more space than the window. All of the controls are embedded in a box control, and if you inspect the autosizing options for that box you will see that they are set to grow with the window.
>
> If you resize the window by typing in new values in the **Window Size** inspector tab, then unfortunately the controls end up growing too, so they are still too big for the window—irritation ensues.
>
> However, if you resize the window by simply moving its drag handle at the bottom right, the embedded controls do not resize, so you get your breathing space.

Once you have resized your window, select the box that is acting as the container for all of the controls. We want to get rid of that: choose the **Layout ➤ Unembed Objects** menu item. Now your user interface should look like Figure 9-8.

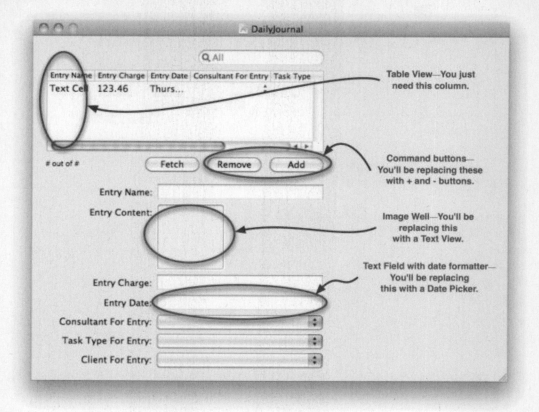

Figure 9–8. *Developing the user interface for the Journal Entries window*

Your user interface may not look exactly like this, but it will be close. The annotations on this figure show some of the main items that need work. You may look at this and think it would have been easier just to build this interface from scratch rather than use the assistant and then put things right. However, one of the nice things that the assistant does is to build all of the data bindings for you. This makes it much easier to do things like replacing one control with another, as you can just reproduce those bindings in the new control.

Let's try that now. You need to replace that Image View with a Text View. So drag a Text View into the window. Now, right-click on the Image Well to see its bindings. Its **Data** value is bound to the `selection.entryContent` property. That means it will display whatever it can from the `entryContent` attribute for the currently selected record in the **journalEntry** entity. So you need to replicate that binding in the Text View. To do this, click in the Text View (remember, this actually selects the Scroll View), then click again. You should see **Text View Bindings** in the **Bindings Inspector** tab if you have selected it correctly. Now use the disclosure arrow to open up the **Data** section, use the pop-up menu to select the Journal Entry Array Controller, and choose **selection** from the **Controller Key** dropdown and **entryContent** from the **Model Key Path** dropdown. The resulting binding should look like Figure 9–9.

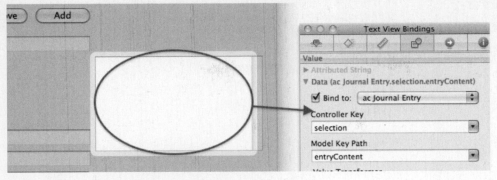

Figure 9–9. *Setting the correct binding for the Text View control*

Now let's make those **Add** and **Remove** buttons look a little more Mac-friendly. Most Mac applications use plus and minus buttons to add and remove items in lists, so let's do that here. Luckily, it's really easy to do. Choose the **Add** button, then look for the **Bezel** attribute in the inspector. Using the drop-down list, change this from **Push** to **Gradient**.

Make it 25 pixels wide by 23 pixels high. Clear the title. Now in the **Media** tab of the **Library** window find the NSAddTemplate image and drag that onto the **Gradient** button. It now has a plus sign (you could have just given it a title of "+," but that doesn't look right). Do the same for the **Remove** button, using the NSRemoveTemplate image in place of the title.

It would be nice if the date control were a Date Picker rather than a Text Field. Drag one of those out of the **Library** into the window. Based on the binding of the current control you know that this Date Picker needs to be bound to the JournalEntry Array Controller selection.entryDate. Make the binding in the same way as you have previously.

Now you can delete the **Fetch** button, the Image Well, and the Text Field with Date Formatter. Tidy things up a little and, though we still clearly have a way to go, it is starting to look a little more like the desired user interface (see Figure 9–10).

A few things deserve mention here. First, I have embedded some of the objects in a box; this helps keep related information together. I set the **Box Type** to **Custom** because I didn't want the usual rounded corners. I gave the box a white fill and 50% white border, which looks about right when compared to the rest of the user interface. Also, I have not used the title attribute of the box, because the font for the title is a bit too small and doesn't match the label that I have used above the **Journal Entries** list. So I have added another label instead, and bound that to the entryName attribute. I gave that label a placeholder title of **Journal Entry**. Then I could delete the entryName Text Field provided by the assistant.

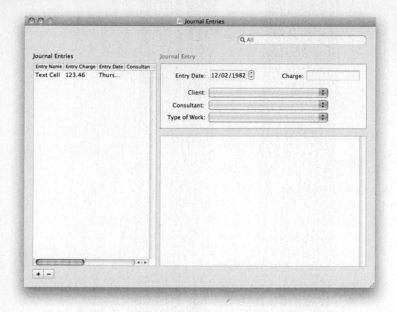

Figure 9–10. *The user interface after a bit of sprucing up*

The TextField for the entry charge has a formatter showing it to be numeric. Delete this formatter and replace it with a Currency Formatter.

I have given the window a title of **Journal Entries** and set it to a minimum size of 800 × 600. I haven't listed the autosizing steps that you need to take to make this window work nicely: it's pretty straightforward, but refer back to Chapter 3 if you are hazy on how to do this.

Tidying Up and Adding the Extra Buttons

The next decision that you need to make is what information to display in the Table View. If you inspect the bindings for the different columns in this control, you will see that it contains columns for all of the attributes of the **journalEntry** entity. You don't want that—this is just a simple list of entries. Earlier I said that the most obvious option is to have just one column with the entryName. But let's think about this—maybe there is some value in having the entryDate as a column as well as the entryName. Remember that one of the original requirements was to know what I was doing on a particular day, so having the ability to look at a list of dates, or to order by date, makes sense. Let's go for a two-column list here. The columns we want to keep are for the entryName and entryDate. Choose each of the other columns in turn (click until the column highlights and you see **Table Column** in the inspector title bar) and press the Delete key. Resize the columns to give them sufficient space. Figure 9–11 shows how things should look now.

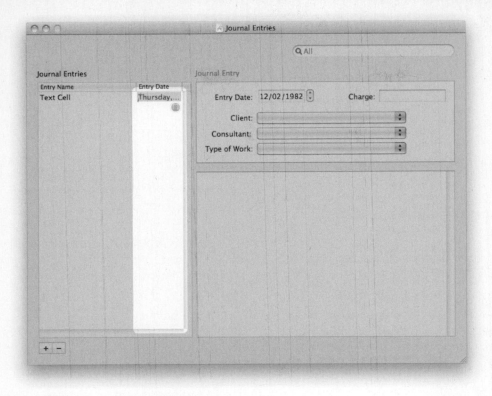

Figure 9–11. *Updated two-column Table View*

While you're at it, actually, change the date formatter for the **Date** column so that it uses the short style rather than the default longer form (Figure 9–12):

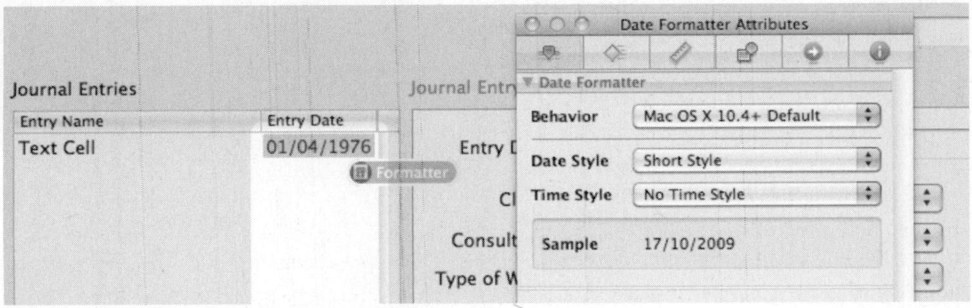

Figure 9–12. *Setting the date format*

The final touch is going to be to provide a way to get to the data-entry windows for managing Clients, Consultants, and taskTypes. For now, add three buttons (I chose Rounded Rect buttons) and give them the title **Manage...** (the ellipsis is a cue to the user that clicking the button will open a new window). See Figure 9–13.

Entry Date: 12/02/1982   Charge:
Client: Manage...
Consultant: Manage...
Type of Work: Manage...

Figure 9–13. *Adding the Manage... buttons*

Later on you will connect these buttons to the appropriate actions. For now this completes the user interface for the **Journal Entry** window.

Creating the Secondary Windows

It's time to create the windows for the **Client, Consultant**, and taskType entities. These are much simpler windows since they deal purely with the business of creating and managing the entity in question. The process is the same for each, so I'll just step through one of them and leave you to do the others.

Let's take the **Consultant** entity. First, create a new window—drag a Window object out of the **Library** into the **Document** window. Call it **wConsultants** and give it the title **Manage Consultants**. Now drag a Core Data Entity object into the window to bring up the assistant. Run through this, choosing the **Consultant** entity and a **Master-Detail** layout. Choose all of the attributes and relationship options (though you don't need a search box this time). The result will initially be a little untidy, but with a little rejigging your window should look like Figure 9–14.

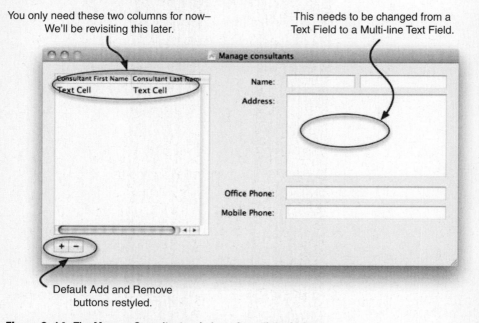

Figure 9–14. *The Manage Consultants window after a little tidying up*

CAUTION: There is an odd bug that sometimes manifests itself when creating new windows in Interface Builder. When you create a window, you should ensure, in the **Window Attributes** tab in the inspector, that the **Release When Closed** checkbox is *not* selected. Leaving this checked—if it is checked to start with, and it isn't always—will cause your application to throw an `EXC_BAD_ACCESS` exception when reopening this window programmatically after closing it. The reason is our old adversary memory allocation. It seems like the memory for the object is released when other components of the application think it is still around, leaving your application confused. Unfortunately, this still seems to throw an exception if you are using garbage collection, so it is well worth a check.

Now repeat for the **Clients** and **Task Types** windows. These follow exactly the same process, and will need a similar amount of tidying. I would advise renaming the windows and array controllers as you go along. The final collection of windows should look something like Figure 9–15.

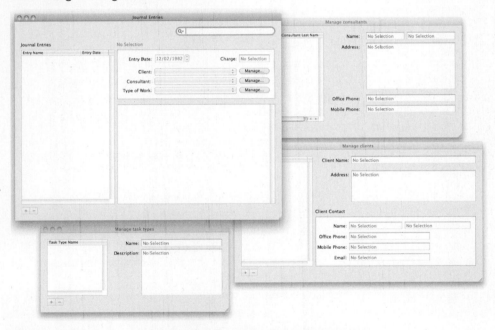

Figure 9–15. *The final collection of windows for the DailyJournal application*

Now that you have all of the secondary windows for the user interface, you need to wire up the connection between the **Manage...** buttons on the **Journal Entry** window and these secondary windows. This is very straightforward. Control-click on the **Manage...** button to the right of the **Consultant** popup and drag it to the **wConsultant** window. From the HUD choose the `makeKeyAndOrderFront:` action. This action, as the name suggests, sets the nominated window as the key window and brings it to the front. Now make the corresponding connections for the buttons to open the other two secondary windows.

Configuring the Search Capabilities

In the **Journal Entry** window there is a search box (assuming that you chose to have one in the assistant). This, like other objects in the user interface, is bound to the array controller. If you select the search box and look at the **Bindings** tab in the inspector, you can see a collection of **Predicates**. These essentially define filters that can be applied to your data to help narrow down searches. With the way that I created this application, there are four predicates, corresponding to three filters plus a catch-all "All" search. Table 9–2 presents their properties.

Table 9–2. *Filter Predicate Bindings in the Journal Entry Window*

Display Name	Predicate Format
All	(entryName contains[c] $value) or (entryCharge.description contains[c] $value) or (entryDate.description contains[c] $value)
Entry Name	entryName contains[c] $value
Entry Charge	entryCharge.description contains[c] $value
Entry Date	entryDate.description contains[c] $value

That all looks a bit strange. It makes sense to search the entryName field, but why did the assistant choose to include entryCharge and entryDate too? Another mysterious piece of behavior from the assistant. However, we don't want those extra searches here, so let's get rid of them. Starting at the bottom, delete predicates 4, 3, and 2. Then edit predicate 1 so that its **Display Name** is **Entry Name** and its predicate format is entryName contains[c] $value. Now when you do a search in the running program it will filter on the entry name.

The obvious lesson from the slightly odd behavior of the Core Data Assistant is not to use it, and once you are comfortable with knowing what bindings to make, you may prefer to create these manually. However, it's important to stress that the assistant definitely has its uses when you are learning about making connections and bindings in the user interface, and on balance I tend to use it to quickly put interfaces together.

MAKING DIFFICULT DESIGN DECISIONS

You might be wondering why I don't have a predicate to search the entryContent field. Well, this is a drawback of using a Binary data type for this attribute—it is not a trivial business to set a predicate to filter such an attribute. A halfway house would have been to have the attribute as a Multi-line Text Field and allow it to use rich text. That would allow for styled (and searchable) text, but not images. Another slight drawback of Multi-line Text Fields is their behavior when a user presses the Return key. Because this is a text-entry field, the standard HCI guidelines behavior is for the editing to end on Return rather than moving the cursor to a new line. You can get a new line in the field by pressing Control+Return, but that is a little counter-intuitive. You can see this in the behavior of the **Address** field in the **Manage Consultant** window.

As often happens in software development, you have to make difficult design decisions: the entryContent field can be feature-rich but not searchable, or have slightly more restrictive features with searchable content. Without a fair amount of coding it is hard to work around this.

Running the Application

Well, the application is now ready to run. Save the NIB file, close Interface Builder and choose **Build and Run** (see Figure 9–16).

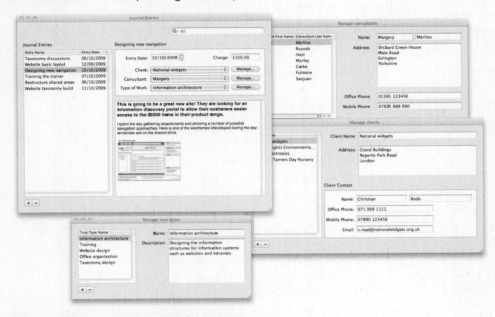

Figure 9–16. *Running the DailyJournal application*

If all has gone according to plan, you should now have a working database application, managing four data entities with a range of relationships between them.

The main window allows you to create and manage journal entries. Each one will refer to a Consultant who is doing the work, a Client, and the type of work done for that entry. There are separate windows to manage each of these other entities. The main window allows you to see at a glance what each Consultant was doing on each day. Once you get beyond a single screen's worth of entries, you can use the search box to filter entries by name.

What to Do if It Doesn't Work

If you encounter problems as you go along, check these common causes:

- If your **Add** and **Remove** buttons don't work correctly, check their bindings to the array controller (for example, for the **Client Add** button this should be `ac Client.canAdd` in the **Enabled Availability** section) and that the button is correctly connected to the add or remove action of the controller (right-click and drag from the button to the controller, and choose the appropriate action).

- Check that your windows are not set to **Release When Closed** in the **Window Attributes** inspector panel.

- If the secondary windows don't open when you click on the **Manage...** button, check that you have connected the button to the `MakeKeyAndOrderFront:` action on the appropriate window.

- If fields on the interface don't display data, or if they display the wrong data, your bindings are wrong. Go back over the details discussed previously and check them through.

Making Improvements

The application works, but already it is plain that there are some clunky features. Let's see what we can do to improve these.

Displaying the Full Name in One Field

One of the clunky features is the way we are handling the Consultant name. In the **Manage Consultants** window we have two columns, holding the `firstName` and `lastName` properties. Since we are probably going to be editing these properties in the text fields rather than the table view, wouldn't it be nicer if we could show the full name in one column? The other place we see this is in the **Journal Entries** window, where we chose to bind the **Consultant** popup to the `firstName` property.

Let's make that work better. To do this we are going to write some code, create a new managed object, and modify the bindings.

Make sure your NIB is saved, and move to Xcode. In the **Detail** panel select the data model, and select the **Consultant** entity. Now choose **File New File...**, and the template chooser will appear. Since you had your data model selected you now have a new option available: **Managed Object Class**. This allows you to build Core Data entities from scratch. Choose this now. In the next window just choose **Next**. You will see a list of the entities in your project: select **Consultant** (actually, it should already be selected if you selected it in the data model earlier). From the checkboxes below the list panel, select **Generate accessors** and **Generate Obj-C 2.0 Properties**. Click on **Finish**.

This has given you a new Managed Object class, which enables you to elaborate the **Consultant** entity—to add your own customized methods and properties. You are going to create a new property to put together a full name from the `firstName` and `lastName` properties. Listing 9–2 shows `consultant.h` with the new property (in bold) that you need to add.

Listing 9–2. *The New Header File for the Consultant Entity*

```
#import <CoreData/CoreData.h>

@interface consultant :  NSManagedObject  {
}

@property (nonatomic, retain) NSString * consultantOfficePhone;
@property (nonatomic, retain) NSString * consultantFirstName;
@property (nonatomic, retain) NSString * consultantStreetAddress;
@property (nonatomic, retain) NSString * consultantLastName;
@property (nonatomic, retain) NSString * consultantMobilePhone;
@property (nonatomic, retain) NSNumber * consultantDayRate;
@property (nonatomic, retain) NSSet* entriesForConsultant;
@property (readonly) NSString *fullName;

@end

@interface consultant (CoreDataGeneratedAccessors)
- (void)addEntriesForConsultantObject:(NSManagedObject *)value;
- (void)removeEntriesForConsultantObject:(NSManagedObject *)value;
- (void)addEntriesForConsultant:(NSSet *)value;
- (void)removeEntriesForConsultant:(NSSet *)value;

@end
```

Take a moment to look over this header file. It contains property declarations for all of the attributes and the relationship defined for the **Consultant** entity in your data model. You have just added one to handle the read-only property `fullName`. Now implement the getter method in the counterpart file `consultant.m` (Listing 9–3):

Listing 9–3. *Implementing the fullName Getter Method*

```
#import "consultant.h"

@implementation consultant

@dynamic consultantOfficePhone;
@dynamic consultantFirstName;
@dynamic consultantStreetAddress;
@dynamic consultantLastName;
@dynamic consultantMobilePhone;
@dynamic consultantDayRate;
@dynamic entriesForConsultant;

- (NSString *)fullName {
    NSString *firstName = self.consultantFirstName;
    NSString *lastName = self.consultantLastName;
    if ((firstName) && (lastName)) {
        return [NSString stringWithFormat:@"%@ %@", firstName, lastName];
    }
```

```
    if (firstName) {
        return firstName;
    }
    if (lastName)    {
        return lastName;
    }
    // we get to here if neither firstName nor lastName is set
    NSString *noName = @"No name";
    return noName;
}

@end
```

This is just making sure that the method returns something: preferably the full name, but failing that, either firstName or lastName, and a fallback in case neither is set.

Now that you have the new Managed Object and the method to create a full name, let's make the necessary changes in the user interface. Switch over to Interface Builder and select the **Manage Consultants** window.

At the moment this window has a Table View with two columns. Recall that these two columns were bound to the ac Consultant array controller like this:

```
ac Consultant.arrangedObjects.consultantFirstName
ac Consultant.arrangedObjects.consultantLastName
```

In the inspector, change the Table View from two columns to one column. Now you need to change the binding for this column to the new fullName property:

```
ac Consultant.arrangedObjects.fullName
```

That will take care of the **Manage Consultants** view, but you will also need to visit another binding: the popup button on the **Journal Entries** window. Find that popup now and take a look at its bindings. It has three, shown in Table 9–3:

Table 9–3. *Original bindings for the Consultant popup*

Item	Binding
Content	ac Consultant for Journal Entry.arrangedObjects
Content Values	ac Consultant for Journal Entry.arrangedObjects.consultantFirstName
Selected Object	ac Journal Entry.selection.consultantForEntry

So the selected object is the Consultant for the current journal entry, the content you need to show is the Consultant object for this journal entry, and the value to display is the first name.

You need to make some changes here to pick and correctly use the fullName property. Clearly the select object is still the same: you need to pick up the right Consultant for this journal entry. But the content and values you need to use come from the Consultant object. So change the bindings to those in Table 9–4:

Table 9–4. *Updated bindings for the Consultant popup*

Item	Binding
Content	ac Consultant.arrangedObjects
Content Values	ac Consultant.arrangedObjects.fullName
Selected Object	ac Journal Entry.selection.consultantForEntry

Save the NIB, then choose **Build and Run**. When you look at either the **Manage Consultants** window or the **Journal Entry** window the full name of the Consultant is now displayed (see Figure 9–17):

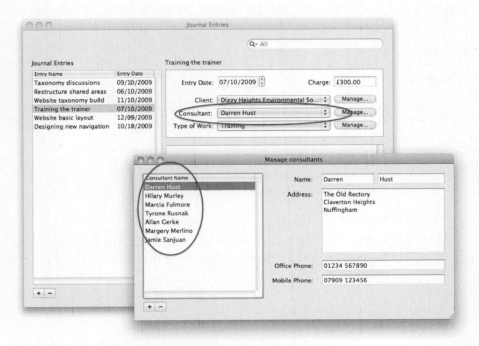

Figure 9–17. *Updated bindings show the generated full name property.*

However, there is still a slight problem. Choose a Consultant in the **Manage Consultants** window and make a change to either the first or last name. Oops... the change is not updated in the **Journal Entries** window. Why not?

The problem stems from the fact that you have created fullName as a *dependent property*. It is generated from the consultantFirstName and consultantLastName properties, but any changes to these need to be communicated using the Key Value Observing mechanism. This is a pretty advanced Objective-C topic and we are not going to discuss it in detail here (Hillegass (*Cocoa Programming for Mac OS X*, Addison-Wesley, 2008) has a good chapter on this), but in summary we need to tell the other objects in the system that the value has changed and needs to be updated. Add the code shown in Listing 9–4 to consultant.m (put it at the bottom, just before @end).

Listing 9–4. *Making the System Aware of Changes to the consultantFirstName and consultantLastNamePproperties*

```
+ (NSSet *)keyPathsForValuesAffectingFullName {
    return [NSSet setWithObjects:@"consultantFirstName", @"consultantLastName", nil];
}
```

Now run the application again. Open the **Journal Entries** and **Manage Consultants** windows and make a change to a Consultant first name or last name Text Field. The updated result will appear immediately both in the Table View in the **Manage Consultants** window and in the **Consultant** popup on the **Journal Entries** window.

Displaying the Total Amount Earned Across the Journal Entries

Each of the journal entries shows the charge that the Consultant is making for that entry. It would be nice to see a running total, wouldn't it?

In Interface Builder, open the **Journal Entries** window. Add two label controls to the bottom of the window. Set the title of one of them to **Total Consultant Charges:**. Add a Currency Formatter to the other. Figure 9–18 shows how it should look.

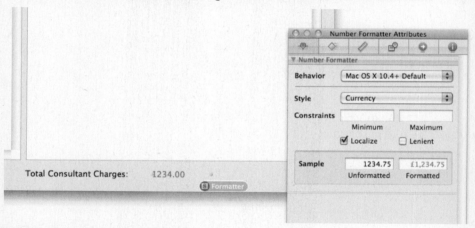

Figure 9–18. *Adding a running total of Consultant charges*

Now you need to provide the second label control with a binding. You need to bind the label's value to the ac Journal Entry array controller. Since you want to aggregate information for all of the entries, you will use arrangedObjects. The attribute you need to use is entryCharge, but you can't put that in as the **Model Key Path** because you want the label to display a sum of the entryCharge values across the whole set of entries. You need to use an *array operator*. These are features that allow you to carry out operations on collections of items. You have access to operators such as @count, @max, @avg, and the one you need here: @sum. The syntax you need to use is Controller.Key.Operator.KeyPath. So now select the label that you want to hold the running total, and bind it to ac Journal Entry with a key of arrangedObjects and a **Model Key Path** of @sum.entryCharge. Save the NIB and run the application again. Try adding new journal entries, deleting existing entries, and changing the charge amount. You should see the **Total Consultant Charge** value change in line with your changes.

As you develop greater skill and greater ambition in your Cocoa development, you will want to develop a good understanding of key-value coding. The Apple documentation on set and array operators (search for the Key-Value Coding Programming Guide) provides all of the detail you would need to make more sophisticated use of these handy operators. It is also more accessible and well-explained than a lot of Apple documentation, so well worth a read.

Where to Take the Application from Here

This application is not complete, but if you look back at the original requirements, you have hit them all. Let's review those priorities:

- I must record the client and the task that I am working on today. *(Done)*

- I must be able to check who I worked for and what I did on any day. *(Done)*

- I should know who owes me for work and how much. *(Partially done, but we have the information to work it out)*

- I should be able to keep track of my clients and their contact information. *(Done)*

- I could do with knowing how much to invoice any client. *(Not done, though we have the raw data)*

- It could be useful to get a profile of my work across clients. *(Not done, but we have the raw data)*

- I don't need to bill my time by the hour—just by the day. *(Done)*

- I don't want an accounting system. *(And we don't have one)*

So where is this application going from here? Well, a few ideas come to mind, particularly looking at the pieces in this list that are not yet done. First, it would be nice to be able to do some more analysis—for example, get a breakdown of earnings by Consultant and client. It might be a good idea to add some enhancements to the features, such as seeing whether you have invoiced a client for a particular piece of work. It might be worth looking at aggregating journal entries into invoicable blocks of work.

However, that will have to wait for another time. This chapter is not about a final polished product, but about getting you to see the development as an iterative process: conceptualize, design, build, repeat. As you move from one iteration to the next you fill in the gaps that are so evident in the first iteration, converging on the product that you are finally going to deliver. In later chapters you will see a number of other steps that support the iterative development process: in particular the use of revision-control repositories and unit testing.

Looking Back and Looking Forward

You have come a long way over the last nine chapters. You should now be comfortable with the core design, construction, debugging, and documentation tools provided by Xcode. The business of how to go about designing and building applications should be becoming clearer. You have seen how the frameworks and patterns built by Apple help you to put together great applications with little work compared to other development environments and allow you to focus your creative energies on the special features of your application rather than on re-creating the wheel.

This is the end of the first section of this book. In the next section's chapters you are moving on from the core tools to visit some of the companion applications that beginners often don't use, but that can be very helpful in the right situations. Over the next few chapters you will learn how to use revision management to protect your investment in your code, how to build automated testing into your development strategies, and how to use Xcode's performance and analysis tools to hunt down problems and wring extra performance out of your programs. It's going to be an exciting trip—turn the page when you are ready to get going!

Part II

Enhancing Development with Companion Tools

Chapter 10

Source-Code Management with Subversion

If you have ever developed software as part of a team, you probably have encountered *version control* (or revision control, or source-code management) systems. Systems like this keep track of the code and ensure that changes are recorded and synchronized to all of the team members who need to know about them. They enable teams to try out alternative branches of code development and to roll back to earlier versions if things are going wrong.

Even if you are developing alone, though, it makes really good sense to take steps to manage your code. Most developers have some sort of process for systematically storing code and naming projects. But good naming conventions and filing policies are only part of the picture. What if you want to work on the same project in more than one place? What if you want to share the code with a colleague to get their help fixing a bug? What if you want to see the way your code was before you tried out that idea—the one that didn't work out? What if—perish the thought—your computer crashes and you lose all of your (non-backed-up—hey, we've all done it) hard work? With a bit of planning and diligence using a source-code management (SCM) system, you can sail blithely through all of those situations.

As a Mac user, you are once again privileged. Your Mac comes loaded with Subversion, a modern, easy-to-use, comprehensive system for managing your code. As you will see, the Subversion server is really easy to set up and run. Even better, the most recent releases of Xcode have had steadily better and better client support for Subversion, meaning that you can do revision management of your projects for the most part without leaving the Xcode environment.

In this chapter you will be getting a grounding in how Subversion works and in installing and configuring a Subversion repository on your Mac. You will also learn about your different options when deciding to use Subversion for source control. After that you will be integrating Subversion into your work cycle, setting up Xcode to use your source code repository, and working through some examples.

There's a lot to cover, so let's get started.

Introduction to Subversion

Subversion is a system for code control and revision management. Think of it as a document-management system for code. Like any document-management system, Subversion keeps your code in a central library (called a *repository*) rather than simply stored as files in the file system. Once you have deposited your files in that repository, you no longer access them directly as files. Instead, you use Subversion's management tools to check out the files you need to work on. Subversion keeps track of the fact that you have a local copy of the files, and when you have finished working on them it allows you to check them back in. As you do this, Subversion monitors whether the files have changed, and if so it creates a new revision of the files, as shown in Figure 10–1. In other words, Subversion provides you with version control.

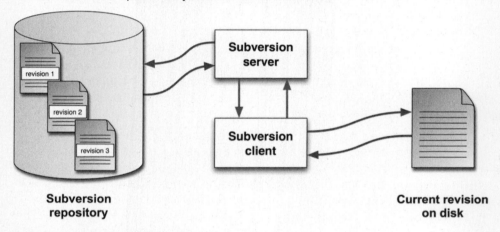

Figure 10–1. *Overview of Subversion*

The most important consequence for you as a developer is that you never lose code: at any time you can return to an earlier revision of your code, either to compare it with another revision or to roll back in the event of problems.

Subversion manages your code in another respect too: it makes it easier to work collaboratively on projects. If more than one person is working on a project, both people can get the code from the same repository. When either of them checks code in or out, Subversion can let them know if the code is out of sync with the version their colleague is using. So if both people happen to edit the same piece of code, Subversion will let them know that there is a code conflict and provide tools to allow the developers to sort out the conflict.

Subversion is a client-server system. That is, there are two components at work: a server component and a client component, which run as separate pieces of software and may be on separate computers. The server component coordinates the storage of different versions of code in a database (the repository) and the communications in and out with the different clients that want to use the content. The client keeps a local copy of code, which may or may not be in sync with the server copy. Periodically the client and server sort out between themselves how to get their copies back in sync.

As far as you, the developer, are concerned, the business of managing the source code is largely looked after by Subversion, provided that you stick to a few basic rules. These rules come down to observing a *work cycle*.

The Subversion Work Cycle

In a Subversion system you keep the gold-standard copy of the code in the repository on the server. The first stage in getting your code under source control is to add it to the Subversion repository. From that point on, any other copy is secondary. Of course, you need code to work on, so you check out a local copy, called a *working copy*, from the repository. That working copy is managed by your Subversion client (in our case, Xcode). The work cycle is simply a systematic way of ensuring that your code moves smoothly back and forth between the repository and the working copy as it needs to.

In practical terms it works like this: At the beginning of a piece of coding work (I tend to do this at the beginning of the working day) you *update* your working copy from the repository. You write code, test, debug, rinse, and repeat. Obviously you save your work from time to time, but it is important to know that when you save you are only saving your files to the local working copy. This copy is out of sync with the server, so needs at some point to be moved over. When you have reached a stable point in your code (this is more important if you are working in a team than if you are working alone, since it is not fun for your colleagues to work on broken code) you use Xcode's Subversion Tools to *commit* your new code back to the repository. The new code is committed as a new revision—a snapshot of the current state of your work. This means that should you need to, you can return to this snapshot in the future. My work practice is to do this at the end of the working day. This work cycle is summarized in Figure 10–2.

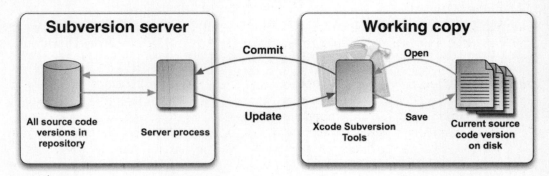

Figure 10–2. The Subversion work cycle

The Xcode Subversion client includes tools to review the version history of your projects and the ability to compare two versions.

Having that gold-standard copy on the server means that (provided the server is accessible) you are able to share a project with others. Each of you follows the work cycle: update the working copy, code, save, commit the new revision. As a result each of you will get all of the changes made by each of you when you update. If you and a colleague have both been working on the same piece of code, then you will get a conflict alert when you do a commit or an update. Subversion has processes to help you resolve conflicts, but undoubtedly this all works better if the various team members divide up the coding so that they don't tread on each other's toes.

We're assuming for the sake of the exercises in this book that you are working alone on your projects, but the repository approach is useful for you too, because it means that you can access your code from more than one computer and make sure that you are always working on the right version. Suppose you work on your iMac at home and your MacBook at the office; by having a code repository on a server, you can use the update, code, commit approach to make sure both computers are kept in sync.

One Repository or Many?

When you are planning your Subversion setup you need to make a strategic decision—whether to have one repository to manage all of your projects or one repository for each project. Both approaches have their benefits and drawbacks, so let's take a look at each in turn.

Using a Single Repository

If you use a single repository, all of your projects will be contained as folders within that repository. This makes management easier at a high level because you only have to go through the process of setting up a repository once. From then on whenever you start a new software project you just import it into your repository. However, the single-repository approach has its drawbacks too, the main one being that Subversion does atomic commits. This means that when you change any file in any project, Subversion creates a new revision of the whole repository. Suppose you are working in a team environment with, say, 5 developers working across 20 software projects in one repository. You make a change to one file in one project and then check in your work. This causes a new revision to be created for the entire repository, with the result that the next time one of your developers makes a change to her code and commits it, she may see quite a jump in the revision number. This doesn't actually interfere with the developers' work, but it does mean that it is likely there will be many revision numbers, and also that revision numbers for any given file may not be sequential. A second disadvantage of a single repository is that everyone in the team is able to take a working copy of every project, with the corresponding risk of someone making changes to the wrong project. Although the revision mechanism will help to sort out any such problems, it's a risk that you can avoid by having separate repositories.

Another consequence of the single-repository approach is that you have to be very disciplined about your use of commit messages. Remember, Subversion stores commit messages with every commit event, and you may have such events spanning all 20 of your projects and from all 5 of your developers.

This is not necessarily as confusing as it sounds, since many Subversion client tools— Xcode's among them—by default show you the history of individual files, but it highlights the importance of including informative messages when you do a commit. Other Subversion clients, however, show a **History** view with commit messages across the repository. As I mentioned earlier, I tend to put a fairly verbose message, following by my initials and the date (for instance, "Fixed problem in TemperatureConverter `Converter.m: convertCToF:` used incorrect formula. IP 20091015."). This may seem a little bureaucratic, especially since Subversion stores your name and the date of the change anyway, but it can be useful later on when you need to *know* what changes happened when to your project. And, if you are working in a team environment, it is absolutely vital to adopt a good commit message policy so that all the team members know what is going on.

It's probably fair to say that the single-repository approach works best for individual developers, and I tend to use this for my own projects.

Using Individual Repositories

If you prefer, you can set up a separate repository for each of your projects. The main benefit of this is clarity, especially if you are working in a team setting: you can determine exactly who has access to what projects. Revision-number changes are a lot clearer.

The main disadvantage to this is that it is a lot of work: for every project you need to go through the business of creating a new repository. For an individual working on just a few projects, it may seem like overkill to have individual repositories.

Where to Get More Information

Subversion is a complex, powerful, sophisticated product that you can configure and use in many ways. We are going to cover the essentials to make it productive for you. If you are interested in learning about Subversion in depth, there is no better resource than the free online book *Version Control with Subversion* (you can see it at: `http://svnbook.red-bean.com`). This is the definitive document on Subversion and a reasonably straightforward read, if a bit technical in places.

OK, that's probably enough theory for now. Let's see how it all works in practice. You are going to set up a Subversion server, add a project, and investigate some of the features of Xcode's Subversion Tools.

Installing a Local Subversion Server

We're going to start by putting the server components on the same computer as you are using for your development. There are good reasons in the real world not to do this (that unexpected system crash springs to mind), but for the purposes of learning how things work it's the easiest way.

First, let's check the version of Subversion that you have on your Mac. Open a Terminal and type svn --version. At the time of writing, Mac OS X Snow Leopard includes v1.6.2, though these instructions are likely to work just fine with other versions. You should see something like the response in Listing 10–1.

Listing 10–1. *Checking That You Have Subversion and Getting Its Version Number*

```
$ svn --version
svn, version 1.6.2 (r37639)
   compiled May 20 2009, 01:36:41

Copyright (C) 2000-2009 CollabNet.
Subversion is open source software, see http://subversion.tigris.org/
This product includes software developed by CollabNet (http://www.Collab.Net/).

The following repository access (RA) modules are available:

* ra_neon : Module for accessing a repository via WebDAV protocol using Neon.
  - handles 'http' scheme
  - handles 'https' scheme
* ra_svn : Module for accessing a repository using the svn network protocol.
  - handles 'svn' scheme
* ra_local : Module for accessing a repository on local disk.
  - handles 'file' scheme

$
```

In the unlikely event that you don't see a message like Listing 10–1, you may have to download and install Subversion for your computer. You can get binary distributions and source code from http://subversion.tigris.org/.

Creating a Repository

Once you have a Subversion installation running, you can create your repository. For the purposes of this chapter let's assume that you will set up just one repository.

There are three locations you need to think about when setting up to use Subversion. We've already covered the repository and the working copy. The third is the original location of the code. You might think that you can simply take an existing project and turn it into a Subversion-managed project. You can do this, but it doesn't work particularly well in practice, and the smoothest way to do it is to think of these as different locations. Let's look at the process (illustrated in Figure 10–3) for a typical project.

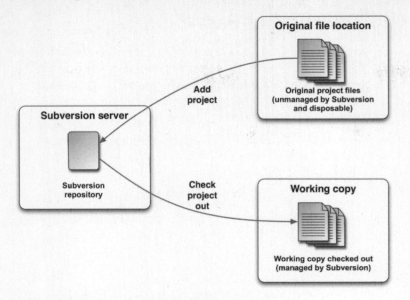

Figure 10–3. *File locations to consider for your repository*

You start with the original project folder containing all of the usual files. You should think of this as a temporary, disposable location. The first step is to *import* that project folder into the Subversion repository. You can set up the repository in any convenient location, but bear in mind that you never use the files in the repository directly—only via the Subversion process and tools. The second step is to do an initial *checkout* of the project to your working copy. Once you have done this, you're finished with the original project folder and can delete this. Actually, you *should* delete the folder in order to not risk any mix-up. From this point on, the working copy is under version control. Subversion manages this local working copy by storing an invisible folder, called .svn, in each folder of the working copy. The Xcode Subversion client adds files to this collection of folders that keep track of all of the changes you make. It's quite important, therefore, that you don't move these folders around or try to change or delete their contents, as bad things can happen. This may all feel a bit kludgy, but in practice it works quite well, and you never see these invisible folders unless you go looking for them.

For this example, you'll create all three locations under your home folder. This is not a realistic location for the Subversion repository, but it avoids the necessity of using sudo or logging in as root (which you would need to do if you put it in a more sensible location like /usr/local/svn).

Create a folder in your Documents folder (that is, the Documents folder under your home folder): call it subversion_work. Create two folders in this folder, called original_projects and working_copy. Listing 10–2 shows these steps (note that the –p flag allows you to create a folder and subfolder in one step).

Listing 10–2. *First steps to create a repository*

```
$ cd ~/Documents
$ mkdir -p subversion_work/original_projects
$ mkdir -p subversion_work/working_copy
```

Now, in the Finder, find the project folder for the project TemperatureConverter from Chapter 6 and copy it to the original_projects folder. You can do this from the command prompt if you are more comfortable working this way.

Go back to the Terminal and type in the svnadmin create command to create your repository:

```
$ svnadmin create ~/Documents/subversion_work/svn
```

You won't see anything in response to this, so to confirm that you actually have a Subversion repository, type the verify command (all of the admin functions in Subversion use the svnadmin command followed by an argument—use svnadmin help to get a list of these).

```
$ svnadmin verify ~/Documents/subversion_work/svn
* Verified revision 0.
```

Notice that it says revision 0. That is because so far you haven't created any revisions (or even imported any content). By the way, you can do most of the things covered in this chapter by use of either the svn or svnadmin commands in the Terminal. We will be working in the Xcode Subversion Tools for the most part, but it is sometimes useful to work from the command line.

> **NOTE:** It is traditional when creating a Subversion repository to create three top-level folders, called branches, tags, and trunk, below the repository name. The trunk folder holds the main folder structure while the branches and tags folders hold information about branches in your revision history and tags that you can assign to specific folders within a revision to give them friendly, easy-to-identify names in addition to revision numbers. I have left these out in this chapter to keep things simple, and actually I rarely use them, but it is very straightforward to add these folders to your repository later on.

Figure 10–4 shows what this repository looks like in the Finder.

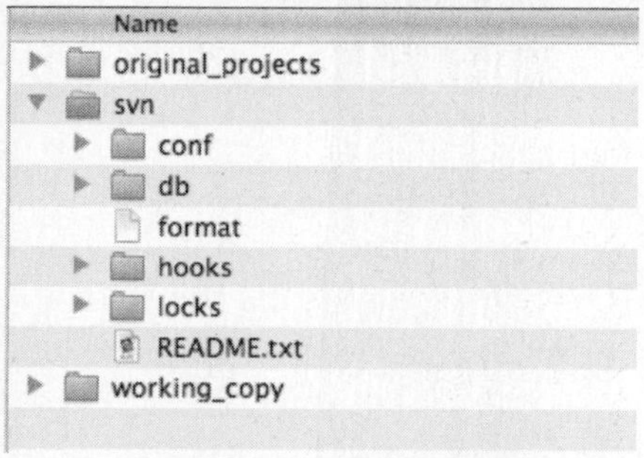

Figure 10–4. *The folder structure for the repository*

This folder structure contains the configuration files for the repository and the database files that are used by the Subversion server to manage revisions. Now close this folder and never open it again! Seriously, it is a bad idea to make any changes directly to this folder, as it could corrupt the database that holds your precious code history. Leave it to Subversion.

Configuring the Repository in Xcode

You have the original files for your project and you have set up a Subversion repository. Now it is time to get the project under source-code management.

Open Xcode if it is not already open. Close any projects that may be open. Find the **SCM** menu and choose the menu item **Configure SCM Repositories...**

This will bring up the **Xcode Preferences** window at the **SCM** panel. Click on the **Add** button to create a new repository configuration: in the drop-down window give it a name like **Local SVN repository**. Make sure that the type of repository is set as **Subversion**; Xcode will also allow source-code management using other systems, such as Perforce and the older CVS, but these are much less common now than Subversion. You then need to add the Subversion settings. In the **URL:** box type in the location of the new repository in URI format; that is, `file:///Users/ianpiper/Documents/subversion_work/svn`. Hit the Tab key, and Xcode fills in the **Scheme** and **Path** boxes automatically (see Figure 10–5).

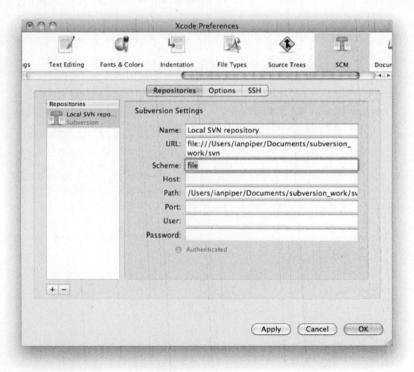

Figure 10–5. *Creating a new Subversion repository configuration*

The other thing to note here is the green light below the list of boxes. As you complete each of the fields, Xcode tests the configuration to ensure that it can connect properly to the repository. That green light confirms that you have a connection since all you had to provide was the file location. When we look at hosted Subversion repositories shortly, you will see how it works when you have to authenticate.

Now choose the **Options** tab and check the box that says **Configure SCM automatically**. This makes it easier to configure your projects when you add them to SCM. While you are on this window you might like to check out the **Comparison Handling** options. When you come to comparing revisions you can use the Xcode Tools or choose an editor such as BBEdit or Apple's own file-comparison utility FileMerge (you'll be looking at FileMerge more closely in Chapter 13). Unless you have a good reason to choose one of these other tools, I'd advise sticking with Xcode for now. Choose OK to finish.

CHECK THE SUBVERSION CLIENT CONFIG FILE

There is just one more step that you may need to take, and at the least it's prudent to check. I've already mentioned that a Subversion installation litters your hard disk with hidden files. In addition to the `.svn` folders in your working copy you will have a `.subversion` folder in your home folder. You can see invisible files and folders in the Terminal by typing `ls -al` rather than just `ls` at the command prompt. In this folder, open the `config` file in a text editor. Scroll down to the `[miscellany]` section and check the `global-ignores` line (in bold here):

```
[miscellany]
### Set global-ignores to a set of whitespace-delimited globs
### which Subversion will ignore in its 'status' output, and
### while importing or adding files and directories.
global-ignores = build *.mode* *.perspective* *~.nib .DS_Store *~
```

This `global-ignores` setting ensures that Subversion ignores the `build` folder. Otherwise Subversion will register a change to the code every time you build the project: more to the point, there is no purpose to doing revision management of these files, as they are generated afresh from your code base and are mostly temporary files anyway. There may be some other file patterns included in the `config` file for your Subversion client installation, but at the minimum make sure that `build` and `*.perspective*` are there.

In my experience this file usually needs to be modified if you are already using another Subversion client for other purposes (so that the `~/.subversion/config` file already exists); sometimes Xcode creates the file only if there is not already one there, which feels like a bug in Xcode's Subversion client implementation.

You now have a usable Subversion repository available to Xcode. The next step is to import your project.

Populating the Repository with Projects

If you open the **SCM** menu again you will see that there is now a second item, entitled **Repositories**. Choose this, and you see the **Repositories** window. This window gives you some useful options for managing your repositories and projects. The first thing you are going to do here is to import the TemperatureConverter project. Click on the **Import** button and use the file browser to locate the project folder in `original_projects`. Before clicking on the **Import** button, add an import message. I use a descriptive message (one that is likely to mean something when I come back to this in six months' time!), my initials, and the date. (In fact, Subversion stores your name and the date of any change, so arguably these last pieces of information are superfluous: it's really just playing very safe, on my part, to put them into the message). See Figure 10–6.

Figure 10–6. *Importing a project and adding a message*

Once you click the **Import** button the process of importing the project begins, and since you are running this as a local repository it will be complete very quickly. Click **OK** on the **Import Complete** message window, and you will see the new project (see Figure 10–7).

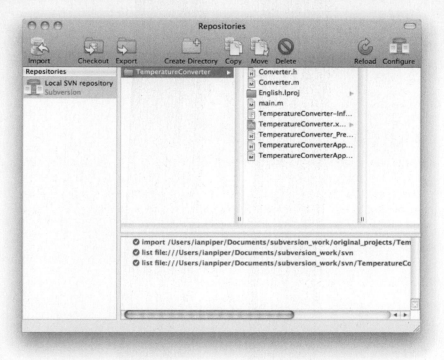

Figure 10–7. *The TemperatureConverter project in the repository*

Notice that you can browse down through the folder structure just as in the Finder. The lower panel shows the equivalent Terminal svn commands.

Now that the project has imported into Subversion you can safely delete the copy of the project folder in original_projects.

Getting a Working Copy out of the Repository

You still need a copy of the code to work on. You have two options here. One is to *export* a copy of the project. This allows you to take a copy of the project out of version control altogether. You may recall that Subversion puts hidden (.svn) marker folders in each folder of the project. If you want a clean copy of the project with no marker folders, then use the **Export** button here.

The other option is to check out the project to a working copy. First select the **TemperatureConverter** folder icon in the **Repositories** window. Then click the **Checkout** button, in the file browser navigate to the working_copy folder, and choose **Checkout**. This will create a Subversion-managed copy of the **TemperatureConverter** project folder and its contents in the working_copy folder. Once it is checked out you will see a message window like Figure 10–8. Click on the **Open TemperatureConverter.xcodeproj** button.

Figure 10–8. *Checkout Complete message window*

This opens the Xcode **Workspace** window for your project.

Before you do any work on this project, briefly refer back to Figure 10–3. This illustrates what you have done so far: imported the original unmanaged project into Subversion, then checked out the project into a managed environment. Let's take a quick look at that managed environment. Open a Terminal window and move to your working_copy folder. Run the commands shown in Listing 10–3.

Listing 10–3. *Exploring the Working Copy*

```
$ cd
$ cd Documents/subversion_work/working_copy/TemperatureConverter/
$ ls -al
total 56
drwxr-xr-x  13 ianpiper  staff .
drwxr-xr-x   3 ianpiper  staff ..
drwxr-xr-x   7 ianpiper  staff .svn
-rw-r--r--   1 ianpiper  staff Converter.h
-rw-r--r--   1 ianpiper  staff Converter.m
drwxr-xr-x   5 ianpiper  staff English.lproj
-rw-r--r--   1 ianpiper  staff TemperatureConverter-Info.plist
drwxr-xr-x   6 ianpiper  staff TemperatureConverter.xcodeproj
-rw-r--r--   1 ianpiper  staff TemperatureConverterAppDelegate.h
-rw-r--r--   1 ianpiper  staff TemperatureConverterAppDelegate.m
-rw-r--r--   1 ianpiper  staff TemperatureConverter_Prefix.pch
drwxr-xr-x   3 ianpiper  staff build
-rw-r--r--   1 ianpiper  staff main.m
$ cd .svn
$ ls -al
total 8
drwxr-xr-x   7 ianpiper  staff .
drwxr-xr-x  13 ianpiper  staff ..
-r--r--r--   1 ianpiper  staff entries
drwxr-xr-x   2 ianpiper  staff prop-base
drwxr-xr-x   2 ianpiper  staff props
drwxr-xr-x   9 ianpiper  staff text-base
drwxr-xr-x   5 ianpiper  staff tmp
$ cd text-base
$ ls -al
total 56
drwxr-xr-x   9 ianpiper  staff .
drwxr-xr-x   7 ianpiper  staff ..
-r--r--r--   1 ianpiper  staff Converter.h.svn-base
-r--r--r--   1 ianpiper  staff Converter.m.svn-base
-r--r--r--   1 ianpiper  staff TemperatureConverter-Info.plist.svn-base
-r--r--r--   1 ianpiper  staff TemperatureConverterAppDelegate.h.svn-base
-r--r--r--   1 ianpiper  staff TemperatureConverterAppDelegate.m.svn-base
```

```
-r--r--r--  1 ianpiper  staff TemperatureConverter_Prefix.pch.svn-base
-r--r--r--  1 ianpiper  staff main.m.svn-base
$
```

Starting with the top-level project folder, there are the expected files that make up the project, and also a hidden folder called .svn. Moving into that folder, there is a series of files and folders that are responsible for managing the project's code. The text-base folder contains copies of the text files in the project (for example, Converter.m.svn-base is a copy of Converter.m in the top-level project folder). At least these files are copies to begin with; as you write code and save changes to these top-level files, Subversion notes that they are out of sync with the versions in text-base. There is a lot more to it, but this is at the heart of the system that monitors your project and knows what it needs to commit back to the repository.

Making Changes and Committing Code

OK, back to Xcode; let's make a simple change to a file. Open up Converter.h and add the line in bold in Listing 10–4, immediately before the @property declaration.

Listing 10–4. *Making a Change to Converter.h*

```
[...]
/**
 The original temperature - may be Centigrade or Fahrenheit
 */
@property (readwrite) float originalTemp;
[...]
```

Now save the file. At the top of the **Detail** panel find the tab bar and choose the **SCM Results** tab. You should see something like Figure 10–9.

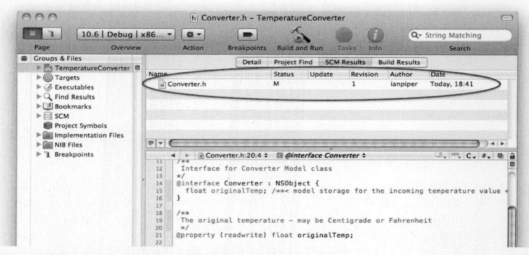

Figure 10–9. *Change in Converter.h reported by Xcode's Subversion Tools*

The status column in the **SCM Results** panel gives an indication of the current state of any project resources that need attention. `Converter.h` has the status **M**, which means *modified*; the content needs to be committed to the repository in order to get everything back into sync. Subversion uses a range of flags to indicate the status of resources: the most common are shown in Table 10–1.

Table 10–1. *Subversion Flags*

Flag	Meaning	Required Action
M	Modified local file	Commit
U	File in repository is more recent	Update
?	File is not under version control	Add
A	File has been added to working copy	Commit
C	File version conflict	Resolve before committing

When the TemperatureConverter project was imported and came under Subversion's control, the revision number was incremented from 0 to 1. OK, let's commit the change to the repository (see Figure 10–10). You can do this in two ways: to commit just one file (which is all we need to do here), select the file and choose **Commit**.... Alternatively, if you have changed a number of files, you can commit the entire project by choosing **SCM Commit Entire Project**....

Figure 10–10. *Committing the first revision to the repository*

Comparing Revisions and Rolling Back

Now let's try something slightly different. Suppose you make an error in the code and need to see what's wrong. In the Xcode Workspace move to the **Detail** tab and choose `Converter.h` again. To get the effect of an error, change the @property declaration to use int rather than float. Save it and commit the change. Now when you run the program you will get a compile error. OK, you know what has caused the problem, and in any case debugging would quickly get you to the bottom of it, but let's just take a look at Xcode's compare tool to help us out. You know you were doing something with `Converter.h`, so select that file in the **Detail** pane and choose **SCM Compare With** ➤

Revision.... The **Version Summary** window that appears (see Figure 10–11) shows the revisions in which changes were noted for that file. Xcode's Subversion tools are quite clever in this respect: if you had chosen, say, `Converter.m`, it would only have shown revision 1 in the summary window, since there had been no changes to that file in any later revision.

State:	Up To Date			Local : 3
Tag:				Latest:

Revision	Author	Date	Message
3	ianpiper	Today, 19:45	Deliberate error added to Converter.h in TemperatureConverter project. float changed to int. IP
2	ianpiper	Today, 19:26	Comment added to Converter.h in TemperatureConverter project. IP 20091019.
1	ianpiper	Today, 18:41	Initial import of TemperatureConverter project. IP 20091019.

Figure 10–11. *The Version Summary window for Converter.h*

You know (especially since there is a big hint in the message—good thing you wrote a verbose message, eh?) that revision 3 is our current version, so let's do a comparison against revision 2, the revision immediately previous to the problem appearing. Select that revision and click on **Compare**. Figure 10–12 shows the result:

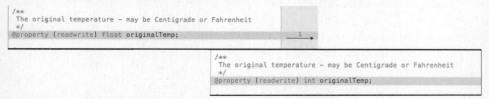

```
/**
 The original temperature – may be Centigrade or Fahrenheit
 */
@property (readwrite) float originalTemp;
```
```
/**
 The original temperature – may be Centigrade or Fahrenheit
 */
@property (readwrite) int originalTemp;
```

Figure 10–12. *Change to Converter.h highlighted in the Compare window*

It's instantly obvious where the change was made (in this case there was only one, but the window would show all differences between the files). Close the **Compare** window. Now you can put that error right with a one-line change in the editor, then test (shame we didn't do that last time!) and commit the now-working code.

In Chapter 13 you will be looking at another tool, FileMerge, that you can use to manage wholesale changes between file versions.

Handling Version Conflicts

Suppose you are working on the same project in two separate locations. You do some work at home, and commit it to your online repository. Then you do some more work on the same project using your notebook computer, and realize that you hadn't committed your work from the previous day. You'd made changes to the same file in the same project. Here's how this might work, and how you would resolve it.

To set up this scenario, I have imported the ColorPal project from Chapter 7 into my local repository. Then I checked it out into two different working copies in different locations. One working copy is the `working_copy` folder that we were using earlier, and the other is called `working_copy_notebook`.

I started by making an edit to the notebook copy of the project: I added a comment to `ColorPalAppDelegate.m`. I saved this but didn't commit the changes. Then I went to the desktop-computer copy of the project and made a different change: a comment in the same file and a comment in ColorPalAppDelegate.h. I saved and committed these changes. So by now I have two versions of my project in different working copies. One is in sync with the Subversion repository and the other isn't. Let's see what happens when I do an update while sitting in front of the "notebook computer" working copy. Take a look at Figure 10–13.

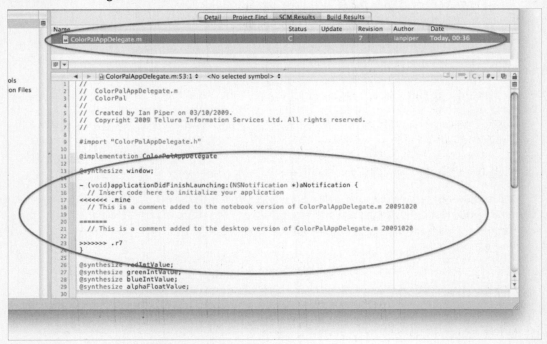

Figure 10–13. *Identifying conflicts in out-of-sync code*

So what does this tell you? First, it identifies that there is a problem with the file ColorPalAppDelegate.m—the **Status** flag is **C**, meaning conflict. The most recent revision is 7. (Remember, Subversion does atomic commits, so even though this project is on its first revision, the repository itself has gone through more with the earlier work on TemperatureConverter. You can see how a multiproject repository soon racks up the revision numbers!) If you look at the code editor, you will see exactly where the conflict is located. First there is an indicator to show my (notebook) local version of the conflict (shown as left-pointing chevrons followed by .mine). Then there is a separator between the "notebook" version and the "desktop" version, and finally a set of right-pointing chevrons followed by .r7 (that is, repository revision 7).

Subversion is a little cleverer than the Xcode Tools allow at this point, and if you are using the command line or other Subversion clients (such as SVNClient) you can issue commands saying one or the other version is correct. The only real option with Xcode's Subversion Tools here is to edit the file to correct the error (make sure you remove the lines containing chevrons and double lines) and then choose **SCM ➤ Resolved**. The **C** flag for the file will be replaced by an **M** flag. You can now commit the file from the "notebook" working copy. When you do an update on the "desktop" working copy it will happily update that to your new revision.

> **NOTE:** Sometimes updates don't immediately show in the Xcode Workspace. Try refreshing the project (**SCM   Refresh Entire Project**). If you still don't see a change to your code when you know there is one, close and reopen the project.

Using an Online Subversion Server

If you want to use Subversion in the most flexible and safe way possible, it makes sense to use a hosted server. This could be on your own server if you are tech-savvy and run your own. Alternatively, your ISP may offer Subversion as a service, or you can take advantage of one of the subscription Subversion services that are now available. The benefit of these, like any Software as a Service (SaaS) arrangement, is that the setup, configuration, backup, and so on are all taken care of for you.

Here is a quick example using a typical hosting service that offers a Subversion service. There are many such services around, and they will mostly work in a similar way to this example; for this reason I haven't identified the service.

Suppose I use my web browser to log into my ISP control panel and choose to create a new Subversion repository. The relevant form on the web page looks like Figure 10–14.

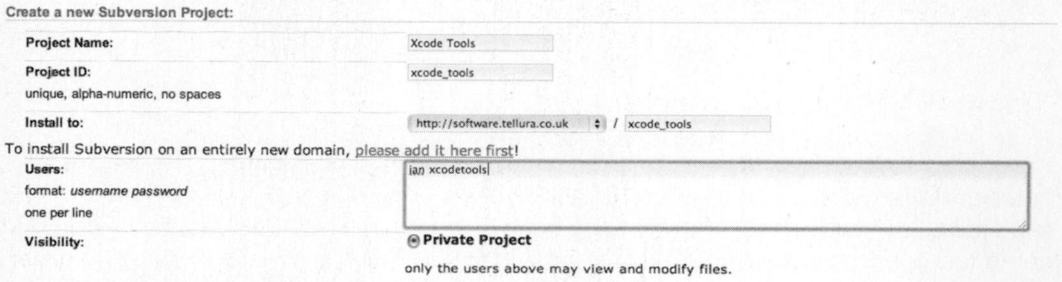

Create a new Subversion Project:

Project Name:	Xcode Tools
Project ID: unique, alpha-numeric, no spaces	xcode_tools
Install to:	http://software.tellura.co.uk ⬍ / xcode_tools

To install Subversion on an entirely new domain, please add it here first!

Users: format: *username password* one per line	ian xcodetools
Visibility:	⦿ **Private Project**

only the users above may view and modify files.

Figure 10–14. *Creating a Subversion repository on a hosted service*

For the purposes of using this service later on from within Xcode, the crucial parameters are the URL for the service (in this case, `http://software.tellura.co.uk/xcode_tools`) and the authentication details. Once those are submitted, I receive some sort of success message. The repository is now available for me to add to my Xcode configuration; Figure 10–15 shows the configuration screen in this case. Note that the main differences from the configuration for the local repository are that the scheme is **http** rather than **file**, and that I have had to add authentication information to enable me to connect.

Figure 10–15. *Configuring an online Subversion repository*

Having created and configured the online repository, I can import projects, check them out, and update and commit my work exactly as you saw earlier in this chapter. The only real difference between this repository and the local repository that I created is that I can get to this one from anywhere that gives me an Internet connection. So I can work from a variety of locations and computers, and I can also share the project with colleagues.

Summary

Using source-code management, and in particular Subversion, involves a small amount of discipline but brings big benefits in terms of preserving your investment in your code. By having an online repository in particular, you gain the security of knowing every revision of your precious code is held safely in a separate location from your local machine. You have the capability of working on your projects on other computers and in other locations, and can share work with others in a well-managed environment. The cost to you is a certain amount of discipline. Observe the work cycle. Always use the Subversion Tools to manage your code, never the file system. Always add verbose messages to your commits. Once acquired, the Subversion habit will stick with you, and your projects will thank you for it—well, they would if they could.

So what's next? You're going to take a look at another underused aspect of software development, and one which, like SCM support, has had steadily increasing support added in recent versions of Xcode. I'm talking about unit testing. Let's get to it!

Chapter 11

Unit Testing in Xcode

If you have spent any significant time in the UK, you may well have encountered Marmite. Marmite is—well, I'd hesitate to call it a food, but it is a substance consumed, usually spread on toast at breakfast time, and almost unknown beyond Britain. If you haven't come across it, there are two things you need to know about Marmite: first, it is generally accepted that consuming it at all is an illustration of British eccentricity; and second, it is one of those things that you either love or hate. There is little ambivalence in people's attitude to its consumption.

Why this talk of the British breakfast-eating habits? Well, like consumption of yeast extract, unit testing is a topic that tends to drive people toward extreme positions: either you are sold on it and use it for all of your development work, or you consider it a waste of effort and avoid it at all costs.

I've often felt that one of the main reasons people don't do unit testing is a lack of knowledge about how to get the best benefit from what is undoubtedly a bigger up-front investment in time and effort than many of the alternative testing approaches. In this chapter, I'm going to try to clear up some of the misconceptions about unit testing, show how you can use it productively in your work, and give you a feel for where it helps and where maybe it doesn't add much. It is not a trivial topic, and some real investment of time and effort is needed to get to grips with it. But by the end of the chapter you will be able to make an informed choice about where—and maybe whether—unit testing is going to help you.

Introducing Unit Testing

To put unit testing into some sort of context, consider for a moment how you do your software development currently. You care about your code, you are proud of your product, and want your users to have a great experience. You have taken care to think about the features of the product and have designed it to be friendly and easy to use. And you have probably tested it. That is, you have confirmed that it doesn't have any obvious bugs and that it works without crashing or losing your files or running amok on your computer. You have probably given it to beta testers and diligently solved the problems that they have uncovered.

For most of us, if we are honest, that's about it. But this approach has some real limitations. The main problem is that it deals with only the day-to-day cases—it assumes that people will use the program in the way that you intended and within the constraints you had in mind when designing it. The chances are that you probably haven't written your program *defensively*—that is, you expected your users not to try to paste a 3 GB data file into a text field. Another problem is that you probably haven't checked the boundary conditions: if you are doing a numeric calculation, what happens if the user provides a very big number, or a negative number? Possibly the biggest problem is that you are too close to your code. You have worked through every line and control and know how everything is supposed to work. Consequently, you will have well-established shortcuts and ways of navigating the features of your program. These can act as blinkers, helping you to avoid making errors that a new user—or an automated test process—would not miss.

A central principle of unit testing is that you cannot be sure that your program works unless you have *proven* that it works through well-designed tests. Those tests should address the most important features of your program and check the functionality using a specially constructed set of known cases. For each case, you make one or more *assertions*—statements about the result that you expect to see when running that piece of functionality. If the function returns the expected result, then you can be confident that that aspect of your program is working in the way you designed it. Running the collection (or suite) of unit tests will give you a set of results that let you know your program is on track.

Ideally, you write your unit tests as you write your code. The reason for this is that it makes it more likely that you design your code well—the argument goes that if you are continually thinking "OK, that's how I think this method should work, but how will I prove it and what will happen at the boundaries?" you are more likely to write solid defensive code. The most extreme form of this approach comes with Test-Driven Development, in which you write your tests first, and then write code that will pass the tests. You won't be going this far in this chapter.

It is more likely, particularly when you start doing unit testing, that you will be retrospectively writing tests for existing code. Of course, the real benefit of this is to automate the process, so that when you build your program you also run the test suite. The incremental effort on your part to monitor the test results is therefore quite modest.

The unit-testing approach is quite different from "normal" development, and it is probably already clear that it involves significant investment, not only in writing and running all these tests, but also in learning yet another principle of software development. So what is in it for you?

- Your code is more likely to work the first time. You are coding more thoughtfully, strategically, and defensively, and, therefore, you're less likely to make significant errors.

- Your application is less likely to suffer from post-launch bugs. The traditional approach to software development involves creating a release and then testing it. That means your development may be a long way down the track before problems emerge—the product may possibly even be launched. The bugs that you find in this way may be deeply enmeshed in your code, giving you a major headache to resolve. Building testing into your development practice at an early stage will reduce the likelihood of your having to send out post-launch fixes to unhappy customers.

- Discovering bugs early is always better than discovering them late! The code is more likely to be fresh in your mind and it is less likely that unpleasant dependencies will have developed with other parts of your code base.

- Unit tests can alert you to sudden changes—particularly useful if you are sharing development with colleagues. If you are regularly running successful tests and suddenly the tests start to fail, you know immediately. Combining unit testing in this way with source-code management gives you an excellent mechanism for managing change and its consequences, particularly in a team environment.

- Taking the time to test can save you time. Really. Fixing a bug that you have just written tends to be much quicker than fixing a bug that you inadvertently wrote six months ago and that has just come to light because a new feature revealed a weakness. The whole business of development also tends to be more rigorous and run more smoothly. The iterative process of design, develop, test, analyze helps your projects keep their momentum too.

- You have supporting evidence that your work is done. If you are writing code for someone else, a complete suite of successful tests is an additional deliverable that will give your customer greater confidence in the quality of your products.

Still interested? Let's look at unit testing in practice. You will be setting up one of the projects from earlier in the book for testing, creating a collection of tests, and reviewing the results.

Unit Testing in Practice

As usual, there is a certain amount of planning and setup to be done. Here is an overview of what you need to do:

1. Add a new target to your project for the testing process. Your unit tests will run only when this target is current.

2. Decide what you are going to test.

3. Create test cases that will be compiled within the test target.

4. Run the tests and check the reports.

The reports that you get back from the tests can be saved as part of the supporting documentation for your project.

As is so often the case with Xcode development, there is a lot more to this topic than you'll be covering here. There is some excellent documentation support, and I'll point you at it as we go along.

Setting Up a Project for Unit Testing

A good candidate for investigating unit testing is our old friend TemperatureConverter. Open this project now (if you have put the project under Subversion control, as discussed in Chapter 10, it's a good idea to do an update to ensure you are up-to-date before starting work).

Create a new target using **Project New Target....** From the **New Target** template window, choose **Unit Test Bundle** (see Figure 11–1).

Figure 11–1. *Choosing a Unit Test Bundle as a new target*

Call it TemperatureTests. Click on **Finish**. Close the **Target Info** window; there are some advanced settings that you could potentially set in this window, but you won't need these in this chapter. Now, in the Xcode **Workspace** window you can see the new target. Figure 11–2 shows this both in the **Groups and Files** list and in the **Overview** pop-up list.

Figure 11–2. *The new target in the Project Workspace window*

In passing, since you were looking at Subversion in the last chapter, notice that the **SCM** status of the project has been set to **M** (since you have just modified it) and there is a new Plist file for the new target (flagged with an **A** to show the file needs to be added to the repository to be brought into revision control). You will see these only if you have the project under Subversion control, of course.

Now use that overview popup, or the **Project ➤ Set Active Target** menu, to choose TemperatureTests as the active target for your project. The effect of choosing this target is that when you compile and run your application, Xcode will run the unit tests as part of the build process, so you will know right away if your tests fail. You will see how this works as the chapter proceeds.

The next step is to add a group to the **Groups and Files** list. This is where your test classes will live. Right-click on the project name and choose **Add ➤ New Group** and call it Tests. Select this group and add a new file. This should be an Objective-C test case class. In the second step call the class TCTests and make sure that you have selected the new TemperatureTests target and not the normal TemperatureConverter target. See Figure 11–3.

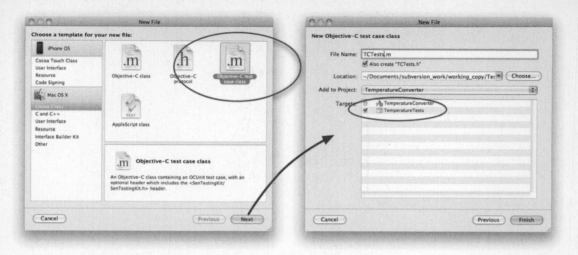

Figure 11–3. *Adding a test case class to the TemperatureConverter project*

Now you should see, in the **Tests Group**, two new files representing your TCTests class. Take a look at TCTests.h first. You will see that it is importing SenTestingKit.h. This is the header for the OCUnit testing framework. This framework was originally created by Sente (http://www.sente.ch/software/ocunit/) but has been included in recent releases of Xcode.

Otherwise, there is nothing much in this file, and nothing either in the counterpart .m file. So you have some work to do.

Writing Unit Tests

You are going to test the functionality of the temperature conversion, so you need to import Converter.h into the TCTests.h file. You also need to declare the Converter object—see Listing 11–1.

Listing 11–1. *TCTests.h*

```
#import <SenTestingKit/SenTestingKit.h>
#import "Converter.h"

@interface TCTests : SenTestCase {
    Converter *testTempConverter;
}

@end
```

The first test you will write will be testing the normal behavior of the code, so it will be asserting that the value 25°C will convert to 77°F. Listing 11–2 shows the code you need to write in TCTests.m.

Listing 11–2. *First Unit Test in TCTests.m*

```
#import "TCTests.h"

@implementation TCTests

- (void)test25ShouldConvertTo77 {
    testTempConverter = Converter.new;
    [testTempConverter setValue:[NSNumber numberWithFloat:25.0]
forKey:@"originalTemp"];
    NSNumber *newTemperatureInF = [NSNumber
numberWithFloat:(float)[testTempConverter convertCToF]];
    STAssertEquals(77.0f, [newTemperatureInF floatValue],
@"Expecting 77.0 : we got %f", [newTemperatureInF floatValue]);
}

@end
```

Let's run through this method. First, the method name must begin with test. This ensures that the OCUnit framework is able to recognize it as a test. The remainder of the name says something about what you are testing: 25°C should convert to 77°F. If you have come from a Rails development background, this exemplifies principles both of opinionated software and of *convention over configuration*, meaning that the environment expects you to conform to particular conventions when naming items in order to make things run more smoothly. Also, test methods should be void (that is, they should not return anything) and should take no parameters.

This test method is designed to confirm that a centigrade value of 25 will be converted by the algorithm into a Fahrenheit value of 77. The method first instantiates a new Converter, then sets the original temperature property for that object to 25.0 (as a float). Next the method runs the object's ConvertCToF method and retrieves the result, also as a float. The last line is where the test is evaluated: STAssertEquals is an OCUnit macro that is used to test the equality of two values. In this case, the macro is *asserting* that the value returned from the ConvertCToF method is equal to the floating-point number 77.0. If that assertion is correct, then the test passes. Successful tests are simply reported as such in the **Build Results** tab: there is no message associated with a test that passes. If the assertion is incorrect, then the test fails and the message in the third parameter is displayed in the **Build Results** tab. This is the fundamental way that all unit tests run in OCUnit.

Running Your First Unit Test

You're nearly ready to run this test, but there's one more thing to do. The TemperatureTests target must include the Converter class. To do this, choose the TemperatureConverter item at the top of the **Groups and Files** list. In the **Detail** pane you will have a list of all the resources used in the project. Make sure that you have set the current target to TemperatureTests, and then select the checkbox for Converter.m in the list (see Figure 11–4).

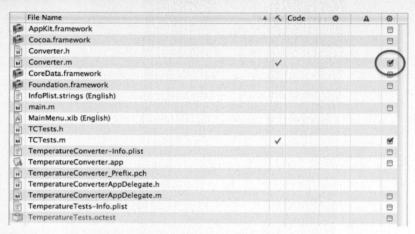

Figure 11–4. *Linking the test class to the Converter class*

OK, now you can run the test. To do this you just need to build the project (press ⌘B or use **Build ➤ Build**, though you can choose **Build and Run** if you prefer.

Assuming your test has worked, you will see a display like Figure 11–5 in the **Build Results** tab.

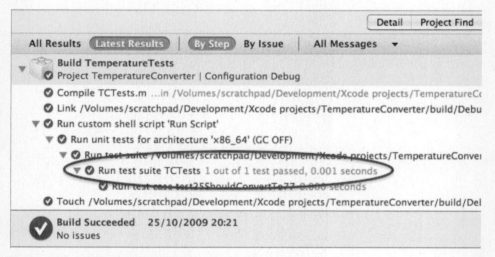

Figure 11–5. *Results from the first successful unit test*

As you can see, it's not terribly informative apart from confirming that the test has passed (see the circled section in Figure 11–5). Later in the chapter, you will see how to get some more detailed information. However, it confirms that your basic algorithm is working for a normal case.

Now let's try writing an assertion for something that we know is wrong. Let's test to see whether the algorithm knows that 100°C is different from 100°F. Add the test method shown in Listing 11–3 to TCTests.m below the first test method.

Listing 11–3. *Adding a Test Designed to Fail*

```
- (void)test100CShouldNotConvertTo100F {
    testTempConverter = Converter.new;
    [testTempConverter setValue:[NSNumber numberWithFloat:100.0]
forKey:@"originalTemp"];
    NSNumber *newTemperatureInF = [NSNumber
numberWithFloat:(float)[testTempConverter convertCToF]];
    STAssertEquals(100.0f, [newTemperatureInF
floatValue], @"Expecting 100.0; we got %f", [newTemperatureInF floatValue]);
}
```

Now run the test again and you will see the first test passed but the new test has failed, as shown in Figure 11–6.

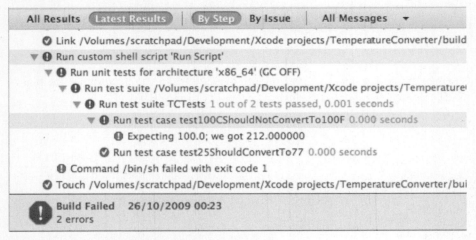

Figure 11–6. *The second test has failed, as expected*

That is as you'd expect, since the two values are different. To get a test that passes, you would ideally need to assert that the values are different, but sadly there is no STAssertsNotEqual macro. However, you can test this by using a different macro, STAssertFalse. Change the method to that shown in Listing 11–4.

Listing 11–4. *A Better Way to Test a "Not Equal" Assertion*

```
- (void)test100CShouldNotConvertTo100F {
    [testTempConverter setValue:[NSNumber numberWithFloat:100.0]
forKey:@"originalTemp"];
    NSNumber *newTemperatureInF = [NSNumber
numberWithFloat:(float)[testTempConverter convertCToF]];
    STAssertFalse(100.0f==[newTemperatureInF
floatValue], @"Result should be %f, not 100.0F",
[newTemperatureInF floatValue]);
}
```

In this case, you are asserting that an expression saying the returned value is 100.0 is false (as it is, since the returned value is 212.0). Run the test, and it should pass. To confirm that this is a valid test, change the assertion line to read as follows:

```
STAssertFalse(212.0f==[newTemperatureInF floatValue],
```

```
@"Result should be %f, not 100.0F",
[newTemperatureInF floatValue]);
```

If you run it again, it will fail (because your assertion is that the expression 212.0==212.0 is false, and it is in fact true).

What about testing body temperature (should be 98.6°F or 37.0°C)? This time, you can test the inverse conversion (that is, feed in a Fahrenheit value and get back a centigrade value). Create a new method to test this conversion (see Listing 11–5).

Listing 11–5. *Testing a Different Conversion*

```
- (void)test98_6CShouldConvertTo37C {
    testTempConverter = Converter.new;
    [testTempConverter setValue:[NSNumber numberWithFloat:98.6]
forKey:@"originalTemp"];
    NSNumber *newTemperatureInC = [NSNumber
numberWithFloat:(float)[testTempConverter convertFToC]];
    STAssertEquals(37.0f, [newTemperatureInC
floatValue], @"Expecting 37.0; we got %f",
[newTemperatureInC floatValue]);
}
```

Save TCTests.m and run the tests (⌘B). They should all run and pass.

STAssertEquals is the most commonly used macro, but there are several others. You can see the full list of macros available in the documentation (you can search for "Unit Test Result Macro Reference" or ⌘⌥–double-click on the **ST** keyword in the code editor), but Table 11–1 presents a summary of some useful macros:

Table 11–1. *Summary of Macros*

Macro Name	Summary Description
STAssertEquals	Succeeds when two values are equal; fails when they are different.
STAssertEqualObjects	Succeeds when [object1 isEqualTo:object2] is true; fails when this evaluates to false.
STAssertEqualsWithAccuracy	Allows you to compare two values within a degree of accuracy. Succeeds when two values differ by less than the accuracy specified.
STAssertNil	Succeeds when the expression evaluates to nil, fails when it does not evaluate to nil (STAssertNotNil is the reverse).
STAssertTrue	Succeeds when the expression evaluates to true, fails when it evaluates to false (STAssertFalse is the reverse).
STAssertThrows	Succeeds when the expression raises an exception; fails when it doesn't.
STFail	Causes an unconditional fail.

What Should You Test?

You would normally create a range of tests to confirm that your application behaves as expected. This is one aspect of unit testing—*rightness*. There is a lot more to take into account in unit testing, though. Here are some of the areas to think about.

Rightness

Rightness is what you have been testing so far. That is, does the program behave correctly when you provide it with the right information? In other words, does it do the right thing when it should? It is a good idea to write a range of tests to cover the expected range of possibilities. Here you have just a couple: 25°C converts to 77°F, and 98.6°F converts to 37°C. Some other values you might like to add include 0°C converts to 32°F, 0°F converts to −17.78°C, -40°C converts to −40°F, and so on. In practice this is a simple linear calculation, so beyond a couple of examples you don't need to keep testing for correct behavior.

Wrong Input

How does your program behave when you give it unexpected input? In your TemperatureConverter program, what happens if you type in alphabetic rather than numeric characters? Let's test that. First, try the program itself (**Build and Run**). Try adding a word (say, **twenty**) in the Centigrade field. Tab to the other field and you will see the Fahrenheit value 32. If you do the reverse and type **twenty** in the Fahrenheit field, you get −17.777 . . . in the Centigrade field. See Figure 11–7.

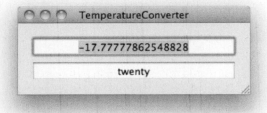

Figure 11–7. *Entering a string into a field that expects a number*

What's happening? Well, your program is trying its best to get a numeric value from the field, and the string you typed in has a numeric value of zero. So the program feeds zero into the ConvertCToF or ConvertFToC method and gets back the corresponding converted temperature.

To reproduce this in a unit test, you need to take a string and extract its floatValue. This is perfectly legal, and in fact Cocoa will try to get a legal number out. So add the test method in Listing 11–6 below the others.

Listing 11–6. *Testing Alphabetical Input Where Numeric is Expected*

```
- (void)testTemperatureAsWordShouldReturnZero {
    testTempConverter = Converter.new;
    NSString *inputString = [NSString stringWithFormat:@"twenty"];
    [testTempConverter setValue:[NSNumber
                        numberWithFloat:[inputString floatValue]]
                                    forKey:@"originalTemp"];
    NSNumber *newTemperatureInF = [NSNumber
numberWithFloat:(float)[testTempConverter convertCToF]];

    STAssertEquals(32.0f, [newTemperatureInF
floatValue], @"Expecting 32.0; we got %f",
[newTemperatureInF floatValue]);
}
```

In this method, you create an input string, then extract its floatValue (which should be 0) and pass that into the ConvertCToF method. The result should be 32.0, and if you run the test it should pass. You might wonder why you should bother with this test at all. Well, in a sense in creating the test you have identified a piece of behavior in your program that should ideally be revisited—perhaps your program should manage the incoming data more gracefully. By having this test on hand you will be alerted when the behavior is fixed, or if something else changes in the program that causes the behavior to change. Figure 11–8 shows how the growing report of successful unit tests looks.

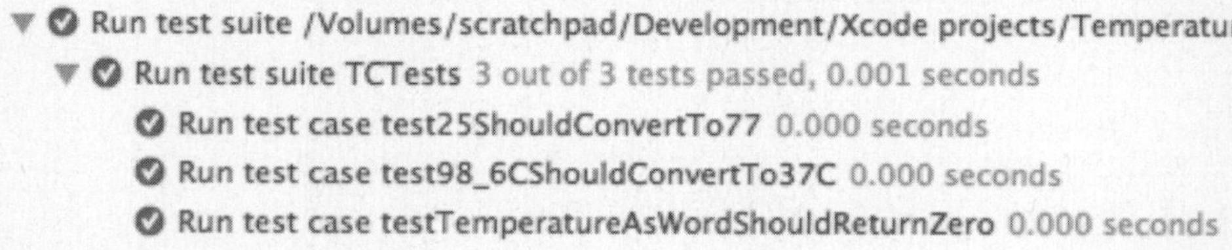

▼ ✅ Run test suite /Volumes/scratchpad/Development/Xcode projects/Temperatur

   ▼ ✅ Run test suite TCTests 3 out of 3 tests passed, 0.001 seconds

      ✅ Run test case test25ShouldConvertTo77 0.000 seconds

      ✅ Run test case test98_6CShouldConvertTo37C 0.000 seconds

      ✅ Run test case testTemperatureAsWordShouldReturnZero 0.000 seconds

Figure 11–8. *Report from a suite of successful unit tests*

Boundary Conditions

How does the program behave at the boundaries? For example, if you have a numeric calculation—say, you are dividing one number by another—what happens when you provide an extreme example, such as dividing a number by zero? What if you put a very large number into one of the fields? Try it again with the real user interface. To save you having to try every possible number, go straight to 1 followed by 39 zeroes: 1000000000000000000000000000000000000000.

Enter this number in the **Centigrade** field and press Tab, and you will see the string "inf" in the other field. This seems to suggest a unit test (see Listing 11–7):

Listing 11–7. *Testing for Infinity*

```
- (void)testVeryLargeNumberShouldReturnInf {
    testTempConverter = Converter.new;
    [testTempConverter setValue:[NSNumber
numberWithFloat:1000000000000000000000000000000000000000.0]
forKey:@"originalTemp"];
    NSNumber *newTemperatureInF = [NSNumber
```

```
numberWithFloat:(float)[testTempConverter convertCToF]];
    NSString *newTemperatureString = [newTemperatureInF stringValue];
    NSString *testString = [NSString stringWithFormat:@"inf"];
    STAssertEqualObjects(testString, newTemperatureString,
@"Expecting %@ and we got %@", testString, newTemperatureString);
}
```

I needed to construct this test slightly differently to extract the string values of the float inf that is coming back from the calculation. This comes back as an NSString. So I need to create an NSString containing "inf" and compare the two NSString objects for equality using the STAssertEqualObjects macro.

Let's look at the results so far. This time, expand the report to show more detail. You can click on the little transcript icon that appears at the right end of any highlighted line in the Build Results tab. Depending on the level you select, you will see more or less detail. Using the disclosure arrows, find and select the line that starts Run test suite.... Then click on the transcript icon. You will see a detailed report on the suite of tests—see Figure 11–9.

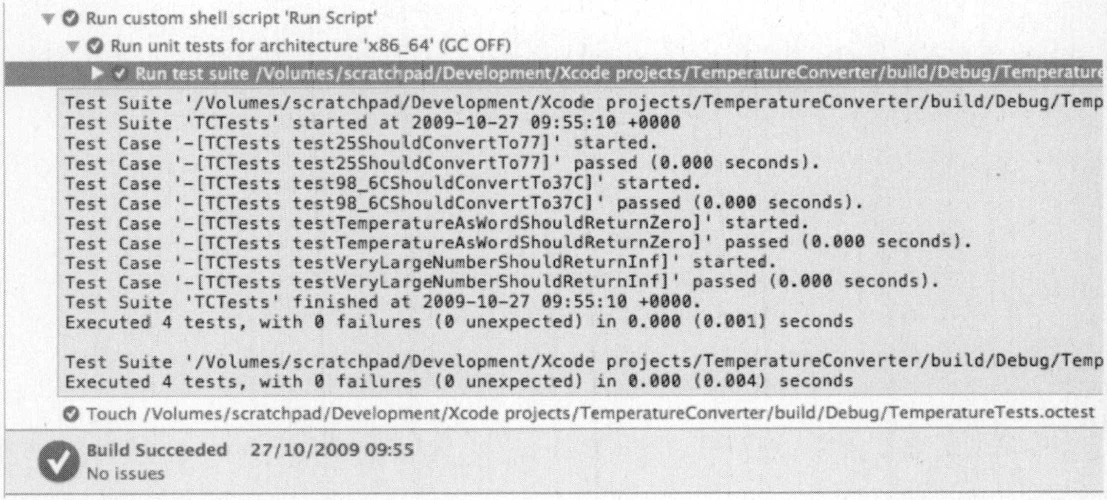

Figure 11–9. *Getting a detailed test report*

You can also open the full transcript text file in the code editor. To do this, right-click on a line in the Build Results tab and choose the menu item Open These Latest Results as Transcript Text File.

Other Factors to Test

Seasoned unit testers will be aware that there are other factors to consider in unit testing beyond rightness and boundary conditions. Here are a few:

- Cross-check: If possible, find more than one way to test an algorithm.

- Performance: You have expectations about how the software will perform, and you might consider designing testing so that it works within those expectations.

- Inverse: If you test, say, an equation A / B should equal C, you might also test that B × C should equal A.

In real life you will no doubt be dealing with much larger and more sophisticated programs. You will be dealing with the same factors, but additional complexity. Some points to bear in mind:

- Approach each function in each class from the perspective of a challenge to your coding. You know that your code probably works; how can you prove that it works as expected? You have some ideas about how the function will work at its limits; what methods can you employ to test those limits?

- Don't feel that you need to test everything. Think about the critical path through your application, the workflow if you like. Where are the points in that workflow where you can strategically put tests?

- Some of the additional complexity arises from the sheer volume of code and number of functions. In a large application these can feel overwhelming. The defensive approach to this is to look at the interfaces between functions: the inputs and outputs at each function you test. What are you expecting to feed into the function? Test it. What are you expecting the function to produce? Test it. Testing the interfaces between potentially unknown and unpredictable functions is a good defensive maneuver.

I believe that pragmatism should rule here; you could spend your life designing unit tests, and indeed test-driven development is becoming a popular approach. Provided that you are taking the trouble to test your code for correct behavior and boundary conditions, you are way ahead of developers who do no unit testing at all.

Making Your Test Suite More Efficient

Taking a look back over the four tests you have written so far, you will see that in each case you are duplicating some code. In each case you instantiate a new `Converter`, and at the end of each you release the object. OCUnit provides you with some shortcuts here. Unit tests that are designed to run as a suite can have `setUp` and `tearDown` methods, which, as the names suggest, do any initial preparation before the tests, and follow those tests with the required cleanup. So let's revisit the code in `TCTests.m` to improve its efficiency. Add the instantiation of `testTempConverter` to the `setUp` method, and release it in the `tearDown` method. Then remove those steps from each of the individual tests (see Listing 11–8—this shows just the first test since you will change the others in the same way).

Listing 11-8. *Adding setUp and tearDown Methods*

```
- (void) setUp {
    testTempConverter = Converter.new;
}

- (void) tearDown {
    testTempConverter = nil;
}

- (void)test25ShouldConvertTo77 {
// testTempConverter = Converter.new; removed from here
[testTempConverter setValue:[NSNumber numberWithFloat:25.0]
forKey:@"originalTemp"];
    NSNumber *newTemperatureInF = [NSNumber
numberWithFloat:(float)[testTempConverter convertCToF]];
    STAssertEquals(77.0f, [newTemperatureInF
floatValue], @"Expecting 77.0; we got %f",
[newTemperatureInF floatValue]);
}
[...]
@end
```

Where to Go Next

The chances are that the level of unit testing that I have covered here will provide most, if not all, of what you need to build this methodology into your work pattern. However, I have only scratched the surface of what is possible with unit testing. If you have used other languages, such as Java, Ruby on Rails, or Windows .NET, then you may have come across other features such as fixtures and mock objects as ways of providing alternative input mechanisms for your tests. These involve significantly more planning, though they may be worth investigation if you are building a large system that has complex data processing.

You may also be aware of automated building as an approach to software engineering. This approach combines a code base, usually using a Subversion or other repository, that is regularly updated from the working copies of developers, with a process for automatically building the software against the suites of unit tests. This build process may be run as frequently as the team needs it (though daily builds are a common practice) and the report that comes back from the build informs the work of the team for the following day.

This is a highly disciplined approach to software engineering and one that is unlikely to appeal to the singleton developer, but, in conjunction with some of the other methods described in this book (notably Agile Development), it can work well in large teams. There is no real infrastructure within Xcode for doing automated builds, but there is some coverage on the Internet (take a look at this resource, for example: http://gusmueller.com/blog/archives/2007/03/me_on_late_night_cocoa.html).

Dependent versus Independent Unit Testing

So far I have not mentioned one major design decision that you are able to make in doing unit testing in Xcode. That is the issue of dependent versus independent tests. The tests you have learned about in this chapter are independent tests: that is, you can build and run them completely independently of the software itself. More to the point, there is nothing preventing you from ignoring your unit tests and simply developing and running using the normal target rather than your test target.

This is where dependent unit tests come in. Building a dependency between your main executable and the test target ensures that your tests run whenever you build your application.

Personally, I tend to keep my unit tests independent: there is less to set up and I like to be in control of when things happen. However, here, in overview, is what you need to do if you want to make your test bundles dependent.

The steps are basically the same as the ones you took in setting up the TemperatureTests bundle. However, you may recall that I skated over the **Target Info** window, alluding to some advanced settings that you didn't need to make. Let's take another look at that window now.

In the Xcode Workspace, find the TemperatureTests item in the **Targets** section of the **Groups and Files** list. Right-click on this and choose **Get Info** (see Figure 11–10):

Figure 11–10. *The Target Info window*

To add a dependency, click on the **Add** button at the bottom of the dependencies panel. Choose the **TemperatureConverter** target (see Figure 11–11).

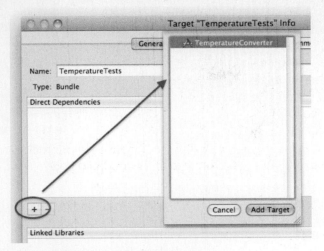

Figure 11–11. *Choosing the dependency*

Next, choose the **Build** tab. On this tab find the **Linking** section, entitled **Bundle Loader**. Double-click in the space to the right of this option to bring up a sheet for editing (easier when typing in a long string) and enter `$(CONFIGURATION_BUILD_DIR)/TemperatureConverter.app/Contents/MacOS/TemperatureConverter`. You would obviously put the executable name for your application here instead. Take a copy of the string before clicking OK, as you will be using it again in a moment. Scroll down to the **Unit Testing** section, click in the space next to **Test Host**, and paste that string in.

Back in the Xcode **Workspace** you can now remove the included **Converter.m** entry in the **Detail** pane (see Figure 11–12 and refer back to Figure 11–4, where you originally set the inclusion):

File Name			Code	⊗	⚠	◉
AppKit.framework						☐
Cocoa.framework						☐
Converter.h						
Converter.m			8K			☐
CoreData.framework						☐
Foundation.framework						☐
InfoPlist.strings (English)						
main.m			4K			☐
MainMenu.xib (English)						
TCTests.h						
TCTests.m			24K			☑
TemperatureConverter-Info.plist						☐
TemperatureConverter.app						☐
TemperatureConverter_Prefix.pch						
TemperatureConverterAppDelegate.h						
TemperatureConverterAppDelegate.m			25K			☐
TemperatureTests-Info.plist						☐
TemperatureTests.octest						☐

Above the table: Detail | Project Find | SCM Results | Build Results

Figure 11–12. *No need to include Converter.m*

Your test classes now depend on the main executable classes, so your main executable will build first, then the test target will build, and then finally the tests will run. As I mentioned earlier, I see little benefit in running dependent unit tests, but at least you know that you have an option. The document **Xcode Unit Testing** in the Developer Documentation has a lot more detail on the pros and cons of dependent versus independent testing. Search for "Unit Testing," and it should be the first hit.

Summary

So that's a brief look at unit testing. It's only fair to mention that not all developers approve of unit testing, and I'm definitely not advocating full-on Test-Driven Development. But any testing is better than no testing or haphazard testing. I use unit tests in my code because I think it helps me to design better code, and it helps me to nail down bugs. It takes a little organization to put meaningful tests in place, but once there they run themselves whenever you use **Build and Run**, so beyond that initial investment they are free.

Another way of checking the workings of your application is to check its performance. Xcode includes some great tools to help with monitoring performance and resource usage. That's where you're heading in the next chapter.

Chapter 12

Monitoring, Analysis, and Performance Tools

This chapter takes a look under the covers at some tools that allow you to understand how your application is performing and where you might be able to improve things.

You could be lucky, of course. If all of your programs perform well and never crash you may never need the tools here. And, frankly, one of the difficulties in writing this chapter is that it is so easy to write well-behaved software in Xcode that it is quite hard to engineer circumstances in which you will need to use these tools! However, by the end of this chapter, you should have a good understanding of where to look in the event that things go awry.

Instruments

Instruments is an analytical tool, and it is clearly the flagship tool in the Xcode toolchest. Use it to monitor your running program and to alert you to issues with, for example, memory leaks, object allocations, and a range of other parameters and problems. In this section, I'm going to focus on using Instruments to locate and help you solve memory-leak problems and to analyze file activity.

Tracking Down a Memory Leak

As with many other modern programming languages, Objective-C v2.0 offers a service called Garbage Collection. Every time a program instantiates an object, it allocates a block of memory space to hold it. As a program progresses, an object may go out of scope (for example, an object created in a loop is no longer needed when the loop is complete) and, therefore, the block of memory is no longer needed. As a good citizen, your computer program should relinquish that memory so that it is available for other purposes (either within the program or elsewhere on your system). The Garbage Collector looks after this, tidying up blocks of memory allocated by your program when you no longer need them.

Before Garbage Collection became available, you as a developer were responsible for allocating objects and releasing the memory when your program had finished with it. Even though Garbage Collection is now available, many developers still prefer the discipline of positively managing the allocation and release of memory. Sometimes that discipline slips and a program may allocate but never release its memory. That is called a memory leak.

Create the Application

It may seem like a slightly perverse thing to do, but in this chapter you're going to write a program that leaks memory (spoiler: you will create a set of objects but never release them). Then you are going to use Instruments to monitor and let you know where it is happening.

In Xcode, create a new Cocoa application (not Core Data- or Document-based). This application is going to be a simple calculator for numbers in the Fibonacci sequence, so call it Fibonacci Fun. Listing 12–1 shows `Fibonacci_FunAppDelegate.h`—you just need to set up a text field to take the output and to declare the function where you are going to do the calculation (see the lines in bold in Listing 12–1).

Listing 12–1. Fibonacci_FunAppDelegate.h

```
#import <Cocoa/Cocoa.h>

@interface Fibonacci_FunAppDelegate : NSObject <NSApplicationDelegate> {
    NSWindow *window;
    IBOutlet NSTextField *outputField;
}

@property (assign) IBOutlet NSWindow *window;

- (IBAction)startCalculation:(id)sender;

@end
```

Now for the implementation. You will want the button click to run the calculation—in fact, to make it work a bit harder I am going to run the calculation 10 times. Each time the calculation works out the first 90 members of the Fibonacci series of integers: each member of the series is the sum of the two previous members of the series, so it goes 1, 1, 2, 3, 5, 8, 13, 21 and so on. The numbers get to be pretty big, which is why you need to declare the `fibValues` array holding the series of numbers to be a long long int. After setting the first two members of the series manually, you go into a loop, setting the nth member of the series to be the sum of the $(n-2)$th and $(n-1)$th members. Then you take the current member of the array and append that to a growing, comma-separated string—actually, since NSStrings are immutable, you are creating a new NSString with the new contents. Each time around the loop, you are putting a space between the lines and adding a number at the beginning of the next calculation.

Then finally you put the outputString into a multiline text field. See Listing 12–2.

Listing 12–2. *Fibonacci_FunAppDelegate.m*

```
-(IBAction)startCalculation:(id)sender {
NSAutoreleasePool *fibPool = [[NSAutoreleasePool alloc] init];
    NSString *outputString;
    outputString = @"1: ";
    for (int x=1; x < 11; x++) {
        long long int fibValues[90];
        fibValues[0] = 0;
        fibValues[1] = 1;
        for (int i=2; i < 90; i++) {
            fibValues[i] = fibValues[i-2] + fibValues[i-1];
            NSString *thisFibString;
            thisFibString = [[NSString alloc]
initWithFormat:@"%lli, ",fibValues[i]];
            outputString = [outputString
stringByAppendingFormat:@"%@", thisFibString];
}
        outputString = [outputString
stringByAppendingFormat:@"\n\n%i: ", x+1];
        [outputField setStringValue:outputString];
    }
[fibPool drain];
}
```

Building the Interface

OK, over to Interface Builder. Add a button to the window and connect it to the
startCalculation: action of Fibonacci_FunAppDelegate. Also, add a multiline TextField
and connect the outputField outlet of Fibonacci_FunAppDelegate to it. Add Autosizing
parameters to enable the TextField to resize when you resize the window and keep the
button at the bottom left (refer back to Chapter 3 if you need a refresher on this). Figure
12–1 shows what the interface should look like at this point.

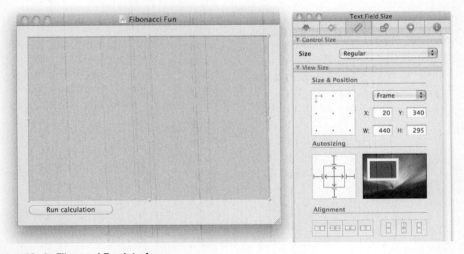

Figure 12–1. *Fibonacci Fun interface*

Now go back to the Xcode Workspace and choose **Build and Run**. Click the button, and you should see something like Figure 12–2.

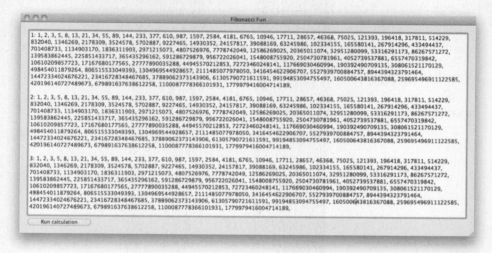

Figure 12–2. *Fibonacci Fun application running*

Monitoring the Application in Instruments

OK, we have a working application. Let's see how it looks in Instruments. You can actually run your application with Instruments from within Xcode (make sure that you build it first, though, using ⌘B—this method just runs the currently built state of the application).

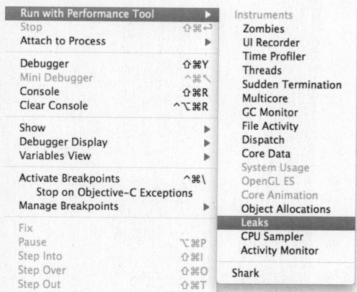

Figure 12–3. *Running an application with Instruments*

As you can see from Figure 12–3, there is a range of analysis tools available within Instruments. You are also able to run Shark from here—you'll be learning more about Shark later in this chapter. For now, Choose the **Run ➤ Run** with Performance Tool Leaks menu item.

You should see the Instruments window come up, together with the window for **Fibonacci Fun**. A timeline at the top of the window starts recording as soon as it loads, showing that it is monitoring your application. Click on the **Leaks** instrument at the top left, then position the **Fibonacci Fun** window so that you can see both. (See Figure 12–4.) Instruments is now monitoring for memory leaks.

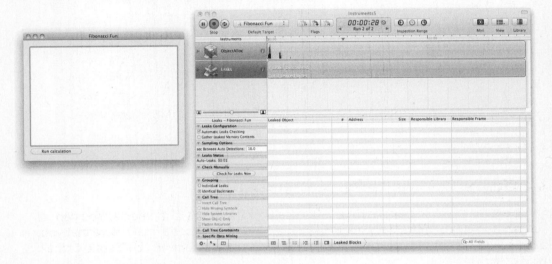

Figure 12–4. *The Leaks instrument monitoring the application*

We'll do a bit of orientation in a moment, but let's first get on with testing the application. You will see that the top timeline (monitoring object allocation) showed a couple of spikes when the application first loaded, then nothing more. The Leaks timeline is clean. Now click the **Run calculation** button in Fibonacci Fun and wait for a few seconds (the Leaks instrument samples every 10 seconds by default, though you can change that). Aha! What's this? There is a red spike in the timeline and then blue lines. This is showing a memory leak. Click the button again, and you should see the same again. Leave the monitoring to run, and you should see a theme: clicking the button causes a memory leak, then nothing else until you click again. Click the record button at the top left of the **Instruments** window; the recording will stop and Fibonacci Fun will quit. The **Instruments** window will look something like Figure 12–5.

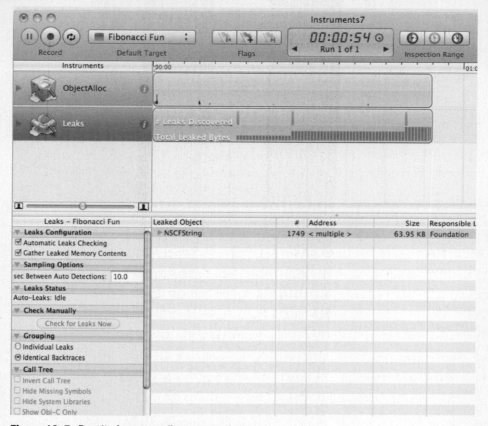

Figure 12–5. *Results from recording memory leaks*

Analyzing the Memory Leaks

Now let's take a closer look at the report. The Instruments window is divided broadly into three sections: the list of instruments with their associated timelines, the Leaks Configuration pane, and the Leaked Object View.

The Instruments list shows all of the instruments that you have chosen to use. You can add other instruments from the Library (you can see the Library using the button at the right-hand end of the toolbar). If you have run the Leaks instrument several times, you can see previous runs by clicking the disclosure arrow to the left of the icon in the Instruments list. The timeline shows the points at which Instruments has discovered memory leaks and indicates the total amount of leakage.

The Leaks Configuration pane allows you to set a variety of parameters for your analysis. For example, you can choose the frequency of sampling or do an ad-hoc check at any point.

The Leaked Object View shows the detailed report on the leakage. The default view (Leaked Objects Block View) is not terribly informative, showing the same leak every time (see Figure 12–6). It does indicate that the problem is something to do with a string, but there is not much more to tell than that.

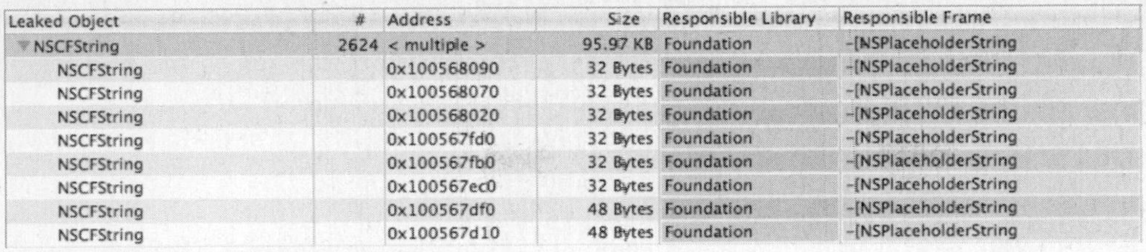

Leaked Object	#	Address	Size	Responsible Library	Responsible Frame
▼ NSCFString	2624	< multiple >	95.97 KB	Foundation	-[NSPlaceholderString
NSCFString		0x100568090	32 Bytes	Foundation	-[NSPlaceholderString
NSCFString		0x100568070	32 Bytes	Foundation	-[NSPlaceholderString
NSCFString		0x100568020	32 Bytes	Foundation	-[NSPlaceholderString
NSCFString		0x100567fd0	32 Bytes	Foundation	-[NSPlaceholderString
NSCFString		0x100567fb0	32 Bytes	Foundation	-[NSPlaceholderString
NSCFString		0x100567ec0	32 Bytes	Foundation	-[NSPlaceholderString
NSCFString		0x100567df0	48 Bytes	Foundation	-[NSPlaceholderString
NSCFString		0x100567d10	48 Bytes	Foundation	-[NSPlaceholderString

Figure 12–6. The Leaked Objects Block View

Luckily, there is a more useful view. At the bottom of the window, click on the **Call Tree View** button (second from left). Open up the call tree all the way down—see Figure 12–7.

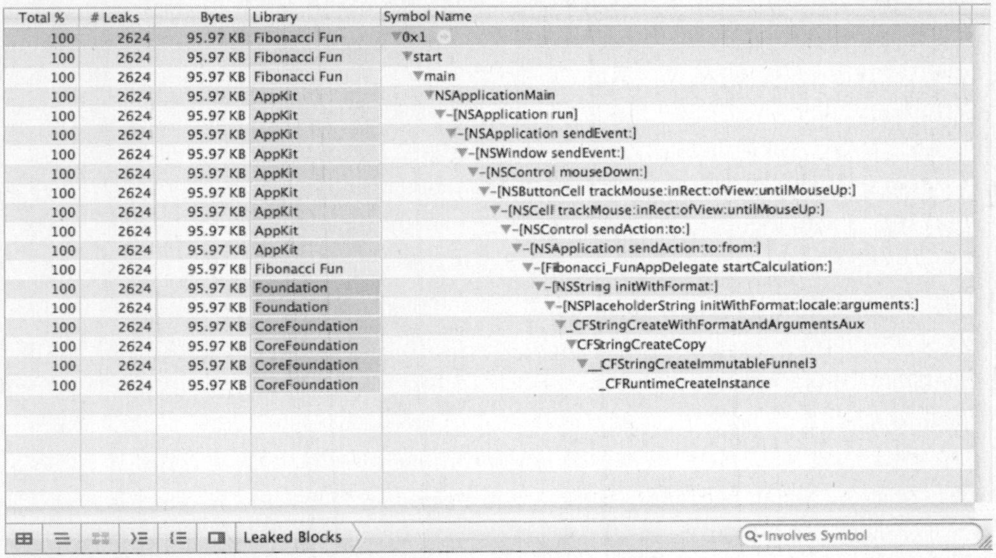

Total %	# Leaks	Bytes	Library	Symbol Name
100	2624	95.97 KB	Fibonacci Fun	▼0x1
100	2624	95.97 KB	Fibonacci Fun	▼start
100	2624	95.97 KB	Fibonacci Fun	▼main
100	2624	95.97 KB	AppKit	▼NSApplicationMain
100	2624	95.97 KB	AppKit	▼-[NSApplication run]
100	2624	95.97 KB	AppKit	▼-[NSApplication sendEvent:]
100	2624	95.97 KB	AppKit	▼-[NSWindow sendEvent:]
100	2624	95.97 KB	AppKit	▼-[NSControl mouseDown:]
100	2624	95.97 KB	AppKit	▼-[NSButtonCell trackMouse:inRect:ofView:untilMouseUp:]
100	2624	95.97 KB	AppKit	▼-[NSCell trackMouse:inRect:ofView:untilMouseUp:]
100	2624	95.97 KB	AppKit	▼-[NSControl sendAction:to:]
100	2624	95.97 KB	AppKit	▼-[NSApplication sendAction:to:from:]
100	2624	95.97 KB	Fibonacci Fun	▼-[Fibonacci_FunAppDelegate startCalculation:]
100	2624	95.97 KB	Foundation	▼-[NSString initWithFormat:]
100	2624	95.97 KB	Foundation	▼-[NSPlaceholderString initWithFormat:locale:arguments:]
100	2624	95.97 KB	CoreFoundation	▼_CFStringCreateWithFormatAndArgumentsAux
100	2624	95.97 KB	CoreFoundation	▼CFStringCreateCopy
100	2624	95.97 KB	CoreFoundation	▼__CFStringCreateImmutableFunnel3
100	2624	95.97 KB	CoreFoundation	_CFRuntimeCreateInstance

⊞ ≡ ≋ ⟩≣ ⟨≣ ▭ Leaked Blocks ⟩   Q- Involves Symbol

Figure 12–7. The Call Tree View

Here you can track through the application events: the purple- and pink-labeled entries show where the leak has been detected (the figure shows only black and white, but you will see the colors on your display).

So what do you know now? First, the leak is something to do with a string. Second, things start to go awry near a statement containing initWithFormat. So let's take a look back at the code to see what is occurring there. There is only one occurrence of initWithFormat, and that is in the code shown in Listing 12–3:

Listing 12–3. *Tracking Down the Source of the Leak—Where Are We Using initWithFormat?*

```
        for (int i=2; i < 90; i++) {
            fibValues[i] = fibValues[i-2] + fibValues[i-1];
            NSString *thisFibString;
            thisFibString = [[NSString alloc]
initWithFormat:@"%lli, ",fibValues[i]];
            outputString = [outputString
stringByAppendingFormat:@"%@", thisFibString];
        }
```

Is there a problem with thisFibString? Well, no. It's being created and populated quite correctly. Each time around the loop you are creating a new instance of thisFibString.

OK... the problem is becoming clearer. You are creating these instances but never disposing of them. In Objective-C, good memory management involves keeping track of your objects and making sure that you get rid of them using the release command when they are no longer needed.

But this function uses an NSAutoreleasePool—shouldn't that take care of releasing objects? It turns out that objects that are created using init are not managed by the autorelease pool. So you do have to explicitly release the memory for such objects. There are two things you could do about this. First, you could create the thisFibString object differently, without using initWithFormat. Second, you could explicitly release the object's memory. Let's take the second option.

Modify the code so that it looks like Listing 12–4:

Listing 12–4. *Releasing the thisFibString Object*

```
-(IBAction)startCalculation:(id)sender {
    NSAutoreleasePool *fibPool = [[NSAutoreleasePool alloc] init];
    NSString *outputString;
    outputString = @"1: ";
    for (int x=1; x < 11; x++) {
        long long int fibValues[90];
        fibValues[0] = 0;
        fibValues[1] = 1;
        for (int i=2; i < 90; i++) {
            fibValues[i] = fibValues[i-2] + fibValues[i-1];
            NSString *thisFibString;
            thisFibString = [[NSString alloc]
initWithFormat:@"%lli, ",fibValues[i]];
            outputString = [outputString
stringByAppendingFormat:@"%@", thisFibString];
            // we're done with thisFibString now, so release
            [thisFibString release];
        }
        outputString = [outputString stringByAppendingFormat:@"\n\n%i: ", x+1];
        [outputField setStringValue:outputString];
    }
[fibPool drain];
}
```

Tracking File Activity

For the second example of monitoring using Instruments, open up the Text Pal application from Chapter 3. This is a Document-based application that can read and write files.

With the project open, choose **Run ➤ Run with Performance Tool ➤ File Activity**. You will see the Instruments window along with the Text Pal program document window (you may also see a password dialog to authorize Instruments to use admin privileges for some instruments). Add some text to the document, save it, close it, read it in again, modify it, and save again. Once you have done this, click on the **Record** button in the Instruments timeline. Text Pal will close and leave you the **Instruments** window, which will look like Figure 12–8.

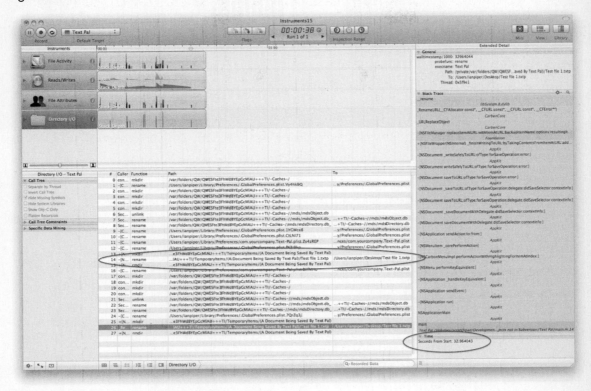

Figure 12–8. *Looking at Text Pal with the File Activity instrument*

There is a wealth of information here, but let's just focus on a couple of items. Click on the **Directory I/O** instrument. First, as with many of the instruments, events are timestamped, so you can get a good idea of the progress of your program. The second item to look at here provides an interesting insight into the process of saving a file. Take a closer look at the three lines highlighted in the figure:

- Event: 13

- Caller: +[NSFileWrapper(NSInternal) _temporaryDirectoryURLForWritingToURL:error:]

- Function: mkdir

- Path: /private/var/folders/QW/QWESFte3FhWdBYEpGcMlAU+++TI/TemporaryItems/(A Document Being Saved By Text Pal)

- Event: 14

- Caller: -[NSFilesystemItemMoveOperation main]

- Function: `rename`
- Path:
  `/private/var/folders/QW/QWESFte3FhWdBYEpGcMlAU+++TI/TemporaryIt ems/(A Document Being Saved By Text Pal)/Test file 1.txtp`
- To: `/Users/ianpiper/Desktop/Test file 1.txtp`
- Event: 15
- Caller: `+[NSFileWrapper(NSInternal) _removeTemporaryDirectoryAtURL:]`
- Function: `rmdir`
- Path:
  `/private/var/folders/QW/QWESFte3FhWdBYEpGcMlAU+++TI/TemporaryIt ems/(A Document Being Saved By Text Pal)`

You can see that Text Pal is not just blindly saving the file. First it creates a temporary directory to hold the file (line 13), then it renames (and in the process moves) the file (line 14), then it deletes the temporary folder (line 15).

Activity Monitor

The last aspect of Instruments that I'll cover here is Activity Monitor. This is quite a simple tool and, unlike the previous two, is designed to give information about the system as a whole rather than just the program under analysis. As a result, it is perhaps best used in conjunction with one of the other tools to provide a picture of the system state as you inspect memory or I/O or other aspects of your program. Figure 12–9 shows detail from the **Activity Monitor** window.

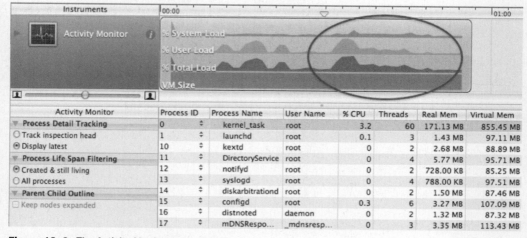

Figure 12–9. *The Activity Monitor instrument*

The circled section in the timeline shows the impact on the system as the Fibonacci Fun calculation runs.

The nice thing about the Activity Monitor instrument is the amount of information you can get not just about your own application (you can use the search filter at the bottom of the windows to narrow down to the application you are interested in) but also about the system as a whole, and not just at a point but also along a timeline.

What Else Can You Do with Instruments?

Instruments offers quite a lot of useful information about your application and environment that can help you get to the bottom of problems. To see the full range, click on the **Library** button. Alternatively, you can start up Instruments from the Finder, and then attach it to a running process. Figure 12–10 shows the welcome window.

Figure 12–10. *The Instruments welcome window*

Having chosen the tool that you want to use, you can attach it to a currently running process or launch an application (see Figure 12–11):

Figure 12–11. *Choosing a process to monitor with Instruments*

In practice, I find that I use Leaks, ObjectAlloc, File Activity, and Activity Monitor, but not much of the rest of Instruments. And I find the easiest way to utilize it is to use the **Run** menu within Xcode.

As you get more accomplished in your Xcode development, you may well find that you make much more use of this tool. Try it out—it can be very revealing and very helpful in refining your software.

Shark

I may as well nail my colors to the mast—I don't use Shark. It is a venerable application and I'm sure professional Cocoa developers use it all the time, but I personally find it a complex interface with not much useful information (by the way, a significant amount of the functionality of Shark is also available in the Time Profiler instrument, and you use it in much the same way as I describe Shark here).

That disclaimer is out of the way; so, what is Shark? In a nutshell, it's a tool for optimizing performance. You can use Shark to home in on parts of your program that represent performance problems or computational pinch points—you can even get Shark to carry out a static analysis that can suggest better ways to approach particular parts of your program.

To give you a picture of how Shark works, let's look at Fibonacci Fun again. Before doing this, it would be a good idea to load up the program a little more so that we get a better picture of what the program is doing. In **startCalculation** change the number of iterations in the main loop from 10 to 100 (see the bold code in Listing 12–5).

Listing 12–5. *Adding More Tterations to the Main Loop in Fibonacci Fun*

```
-(IBAction)startCalculation:(id)sender {
    NSAutoreleasePool *fibPool = [[NSAutoreleasePool alloc] init];
    NSString *outputString;
    outputString = @"1: ";
    for (int x=1; x < 100; x++) {
        long long int fibValues[90];
        fibValues[0] = 0;
        fibValues[1] = 1;
        for (int i=2; i < 90; i++) {
            fibValues[i] = fibValues[i-2] + fibValues[i-1];
            NSString *thisFibString;
            thisFibString = [[NSString alloc]
initWithFormat:@"%lli, ",fibValues[i]];
            outputString = [outputString
stringByAppendingFormat:@"%@", thisFibString];
            // we're done with thisFibString now, so release
            [thisFibString release];
        }
        outputString = [outputString
stringByAppendingFormat:@"\n\n%i: ", x+1];
        [outputField setStringValue:outputString];
    }
[fibPool drain];
}
```

Having made that change, **Build and Run**. Once the program is running (but before you click the button) start up Shark. You will see the initial interface window (see Figure 12–12).

Figure 12–12. *Initial interface for Shark*

You can choose from a variety of analysis types, ranging from **Time Profile** for the current application through to an entire **System Trace**. Leave the selection as **Time Profile**. Similarly, you can choose to analyze a process or a file or everything (which seems a little draconian to me, and I can't envision when you would choose it!). Leave this popup as **Process**. If the currently selected process is not **Fibonacci Fun** then use the final popup to select it. Then click the **Start** button or press ⌥Esc (this both starts and stops the analysis). Shark makes a little popping noise when it starts or stops analyzing. As soon as it has started, move to Fibonacci Fun and hit the **Run calculation** button. You will see the message "Sampling..." in the Shark window as it does its work. Once the calculation window is populated, you can quit Fibonacci Fun, then click on Stop (or press ⌥Esc) in the Shark window. Shark does a brief analysis then shows the Time Profile results window (see Figure 12–13).

The most obvious information in this window is that over 90% of the processing time in Fibonacci Fun is spent on handling text data. Open the disclosure arrow for the highest percentage entry (at the top). You can trace the symbols right back up to the start of the program (see Figure 12–14):

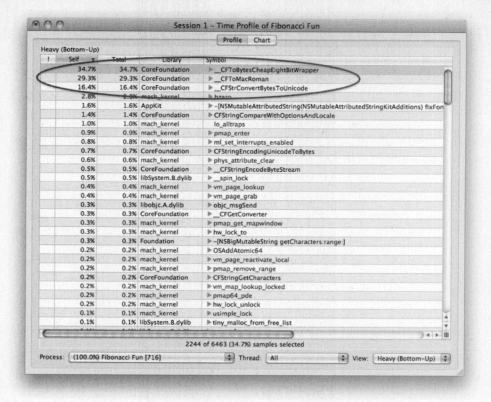

Figure 12–13. *Time Profile view of Fibonacci Fun in Shark*

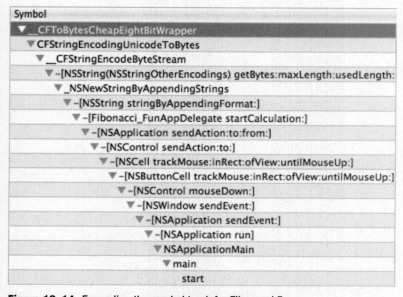

Figure 12–14. *Expanding the symbol track for Fibonacci Fun*

You will see that the highest numbers are from NSNewStringByAppendingStrings onward. Again, this is probably not surprising, since the size of the string being handled is steadily increasing during each trip around the inner loop. You can get some more information out of this analysis. If you double-click on the line in the report for the startCalculation: method it opens a new window enabling you to analyze this method. To get the best from this window, you need to turn on the **Advanced Settings** option (under the **Window** menu in Shark) and choose the **Show Total Column** checkbox (it's surprising that this isn't on by default). Once enabled, this option shows you a line-by-line view of the method with a color-coded performance analysis. If appropriate, you will also see comments and code-tuning advice in the columns to the right. (See Figure 12–15.)

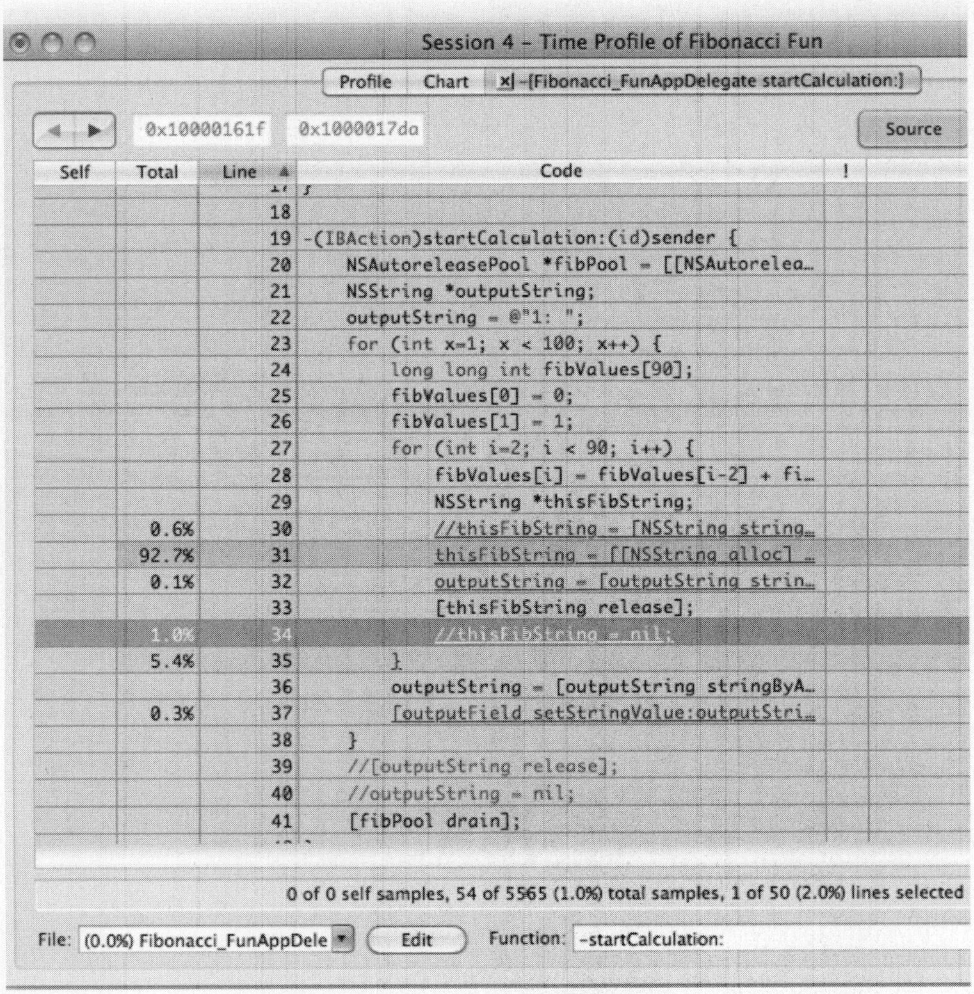

Figure 12–15. *More detailed information on the performance breakdown*

Shark also provides a chart interface that shows the same information graphically. You can zoom in the chart to see each sample. (See Figure 12–16.)

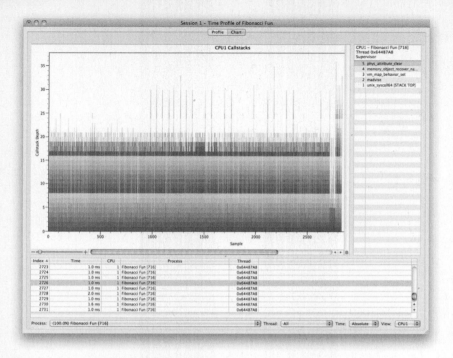

Figure 12–16. *Shark Time Profile for Fibonacci Fun*

There is a lot more to Shark (the Developer Documentation for it is over 300 pages!) but in my view the average software developer is only rarely going to make use of it. Time spent learning Instruments thoroughly will be more rewarding, especially as some of Shark's functionality is also available in Instruments (take a look at the Time Profile instrument).

BigTop

Unix veterans will instantly recognize BigTop as a graphical version of top. top is a command-line utility that gives you a regularly updated summary of the processes running on your computer. To run it, just type **top** at the command prompt, and to stop it press Control+C (see Figure 12–17):

```
Terminal — top — 116×33
○ ○ ○
Processes: 77 total, 3 running, 74 sleeping, 380 threads                          22:44:40
Load Avg: 0.15, 0.18, 0.17  CPU usage: 4.22% user, 7.51% sys, 88.26% idle
SharedLibs: 5916K resident, 4616K data, 0B linkedit.
MemRegions: 12333 total, 861M resident, 26M private, 436M shared.
PhysMem: 276M wired, 1528M active, 259M inactive, 2063M used, 1008M free.
VM: 170G vsize, 1039M framework vsize, 376788(0) pageins, 376479(0) pageouts.
Networks: packets: 209272/131M in, 163049/48M out. Disks: 435563/6455M read, 119183/5658M written.

PID  COMMAND      %CPU TIME      #TH   #WQ #POR #MREG RPRVT RSHRD  RSIZE  VPRVT  VSIZE  PGRP PPID STATE    UID
987  screencaptur 1.1  00:00.04  3     2   42   83+   472K- 8872K- 2972K+ 4692K- 2537M+ 191  1    sleeping 501
983  top          6.0  00:00.94  1/1   0   25   33    1216K 264K   1792K  17M    2378M  983  963  running  0
980  mdworker     0.0  00:00.04  3     1   49   60    1420K 9588K  3780K  31M    2412M  980  1    sleeping 89
970  quicklookd   0.0  00:00.27  6     2   80   85    3560K 6172K  11M    47M    2924M  970  174  sleeping 501
963  bash         0.0  00:00.01  1     0   17   25    364K  244K   1032K  17M    2378M  963  962  sleeping 501
962  login        0.0  00:02.87  1     0   22   53    472K  244K   1580K  18M    2379M  962  960  sleeping 0
960  Terminal     1.3  00:07.77  6     2   110  123   4620K 20M    14M    34M    2580M  960  174  sleeping 501
896  Fibonacci Fu 0.0  00:06.95  2     1   74   106   18M   15M    125M   133M   2674M  896  888  sleeping 501
888  gdb-i386-app 0.0  00:00.03  3     0   40   41    1080K 240K   3012K  21M    2396M  888  332  sleeping 501
886  imklaunchage 0.0  00:00.02  2     1   39   59    1168K 4076K  1936K  40M    2404M  886  174  sleeping 501
879- pilotfish    0.0  00:02.07  4     1   74   203   42M   6416K  28M    153M   764M   879  1    sleeping 0
877- Shark        0.0  00:06.70  4     1   164  350   31M   31M    44M    68M    838M   877  174  sleeping 501
867- EyeTV        4.6  01:52.15  15/1  1   442  373   46M   30M    80M    99M    935M   867  174  running  501
849  mdworker     0.0  00:00.95  3     1   75   104   6488K 8856K  18M    39M    2419M  849  1    sleeping 501
641* mysqld       0.0  00:00.11  6     0   53   111   2860K 3460K  5860K  93M    686M   641  637  sleeping 501
637* Acrobat      1.0  01:46.75  11    0   168  725   87M   32M    130M   641M   1516M  637  174  sleeping 501
524  Mail         0.1  00:47.33  10    5   268- 369-  20M-  42M    71M-   43M-   2679M- 524  174  sleeping 501
341  ssh-agent    0.0  00:00.09  3     2   35   61    1056K 504K   2496K  33M    2401M  341  174  sleeping 501
332  Xcode        0.0  00:56.50  30    2   364  943   189M  69M    232M   456M   13G    332  174  sleeping 501
308  Preview      0.0  00:06.06  2     1   108  183   13M   22M    54M    52M    2624M  308  174  sleeping 501
305- Microsoft AU 0.0  00:00.11  2     1   59   71    608K  620K   1880K  30M    727M   305  174  sleeping 501
304- Microsoft Da 0.0  00:03.55  3     1   79   177   2236K 11M    7976K  31M    801M   304  174  sleeping 501
298- Microsoft Wo 0.2  03:29.03  9     1   148  723   182M  61M    246M   208M   1161M  298  174  sleeping 501
284  check_afp    0.0  00:00.14  4     1   34   43    552K  244K   1056K  29M    2389M  284  1    sleeping 0
```

Figure 12–17. *The top utility running in the Terminal*

The key thing about top is that it lives in the moment. It will tell you how things are now—each current process is a row, and each parameter measured is a column—but not how things change over a period of time. That's where BigTop scores.

You can find BigTop in /Development/Utilities. Start it up and you will see a window like Figure 12–18.

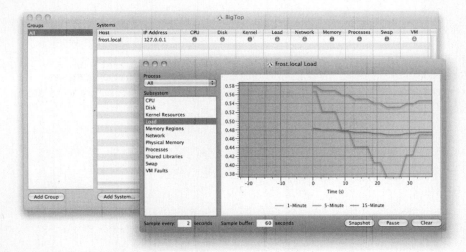

Figure 12–18. *The BigTop user interface*

The subsystem list to the left shows the different parameters that you can measure with BigTop, and you can choose the processes that you want information on using the popup. Figure 12–18 shows the system load across all processes over a 30-minute period.

Let's take a look at Fibonacci Fun running with BigTop. If you didn't make the changes to Fibonacci Fun in Listing 12–5, make them now. Now start up BigTop and choose Fibonacci Fun from the **Processes** popup. Try clicking the **Run calculation** button a couple of times. Since you are now running the loop many more times, it will take longer (about eight seconds on my Mac). If you look at the CPU load trace, you will see bursts in CPU activity each time the calculation runs (see Figure 12–19).

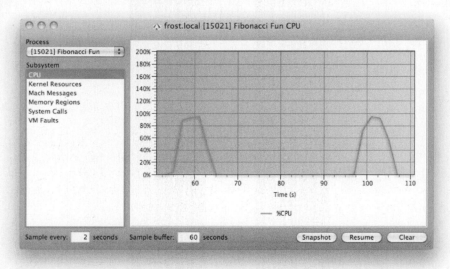

Figure 12–19. *Monitoring activity in Fibonacci Fun using BigTop*

That's about it, really. BigTop is a useful tool to keep running while you are testing, particularly if you think your software is performing a little sluggishly. It's worth mentioning that many of the features are also available within Instruments.

Spin Control

The final tool I'll describe in this chapter is Spin Control. It has just one function—to look out for conditions in running programs in which a hang occurs. It then gives an analysis which in principle allows you to see what is going wrong in your application.

Once again, you need to modify the startCalculation method in Fibonacci Fun. To give us a good chance of getting a beachball (the spinning nonresponsive cursor state familiar to most Mac users), raise the number of iterations around the outer loop again, this time to 200. Then **Build and Run** but don't press the **Run calculation** button yet. Find Spin Control in /Developer/Applications/Performance Tools and start it up. The interface is unassuming (see Figure 12–20):

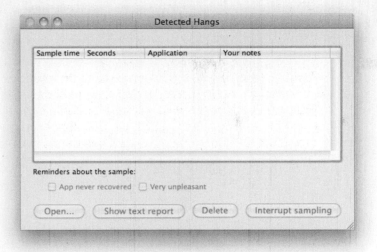

Figure 12–20. *The Spin Control interface*

Once both programs are running (position them side by side so you can monitor them), click the **Run calculation** button. All being well, after a few seconds you should see a beachball. Straight away Spin Control will show the message "Fibonacci Fun is unresponsive." Some time later, the calculation will finish and the Spin Control message will change to "Fibonacci Fun is responsive again." (See Figure 12–21.)

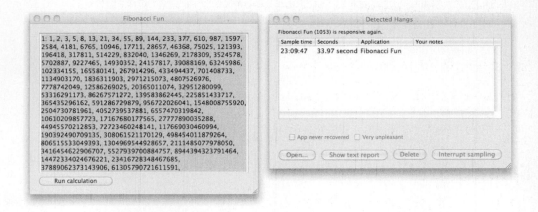

Figure 12–21. *Fibonacci Fun was unresponsive but is responsive again*

From this you can get two reports. One is a text report. This shows a hierarchical call trace, but I don't find this a very helpful view as a developer. It probably is useful in the event of having to submit a bug report for software that you are testing. The other report is the Call Graph View. To get this, select the **Sample report** line in the **Detected Hangs** window and click the **Open...** button. This shows two tabs (see Figure 12–22), giving access to a more useful hierarchical view.

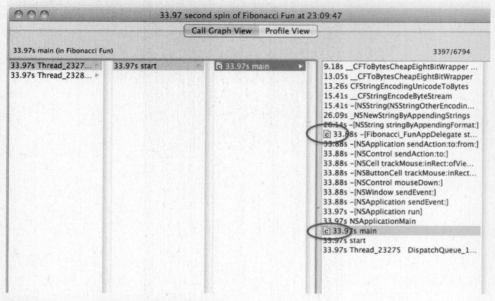

Figure 12–22. *Call Graph View in Spin Control*

Take a look at the times in the rightmost column. You can see the steps that are taking the most time—those string handling steps. One other interesting feature in Spin Control is that where you see the little code icon (circled in Figure 12–22) you can double-click to bring up a code view, revealing the location of that step in the original code. As with BigTop, you can get access to similar features to those of Spin Control using Spin Monitor within Instruments.

Summary

Those are the best known of the Xcode tools for program monitoring and analysis. Try them out—you are almost certain to find a use for Instruments, but perhaps less likely to use the others, especially as many features from the other utilities are now available within Instruments.

Actually, while making use of Xcode, Interface Builder, and Instruments, many developers never venture any deeper into the Xcode Developer Tools chest. And that's unfortunate, because there are some gems waiting there to be discovered (and to enhance your life as a developer, into the bargain). Follow me into the next chapter, and you will discover some of them for yourself.

Part III

Supporting Tools

Chapter 13

Support Tools for the Busy Developer

Take a look in the Xcode Developer Tools folder and you will see quite a collection of programs, most of which we haven't covered. And indeed from talking with other Mac developers it seems that many of these hardly get used at all. Some, such as the OpenGL graphics audio tools, are specialist utilities that are of interest mainly to developers working in these areas. Others, like USB Prober, IORegistryExplorer, Syncrospector, and iSync Plug-in Maker are advanced utilities aimed at developers who are writing software to communicate or synchronize with external hardware. Those utilities are unlikely to be of interest to you as a learning developer and I won't be covering them here. Still others are what I call Cinderella utilities: high-quality, useful programs that somehow don't get the exposure that they deserve.

In this chapter you'll be looking at a grab bag of Cinderella utilities that, although often overlooked, provide really useful support for any developer creating software for Mac OS X or iPhone. There is no common theme to these—apart from being useful, that is— and so, in no particular order, here are my favorite support tools.

Icon Composer

The icon is arguably the first thing your users will see of your product. It's also going to be sitting there in your user's Dock (at least while it's running) alongside your other applications. It ought to look good, bearing in mind the company it will be keeping. Some application icons are things of photorealistic beauty, but the best icons are more than just that. A good icon also carries the brand for the application. Interestingly, an icon doesn't necessarily have to pictorially illustrate what the application is for—actually, some of the best-known applications have quite abstract icons. Figure 13–1 shows some instantly recognizable and memorable application icons: I don't need to tell you which applications they are, do I?

Figure 13–1. *Some instantly recognizable application icons*

So it makes good sense for you to devote some effort to making an attractive and memorable icon for your application. Inevitably you need to bring some graphic-design expertise into your work here—if you don't have that expertise, talk to someone who does.

Adding an icon to your application involves creating a special type of resource file called an icns file. The easiest way to create one of these is using Icon Composer. You import images into Icon Composer and then generate the icns file. Finally you add the icns file as a resource to your Xcode project.

Let's add an icon to the Daily Journal application.

Creating the Basic Image for an Application Icon

You also need to have access to a good graphics package to create the basic image for your icon, and Apple doesn't supply one of those for free in the Xcode Tools (hey, what did you expect?). There are many great tools to choose from, including free tools such as the GIMP. I use Photoshop because I know my way around it. I'll just go through the process briefly here: obviously the detailed processes for image manipulation will vary from one image-editing application to another, so I won't go into unnecessary detail.

I started with a stock image—a photorealistic image of an open book with a pen. I made this image big enough to look good at 512 x 512 pixels, as this is the largest icon size used in Mac OS X. I used the various lasso tools to cut out the image from the background, and then added a drop shadow and some text. I shaped the text so that it followed—more or less—the curve of the page. This gave me the image shown in Figure 13–2.

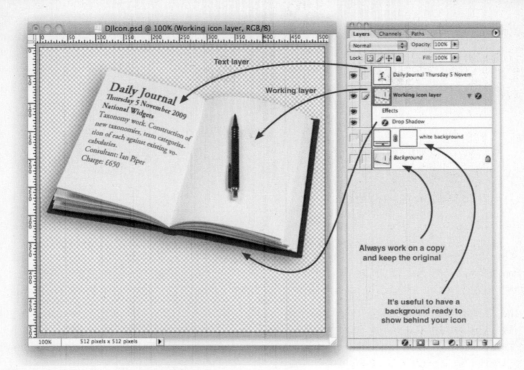

Figure 13–2. *The stock image after manipulation in Photoshop*

Notice that I kept a layer with the original untouched image file. This is prudence born of experience—it's always a good idea to leave the original and work on a copy, because you *will* make mistakes! Notice also that I have a layer that just provides a white background for the image. Since the icon will have transparency and shape, you can use a background layer here to make sure that you have properly cut out the original background and that the drop shadow works OK. Try a few different background colors.

Having saved the Photoshop image, I exported it as a transparent Portable Network Graphics (PNG) file. This is a good format for bringing in to Icon Composer.

Creating the Icon in Icon Composer

If you want to follow along with this next section, you can use your own PNG file or the one provided in the download for this Chapter (it's called DJIcon.png).

Start up Icon Composer (it's in /Developer/Applications/Utilities/). The program window shows a set of image wells representing different sizes, ranging from 16 pixels square to 512 pixels square.

Now find the 512 × 512 pixel PNG icon image file and drag it over the largest image well. You should see something like Figure 13–3.

Figure 13–3. *Icon Composer with DailyJournal icon image at 512 pixels*

The good news is that if you have provided a 512 x 512-pixel icon you probably won't need to supply any of the others. The display system in Mac OS X will handle the resizing to give you the other icon sizes. You can see the effect in the Preview panel, which lets you see how your icon will look at different sizes.

However, because the icon is being resized programmatically it won't always look right. Smaller sizes particularly can look blurred and lose edge definition. If your icon looks ugly or indistinct at different sizes, you can provide a refined image at the appropriate size and drop it into the corresponding image well. The most common case is for the 16-pixel icon.

Icon Composer has two other panels: **Masks** and **Preview**. Check out the **Masks** panel first, in Figure 13–4.

Figure 13–4. *Icon Composer has generated a mask for the icon image.*

You may be wondering why you need a mask—what is it for? In the old days of small, simple, rectangular icons there was no need for them. Masks are used where the edges of images need to be displayed in a more refined fashion, particularly in terms of shapes and aliasing. Take the icon we are creating here: an open book with a drop shadow. Ideally we would want the icon's outline to follow the outline shape of the book itself so that the background shows through correctly when the icon is seen against a colored or image-based background (see Figure 13–5). Additionally, the icon has a drop shadow. This has a soft edge blending out to the background, so we need a way to manage that in the display of the icon. Those two needs are satisfied by having a mask. It can be very difficult to create precise masks manually, so it's great to know that Icon Composer just does this automatically for you (if you really want to, you can create your own mask image and drag it into this pane, but in my experience Icon Composer does a great job).

Figure 13–5. *The Icon Preview pane helps you to see the image against a variety of backgrounds.*

As mentioned previously, the **Preview** pane allows you to see the icon at a range of sizes and against different backgrounds. You can also see how your icon will look in the Dock (**View ➤ Preview in Dock**, or ⌘D, and your icon will replace the standard Icon Composer Dock icon).

You can create the icon resource file now. Choose File ➤ Save and put the file in a suitable location. That's it—you have created the icon resource file.

Now open up the DailyJournal project. Drag the `DJIcons.icns` file that you just created into the `Resources` folder. In the drop-down dialog window that appears, check the box **Copy items into destination group's folder** and click the **Add** button. Next, choose the `DailyJournal-Info.plist` file in the **Detail** pane. In the editing pane, look for the **Icon file** item and enter the name of the new file (see Figure 13–6). As usual with Xcode, there is another way to set the icon file. You can bring up the **Get Info** window (right-click the **DailyJournal** target and choose **Get Info**). Then choose the **Properties** tab and enter the icon file name in the **Icon File** field.

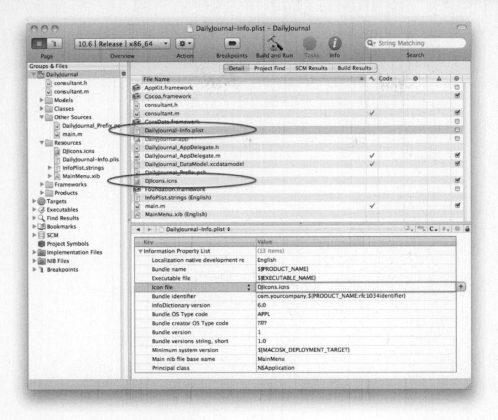

Figure 13–6. *Configuring the icon in Xcode*

Now **Build** (⌘B) the application, then find the executable using the Finder (it will be in your project folder, under build/Debug/). Look at the icon at a range of sizes to check that it looks okay (see Figure 13–7).

16   32   64   128   256   512

Figure 13–7. *The final icon at different sizes in the Finder*

And that's it; you're done. It looks good, doesn't it? Using Icon Composer makes it easy for you to create professional-quality icons for your applications.

Pixie

It's easy to overlook Pixie as a lightweight and not very useful utility—on the face of it, it simply provides a magnified view of the display. Actually, though, it is a remarkably useful tool, and I use it in most of my projects. Here is a quick tour (I have to admit that there is no tour other than a quick tour for Pixie—even the help-file content is only two lines long!).

Start up Pixie (/Developer/Applications/Graphics Tools), and you see the magnified view of your current mouse location (see Figure 13–8; in this figure the mouse pointer is over the three **Manage...** buttons in the **Journal Entry** window):

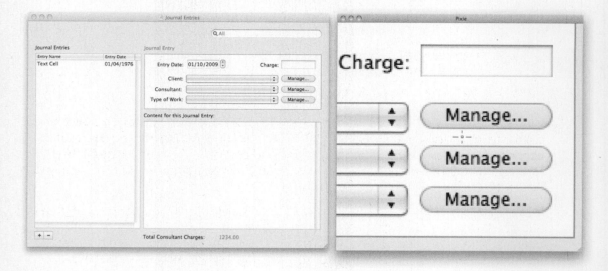

Figure 13–8. *Pixie in action*

If that were all Pixie did, it would be a little dull. However, there is more to it: you can change the size of the inspection window and set the magnification (Use the **Magnify** menu, or ⌘+ and ⌘-, or use ⌘1-⌘9). You can also lock the window using horizontal (⌘X), vertical (⌘Y), or both (⌘L) axes. Open up the **Preferences** window to see a wider range of options (see Figure 13–9).

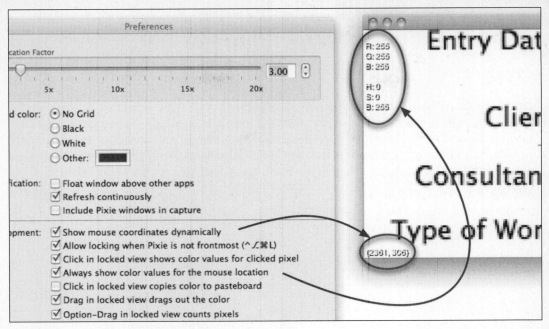

Figure 13–9. *Detail showing some Pixie configuration options*

I find this view useful for various purposes. By checking the options labeled **Show mouse coordinates dynamically** and **Always show color values for the mouse location** you can see continuously updated values for the location and color of the mouse pointer. The typeface used for displaying these values is sadly not very readable, but the close-up in Figure 13–9 shows where to find them.

If you want to know the precise size of an object, you can use Pixie to select an area and count the pixels bound by the selection. When you need to know the color of an object in a window, you can copy the color under the mouse pointer to the clipboard (Pixie calls this the "pasteboard") and it will be stored there in the form [NSColor colorWithCalibratedRed:0.400000 green:0.647059 blue:0.015686 alpha:1.0], which you can use directly within Xcode. To do this, select the checkbox entitled **Click in locked view copies color to pasteboard**, then lock Pixie's viewport so it contains the colors you are interested in. Finally, click on a colored pixel in the viewport. You can now paste the color string in your editor. Or you can drag a color into a system color well for use in other applications. In each case you would simply select the relevant option in the **Preferences** window.

One or two options don't work as well as they might. The grid, though potentially very useful for alignment purposes, seems to come and go in slightly unpredictable ways. The option to show Pixie in the capture is most strange: by default Pixie's own window is invisible to itself, so when you mouse over it you actually see the underlying window as if Pixie were not there. If you check the option to show the Pixie window, then Pixie also captures its own window. This can lead to some interestingly bizarre recursive capture effects, which can be briefly engaging, but frankly there is no obvious application for this option.

Well, that about wraps it up for Pixie. Small but well formed, a sadly neglected but very useful utility.

FileMerge

Here is the scenario: I had a copy of the DailyJournal project stored on the network. I took a copy off to my desktop and did some work on it but forgot to copy it back. The next day I connected my notebook to the network and took a copy of that project to work on it. I added an icon to the desktop copy, and an installation package document to the notebook copy, and made changes to the same class code file in both.

Oops. I now have three copies of the same project, completely out of sync. Oh, and I had neglected to read Chapter 11 of this book and so none of these folders was under Subversion source-code management. What a mess. I could work painstakingly through each folder to figure out the differences, but that's what computers are for, isn't it? Let's see what FileMerge can do to help.

The first thing to do, in the interest of safety, was to copy all three folders somewhere where I could work on them. For clarity I gave the three project folders different names: `Network copy`, `Desktop copy`, and `Notebook copy`.

Next I started up FileMerge. This utility starts up with a small interface window: its default operation is to compare two files or folders, so that is what you see. However, if you expand the window a little vertically, it pops open to show some additional options that suit what we want to do here; see Figure 13–10.

> **NOTE:** FileMerge is a bit of an oddity from a usability perspective. This "popping open" behavior, for example: why didn't the developer use a disclosure arrow, or **More/Less** buttons, either of which would be more Mac-like? FileMerge also uses a drop-down list to launch a new window where you would normally expect just to make a choice between options in the same window. To me this breaks the cardinal usability rule of not surprising your user. We'll be returning to the topic of usability in a lot more detail in the next chapter.

FileMerge allows you to compare the contents of two child folders against a common original folder (called an ancestor). I entered the location of the Network copy as the ancestor, and the Notebook and Desktop copies as respectively the Left and Right derived versions. The use of "Left" and "Right" as descriptions here is quite arbitrary, by the way (another usability flaw): they are flags that identify the two versions that you want to compare. These also identify the two panels in the comparison view, which you will see a little later.

The final thing to consider was what to do once I had figured out where the most relevant files belonged. FileMerge has the option of a merge folder that holds the correct

version of each file as the result of the compare operation. I created a new folder called
`Fixed copy`. The final FileMerge setup looked like Figure 13–10:

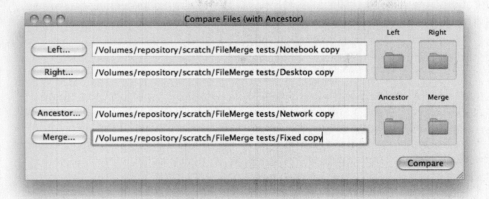

Figure 13–10. *FileMerge window ready to carry out compare and merge operations*

OK, ready to go. I clicked the **Compare** button. After a short pause I saw the result (see
Figure 13–11).

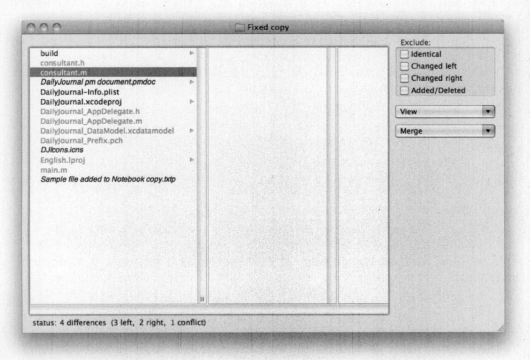

Figure 13–11. *FileMerge report from comparing folders*

This report carries a lot of information. Files and folders shown grayed-out are identical. Those shown in normal text indicate a difference between the left and right versions (I could safely ignore any differences in build, since that folder's contents are rebuilt at compile time anyway). Those shown in italics indicate a file added or removed. Selecting any entry shows a brief message in the status area (at the bottom of the window) describing the change or difference. If there are a lot of files and folders, you can use the **Exclude** checkboxes to narrow down the list displayed.

OK, the file `consultant.m` shows some significant differences, so I decided to take a closer look. I selected that entry and then chose **Comparison** from the **View** dropdown menu (here's that bit of poor usability). The file-comparison window that appears shows the left and right files with the differences highlighted (see Figure 13–12).

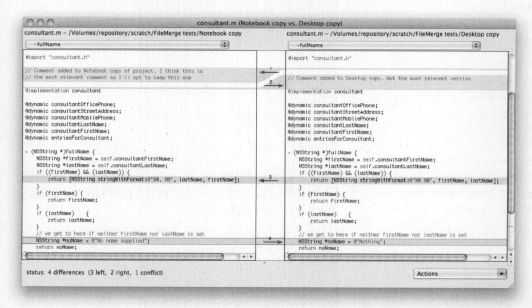

Figure 13–12. *FileMerge side-by-side comparison*

The highlighting in this window shows not only the differences but also how they compare to their ancestor file. Looking down the file contents, the first difference is a comment added to each file. These comments (differences 1 and 2) don't actually conflict with each other, and FileMerge simply indicates where the content departs from the ancestor.

The next difference (3) is highlighted in gray. The arrow pointing to the left indicates that the left file has changed with respect to the ancestor file. The final difference is highlighted in red to show a conflict. This means that both copies of the file have had the same line of code changed from the version in the ancestor file.

In each case you can choose which version is valid for the final merge file, and in fact you can see how the merge file will look by pulling up the splitter handle near the bottom of the window.

I chose to keep the left-hand version of difference 1 and difference 2 (this means that I effectively delete the comment from the right-hand version. I decided to unwind the change made in the left-hand copy revealed in difference 3 and to choose the right-hand version in difference 4.

> **CAUTION:** When you are choosing actions you might think (at least, I did) that choosing the **Neither** option in the **Actions** drop-down list would result in the file reverting to the ancestor copy. Sadly, it doesn't. It literally chooses neither the left nor the right version, and you end up with no code at all for this line in the merge file! Use this action with caution.

The final step here was to save the merge file (**File ➤ Save** or ⌘S). The file was saved in the `Fixed` copy folder. When I closed the compare files window I could see that there was a checkmark against the file `consultant.m`.

For the other files there were no conflicts, simply files added to one side or another or changed on one side or the other. In each case, the thing to do was to select the file and choose the appropriate action from the **Merge** drop-down list. Where a file had been added to one copy but not the other I chose the copy with the added file. Where a file was on both copies and had changed on one copy but there were no conflicts, I chose the changed copy. In each case the message at the bottom of the FileMerge window showed which copy was which, and FileMerge duly put the appropriate file into the `Fixed` copy folder. In the case of the grayed-out folders I simply chose the left file (it could have been either since they are identical) and I left the build folder alone (I chose the **Merge** action **Remove**) since it would get rebuilt by Xcode.

There remained one slight complication: the xcodeproj project/folder. When I looked at that I noticed that there were quite a number of issues. I had `.pbxuser` and `.perspective3` files for the user accounts on both computers and a single `project.pbxproj` file. I could choose **Remove** for the `.pbxuser` and `.perspectivev3` files since these are regenerated when needed. Looking at the `.pbxproj` file it was clear that the main changes were due to the addition of **DJIcons** to the right (desktop) copy. That fit well with what I knew I had done, so I reckoned it was safe to use the right copy of this file.

At the end of this process I had a new **Fixed** copy folder that held the files containing the correct versions. I opened the project and checked that all was well.

FileMerge is a sophisticated and capable utility, if a little quirky in usability terms. If you need an effective method to manage the business of comparing and merging the contents of folders and text files, it's there waiting for you.

Property List Editor

In a sense you have already encountered the Property List Editor. When you choose a Plist file in the **Detail** pane in the Xcode Workspace you will see an editor that shows a structured view of your plist file. In fact, this file is an XML file and can also be read into a text editor like TextEdit. (However, I prefer a more sophisticated editor like TextMate for its color-coding. I also like the code-folding feature that allows you to collapse and hide parts of the plist structure that you don't want to look at. You can get a trial copy of TextMate from `http://macromates.com/`.) Figure 13–13 shows the `DailyJournal-Info.plist` file in both the Xcode view and in TextMate.

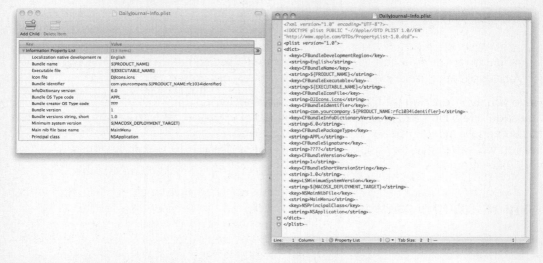

Figure 13–13. *DailyJournal-Info.plist open in Property List Editor and in TextMate*

Both views have their advantages (I am a great fan of plain-text views—it's harder to hide problems in plain text!). Actually, the standalone Property List Editor offers few real advantages to the Xcode developer over simply using the editing panel in Xcode Workspace. However, it has one feature that you may find useful—the ability to open binary `.plist` files. For reasons that seem to have to do with performance, Apple chose back in version 10.2 of Mac OS X to start generating `.plist` XML files in a binary format. Anyway, if you were to look at the plist file for a program such as TextEdit, you would find that it looks like Figure 13–14 in TextMate:

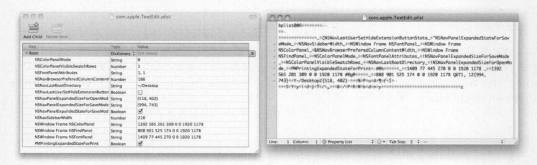

Figure 13–14. *TextEdit's plist file is in binary XML format*

That's not much use if you like a hierarchical view, or even a plain-English view. That's where Property List Editor is useful. Having read in a binary file such as this one, you can save it in normal text-based XML format (use the File ➤ Save To... menu item and choose XML Property List from the File Format popup). Then you can read it into any text editor.

Adding Help Functionality

The last utility you'll be looking at in this chapter is the Help Indexer. But you'll be learning a bit more than that: this section is about building an HTML-based help system for your application, and the Help Indexer is part of that process.

Have you ever reached for the Help menu in an application, only to see the terse message "Help isn't available for [insert name of application here]"? Personally, I find it a tad unfriendly. While Mac software has an inbuilt advantage when it comes to usability (as you will see in the next chapter) it does no harm to include some helpful hints for your user about how to get the best out of your killer application.

Help in Xcode-based Applications

The collection of help pages for your application is really just a collection of web pages, in XHTML format. You can create your help system using any tool you like to make a local collection of static XHTML pages. These can include text, images, and even multimedia resources. There are great resources available in the Developer Documentation: search for "Apple Help Programming" for a good entry point. For this section I am going to focus on enhancing the DailyJournal application by adding a set of help pages with text and images and making them available through the Apple Help mechanism.

Creating the XHTML Pages

You can use any tool to create your pages. I use RapidWeaver, which is a great application for quickly putting together professional-looking websites. You could just as easily use Coda, BBEdit, TextMate, iWeb, or any of a host of similar tools.

As always, there is some planning and setting up to do. First, here is the page layout that I decided on: there is a welcome page that describes how to create a new journal entry, and a simple menu leading to three further pages dealing with the three secondary windows (see Figure 13–15):

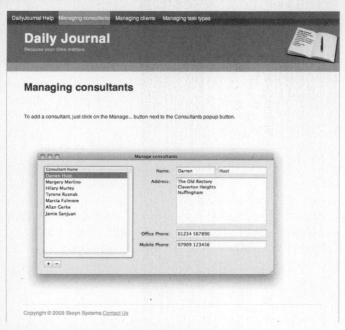

Figure 13-15. *Web page layout for DailyJournal help*

Obviously you need to add some help content—text, images, and so on—to these web pages. Good writing for web pages is a discipline in and of itself, and a detailed description is way beyond the scope of this book. However, there are a few points to bear in mind when writing help web pages:

- Keep the pages short unless a long description is really necessary.

- Put the salient points near the top of the page—many people never venture below "the fold" on a web page.

- Use diagrams only where they add to the message, and keep them small.

- Make the page title as meaningful as possible—this is the text that will show up in a help search later on. You can use the meta-description tag to provide a more verbose description that will show up as a tooltip and as the second line in any search results (see Listing 13-1 and Figure 13-20).

Adding Meta Tags to the Welcome Page

The next thing you need to do is add some meta tags to the `<head>` element of the welcome page: these help to identify that page to the Help Indexer and Xcode as the entry point for help. See Listing 13-1—much of the `<head>` element has been omitted for clarity, indicated by [...].

Listing 13–1. Meta Tags in Index.html

```
<!DOCTYPE html PUBLIC "-//W3C//DTD XHTML 1.0 Strict//EN"
"http://www.w3.org/TR/xhtml1/DTD/xhtml1-strict.dtd">
<html xmlns="http://www.w3.org/1999/xhtml">
    <head>
[...]
        <meta name="AppleTitle" content="DailyJournal Help" />
        <meta name="AppleIcon"
          content="DailyJournal/DailyJournalIcon16.png" />
        <meta name="description"
          content="Online help for the Consultant's Daily Journal application" />
[...]
</head>
[...]
```

The `AppTitle` meta tag is used, as you will see shortly, to identify the entry point into our help pages. The 16-pixel PNG image will be used in the **Help** menu—of course, there has to be an image file at this location. The `description` tag provides text that will appear as a tooltip when doing help searches. For this reason you should add `meta name="description"` tags to each of the HTML files in the collection of help web pages.

Running the Help Indexer

Once you have created and configured the welcome page and other pages, it's time to run the Help Indexer. To do this, start up the program in `/Developer/Applications/Utilities/`. The interface is very simple, asking for a help folder location. The folder in this case is the folder that contains the `index.html` and other files (see Figure 13–16):

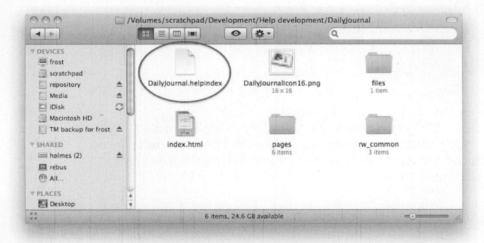

Figure 13–16. *Web page files complete with help index for use in the DailyJournal application*

The Help Indexer acts in much the same way as a search spider on a conventional web page: it reads the textual content of each web help page and follows any links that it finds to other pages. It uses the meta AppleTitle tag to identify the home page out of the collection of web help pages. All of this information is then packaged up into the index that is used by the help search function and stored in this folder with the name DailyJournal.helpindex. The application's Search Help function is able to read this index and point to the relevant location in the help page collection.

Adding and Configuring the Help Files Within the Xcode Project

The next step is to add this complete folder to the DailyJournal project. Open the project in Xcode, select the **Resources** item in the **Groups & Files** list, right-click, and choose **Add ➤ Existing Files**. Choose the DailyJournal folder that contains the help files (in the preceding example this folder is /Volumes/scratchpad/Development/Help Development/DailyJournal). In the drop-down window that appears check the **Copy items** checkbox and also the radio button labeled **Create Folder References for any added folders** (see Figure 13–17), then finally click **Add**.

Figure 13–17. *Adding the help files to the DailyJournal project*

This should give you a project window like the one in Figure 13–18. The final step is to edit the DailyJournal-Info.plist file so that it links to the help folder and the welcome file. Choose the .plist file in the **Detail** pane so that you have the content in the code editor window. Next, right-click on the **Information Property List** title and choose **Add Row** from the contextual menu. This adds a blank row to the .plist file and pops up a menu of available .plist keys. Choose **Help Book directory name** and add the value DailyJournal (as that was the name of the folder containing help content). Add another row with the key **Help Book Identifier**, and set the value of this to DailyJournal Help. Note that this is the same as the value that you put into the meta tag for AppleTitle in the help welcome page (look back to Listing 13–1).

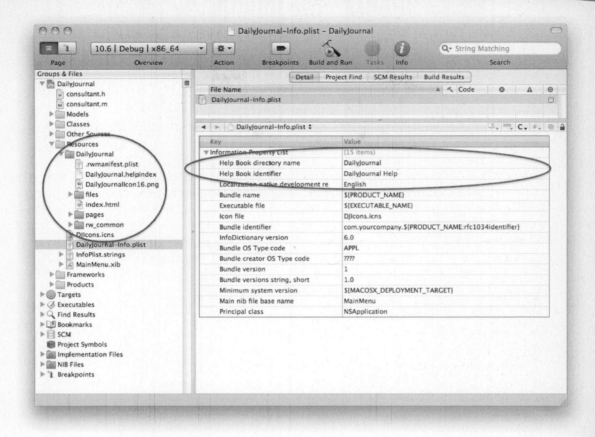

Figure 13–18. *The DailyJournal project after adding and configuring the help files*

Let's review Figure 13–18. The **Resources** item now has the help folder (DailyJournal) and this is also configured in the DailyJournal-Info.plist file as a directory named Help Book. The help index has been generated and is also embedded in the project. The welcome page, index.html, has meta tags with content that mirrors the identifier in the .plist file.

Testing the New Help Function

Now, to test our work. If you are following along with the downloaded project, start up DailyJournal. Choose **Help** ➤ **DailyJournal Help** (note that this is the entry-point name you originally chose), and you should see our nice **DailyJournal Help** window (see Figure 13–19):

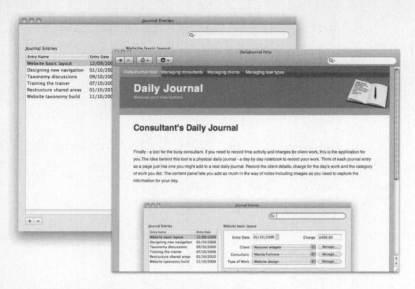

Figure 13–19. *DailyJournal has a real help function now.*

Check that you can navigate between the different pages using the top menu. Now, try a search. Type the word **client** into the search box and press Return. You will see a set of results. For each result the page title is shown, and beneath that is the text that was entered as the meta description tag. This also appears as a tooltip if you hover over the result. Click any result to see the page. See Figure 13–20.

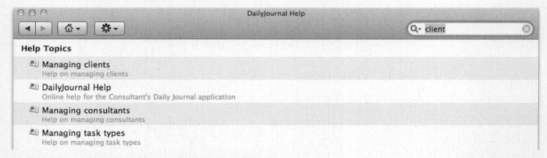

Figure 13–20. *Searching the help index for DailyJournal*

Adding a Help Button Linked to a Help Page

As a final step, let's add a **Help** button to one of the user interface windows and link it to our new help pages.

We'll start with the code. The first thing to do is to create an IBAction declaration and implementation. You'll need this to connect the **Help** button when we create it. Listing 13–2 has the declaration (you will need to add the code in bold).

Notice that we are importing Carbon libraries here (the Apple Help functions are held in Carbon.framework), so the next thing to do is to add this framework to the project. In summary, you do a right-click on **Other Frameworks** in the **Groups & Files** list, then choose **Add ➤ Existing Frameworks...** and choose Carbon.framework.

Listing 13–2. *DailyJournal_AppDelegate.h*

```
#import <Cocoa/Cocoa.h>
#import <Carbon/Carbon.h>
@interface DailyJournal_AppDelegate : NSObject
{
    NSWindow *window;

    NSPersistentStoreCoordinator *persistentStoreCoordinator;
    NSManagedObjectModel *managedObjectModel;
    NSManagedObjectContext *managedObjectContext;
}

@property (nonatomic, retain) IBOutlet NSWindow *window;

@property (nonatomic, retain, readonly)
NSPersistentStoreCoordinator *persistentStoreCoordinator;
@property (nonatomic, retain, readonly)
NSManagedObjectModel *managedObjectModel;
@property (nonatomic, retain, readonly)
NSManagedObjectContext *managedObjectContext;

- (IBAction)saveAction:sender;

OSStatus MyGotoHelpPage (CFStringRef
pagePath, CFStringRef anchorName);
- (IBAction) loadHelpForJournalEntry:(id)sender;

@end
```

The implementation of the action in DailyJournal_AppDelegate.m calls a local function called MyGotoHelpPage (I took this directly from the Developer Documentation). This function in turn calls the help function AHGotoPage.

> **NOTE:** The relevant help page with the example code is actually quite hard to find, so here is how to get to it. Search for AHGotoHelpPage (note the lowercase to; It's easy to get this wrong, particularly as GoTo seems correct on the face of it!) and in the results list look for a Full Text result entitled **Opening your Help Book in Help Viewer**. Select that item. Now, in the table of contents open **Opening Your Help Book in Help Viewer** and then click on **Loading a Help Book Page**.

Our IBAction passes in the name of the HTML page that we want to load. That's it (there are other options available—check the Developer Documentation as suggested previously). The function and action are shown in Listing 13–3, with the new code in bold (most of the rest of the class code has been omitted for clarity, indicated by [...]).

Listing 13–3. New Code in DailyJournal_AppDelegate.m

```
[...]
/**
 Implementation of MyGotoHelpPage
 Taken from Apple Developer Documentation
 */

OSStatus MyGotoHelpPage (CFStringRef pagePath, CFStringRef anchorName) {
    CFBundleRef myApplicationBundle = NULL;
    CFStringRef myBookName = NULL;
    OSStatus err = noErr;
     myApplicationBundle = CFBundleGetMainBundle();
    if (myApplicationBundle == NULL) {
        err = fnfErr;
        goto bail;
    }
    myBookName = CFBundleGetValueForInfoDictionaryKey(
        myApplicationBundle,
        CFSTR("CFBundleHelpBookName"));
    if (myBookName == NULL) {
        err = fnfErr;
        goto bail;
    }
    if (CFGetTypeID(myBookName) != CFStringGetTypeID()) {
        err = paramErr;
    }
    if (err == noErr) err = AHGotoPage (myBookName, pagePath, anchorName);
bail:
    return err;
}


/**
 Action calling the MyGotoHelp function with the correct help page
 */

- (IBAction) loadHelpForJournalEntry:(id)sender {
    MyGotoHelpPage(CFSTR("index.html"), NULL);
}
[...]
```

Now move to Interface Builder and open the **Journal Entries** window. Add a help button (the small circular button with a question-mark image). Position it next to the **Add/Remove** buttons below the **Journal Entries** list. We're just going to point this button at the welcome page in the help pages. Right-click on the new button, drag to the DailyJournal_AppDelegate controller, and choose the action loadHelpForJournalEntry:. Once again I am not going to spell this out—you are way past that! Save the NIB and return to Xcode, Build and Run. You should see the new button in your main window. Click on this, and you should see the help window (see Figure 13–21).

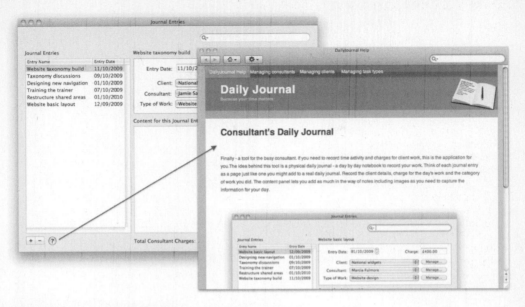

Figure 13–21. *The new help button in the Journal Entries window*

If you wanted to extend this idea to add other help buttons pointing at different help pages, the simplest way would be to have a number of `loadHelpFor...` methods, but that approach would be inelegant and begging for refactoring. Another approach would be to change the `loadHelpForJournalEntry:` method into a general-purpose `loadHelpForTopic:` method, and check within the method for the sender in order to determine which help page to load. I'm not going to give you the line-by-line detail of how to do this, but have a look at the `TemperatureConverterAppDelegate` class in the TemperatureConverter project (first introduced in Chapter 6 but revisited several times since). In the `convertTemperature:` method you can check which `NSTextField` supplied the starting temperature, and that determines which calculation the method then runs. You could use this approach, with some adaptation, to determine which of a variety of help buttons was clicked and thus which help page needs to be loaded.

Summary

Well, I hope you enjoyed that trip off the beaten track, and I hope you are sold on some of these lesser-used utilities and tools. I think they generously repay the modest effort that you put in to learn them.

In a sense, you'll be staying on the back roads in the next chapter, when we take a look at usability and accessibility—two hugely important topics but ones that rarely get an outing in Mac developer books. In the next chapter, you'll learn how you might make your application more usable in general or more usable by users with impairments. I hope you'll stick with me, and turn the page to Chapter 14.

Chapter 14

Usability and Accessibility

Once upon a time I worked in a large corporation in the (at that time) novel capacity of a usability specialist. I had a hard time of it. For one thing, the very idea of building systems whose behaviors conformed to common standards was novel. PC software was gradually emerging from the prehistory of the DOS command line and character-based user interfaces into the comparatively modern world of Windows. In those days the use of a graphic user interface *per se* was deemed to make a program user-friendly. Often repurposing an application for Windows involved literally presenting the character-based interface, together with its bespoke key controls, into a window. I frequently had conversations with developers whose aim was to focus on the features of the software, with the only nod toward usability being an offer to "make it look pretty at the end." Convincing such developers that in fact usability is a systemic issue—that you should design your software from top to bottom to be usable, rather than putting lipstick on a pig—was a long and tough task.

Fortunately for me I was also, in my spare time, a Macintosh user. This exposed me very early on to the benefits to be had from designing software that didn't just "look pretty" but also had well-defined, predictable behaviors, and structures and workflows that conformed to expectations. It also gave me good examples of consistent design to draw on, and gradually things improved.

Nowadays software developers don't need much convincing—the value of consistent, well-designed, and above all usable software is clear, and no one sets out to write unusable systems. Still, there is always the temptation to just get coding, and in doing so it is possible to miss out on some of the opportunities to enhance the usability of a system by understanding and applying some of the basic principles of human-computer interaction.

In this chapter you will cover those basic principles and see how Xcode's tools help you to make usable software. You will also be exploring the relatively unknown territory of *accessible* software, and see how, with a modest investment of effort, you can make your products both usable by and accessible to all of your potential users.

Overview of Usability

Usability is about making computer systems that do the job they are designed to do and that make the experience a pleasurable one. It is also about making computer systems that are easy to use. This should never be taken as an insult to the intelligence of your user—it's more an understanding that systems *just shouldn't be hard to use*, and that your users have better things to do than to try to interpret your view of how the system should work. A user of your program will already be familiar with the environment in which it will run, and will use other programs in that environment already. Your program ought to be a good citizen and work in the way your users expect based on their experience.

Usability has a number of components that are worth exploring and that help in designing usable computer programs from the start. Let's look at a few of these: consistency, affordance, and the mental model.

Consistency

A major purpose behind *consistency* in design is to not surprise your user. If you have a thing that looks like a button, then it should *always* behave like a button. By the same token, everything in your user interface that behaves like a button should look like one. If you have image buttons, it makes sense to have them conform to a common design with a common approach to imagery since that removes the need for the user to stop and think what this control is for.

Consistency applies not just within your program, but across your user's environment. Let's take a simple example. Mac users will be comfortable with the fact that there are certain keyboard shortcuts that work across the Mac. For example, you can always copy and paste content using ⌘C and ⌘V. Your users are going to expect the same from your software, and so you would need a really good reason to map different keystrokes to copy and paste or to use ⌘C and ⌘V for other purposes.

To take a slightly more complex example, where should the menu go? If you are a pure Mac user this is simple—where else would a menu go but at the top of the screen?—but for developers who have come from the Windows world it is far from easy. In a typical Windows program, the menu is placed at the top of each window. This is more than simply a visual design decision: the metaphor in use in a Windows application is that the window is the application container. Typically when you close a window you close the application too. Hence it makes sense to have the menu at the top of the window where you are working.

Mac OS X takes a completely different metaphorical approach: an application runs on your Mac whether or not there is a window visible (this cuts both ways, of course—the idea that an application like Microsoft Word is still running even though you have closed all documents drives some newcomers to the Mac batty!). A window is a container through which your application communicates with the user. As a result, Mac programs universally have the menu bar at the top of the display and not in the window. The menu bar on display at any time is the one for the current application.

MENU BARS BELONG AT THE TOP OF THE DISPLAY

There is another good usability reason for having the menu bar at the top of the display: findability. When you run your mouse up to the top of your display, you don't have to worry about overshooting in the vertical dimension—you know your mouse will stop at the top. This means that when seeking a particular menu item, you have only to worry about precision in the horizontal dimension: the vertical is taken care of by the screen. In contrast, you need to be quite precise about both x and y coordinates when finding a menu bar in a window.

Affordance

Affordance means the degree to which a control reveals its purpose to the user. A button control should look like something that can be pressed, and when you press it it should behave like it has been pressed. Scroll bars have defined handles that leave you in no doubt that you can grab and move them, and their behavior when you do should fit the expected action. A well-designed user interface has controls that spell out for the user exactly how they should be used. The other factor to bear in mind in designing controls with good affordance is that they should invite and reward exploration. A slider control should look and behave like one, and give clear feedback about the consequences of changing its setting.

AFFORDANCE IN THE REAL WORLD—DOOR HANDLES

Think for a moment about a common real-world object such as a door handle. As you walk up to a door you will often see a handle on one side of the door and a push-plate on the other. That is great affordance. The door *tells* you which handle you should pull and which you should push. Now, how often have you seen a glass door that has a pull handle on both sides? Watch people using that door, and you will often see them pull when they should be pushing. That's bad affordance.

Mental Model

A *mental model* is the construction that your user builds in his mind to describe and predict how your software works. For example, a word-processing system provides a mental model to the user of a space in which to create nicely formatted text content, perhaps with pictures. A word processor that didn't support a readily identifiable model would be more difficult to learn, since the user would have no familiar frame of reference in which to approach the program. The mental model that you would be trying to support in writing a word processor would be one involving the creation of a new document (a blank sheet of paper in the real world), tools to put text and images down on the page (a pen or even a typewriter, with a pastepot to glue in a picture), tools to construct the document (more pages when you need them), and some mechanism to store it at the end of the process (folders in a filing system).

An appropriate mental model can be difficult to define, as many factors may influence the user's mental model of your system. Still, it's worth the effort. A well-designed system makes no assumptions about the user's prior knowledge, but provides the appropriate visual scaffolding and other cues that steer the user toward the mental model that you intend for the system. There should ideally be just one mental model—a poorly thought-out system design may allow your user to choose from a variety of mental models, which is a sure recipe for confusion. It is worth taking the time to consider the model that you intend and to provide all of the cues that you can to support that model.

Usability Considerations for Mac OS X

It would be easy just to say "Read the Human Interface Guidelines." After all, Apple has gone to enormous trouble to make sure that developers understand the purpose of every element in application design. And the guidelines are well worth reading (just search for "Human Interface Guidelines" in the Developer Documentation). At around 400 pages (plus another 130 or so for the iPhone HI document) they are a big read, though, and so this section is an introductory overview—just enough usability to get you started.

Writing your applications using Xcode and Cocoa frameworks such as AppKit and UIKit help hugely in building consistency and affordance into your applications. Let's look at some general usability considerations in designing programs (most of these are as true for development in any other computer system) and then some of the tools provided in Interface Builder to aid usability.

Program Design Considerations for Good Usability

Designing for usability is really just good system design. The same principles apply, and you may detect echoes here of the principles of Agile Development ((see Chapter 9):

- Understand the purpose of the program and the tasks you user will conduct, and fit the features and workflow to them.

- Keep the application focused on the fundamentals and avoid unnecessary features, as these could distract the user from the main purpose of the program.

- Keep themes and controls consistent: if you have command buttons, use the same type throughout; if you have image buttons, adopt a consistent visual design for them.

- Don't surprise your user. Support keystrokes that your user already knows (like ⌘C) and ensure that these meet their expectations.

- Support the workflow of your application by including visual cues to show what can and cannot be done. If a particular function accessed by a command button is not available, then make the button unavailable (grey it out).

- Don't leave your user hanging around. Many applications have an introductory splash screen—in some cases this is purely for marketing purposes and in others it is a way of distracting the user while loading data. Either way it is to be avoided where possible, as your program is essentially telling your user to wait until it is good and ready to start working. It is always better to put up something useful as soon as possible. If you must have a splash screen, then offer your user an option to not display it.

- Avoid modal behavior. Modality occurs when you have a window or other control that refuses to allow the user to move to another window or control until the user has carried out some interaction with that control. This is most often seen in dialogs that prevent your user from returning to the program until she has dealt with the dialog's message. While there are circumstances—a critical error, for example, or some print or save dialogs—where you might need to do this, use modal behavior sparingly.

- Don't expect your user to think too much. Remember that this is not to insult your user's intelligence; rather, the best programs act as windows into the underlying functionality. Anything that gets in the way of that—like an ungainly interface or an inconsistent use of controls—will detract from the usability of your system.

- Don't expect your user to *have* to use help, but provide focused, context-sensitive help where it is likely to be needed. Use of tooltip help is also a good idea, though sparingly, as flashing tooltips all over the user interface can be distracting and annoying.

Autosizing and Auto-Positioning

Apple has invested a huge amount of effort over the decades in understanding good visual layout. The autosizing and auto-positioning tools in Interface Builder enable you to lay out controls to help you use white space well and get the optimum spacing and sizing behavior for your program. Take a quick look back at Figures 3-5 and 3-8 in Chapter 3 to see how these work.

Consistent Visual Design

The stamp of consistency in the design of the user interface controls available within Interface Builder is clear. Figures 14–1 and 14–2 show the tools available for Mac OS X and iPhone applications.

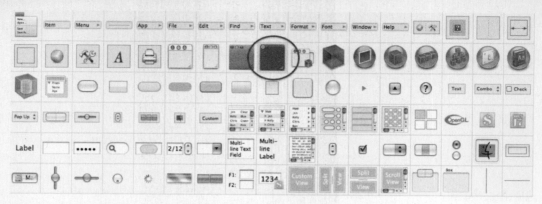

Figure 14–1. *Visual design of UI components for Mac OS X applications*

Figure 14–2. *Visual design of UI components for iPhone applications*

The one area of slight inconsistency is the presence of the HUD window (circled in Figure 14–1). This gray, semitransparent window is a recent introduction and is reminiscent of the UI of Apple's professional applications, such as Aperture. Does this perhaps indicate a move to a wider choice of user interface options for the developer? Time alone will tell.

Affordance Revisited

You have just seen the range of controls in Interface Builder, so there is probably not much point in describing these in detail. Let's just have a look at the controls we used in the Daily Journal application. Figure 14–3 shows the main **Journal Entries** window:

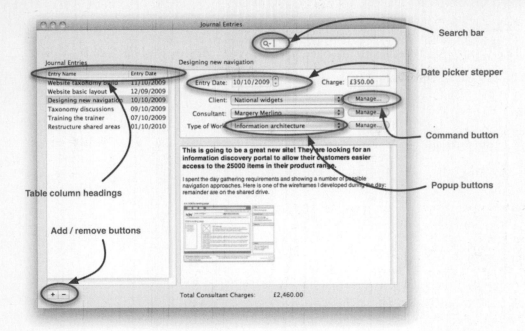

Figure 14–3. *Affordance in Mac OS X controls in the DailyJournal application*

Notice that all of the controls you are likely to interact with have a slightly beveled, 3-D appearance. They have a consistent feel about them: they seem to invite the user to interact with them. Even the table column headings (which you can click to order the data by that value) have the same effect. Now let's look at two of these controls that seem at first glance to be quite similar: the date picker stepper control and the pop-up button. Both have similar up and down arrows: what makes them different? Well, the stepper control has the up and down arrows encapsulated in a buttonlike construct that disconnects it slightly from the date display, whereas the pop-up button is clearly part of the overall control that includes the pop-up menu text. This provides subtle visual cues that tell you that the pop-up control is part of the menu, whereas the stepper control is somehow separate from the date display as a whole (though it is used to manage each component of the date).

The user interface controls available in the iPhone tools have been particularly well-designed in terms of affordance. Take a look at the controls in Figure 14–4. Do they leave you with any doubt about their different purposes?

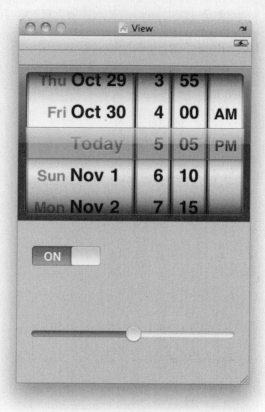

Figure 14–4. *Affordance in the iPhone user interface*

Furthermore, users of the iPhone pick up both the touch-screen display and the gesture control metaphor extremely quickly (it is, after all, the only way to use it!), and so controls like this suggest to the user the way in which the controls should be manipulated (this is known in usability circles as a *direct-manipulation interface* because you interact directly with the control in a realistic fashion).

Tab Order

The tab order, as the name suggests, is the order in which your controls take the focus when you load a window and use the Tab key to navigate around it. Setting your tab order is a matter of setting the `firstResponder` (the control that first receives focus when the window is loaded) and the `nextKeyView` for each of the controls to which you want to be able to tab. Think about the likely workflow for a user of your application—where would you expect them to start, and where would they go from there? Setting the tab order is as important for accessibility purposes as it is for usability: when your user has a visual impairment, it is important to provide a logical progression around your user interface to help them in framing the mental model for the program.

Special Usability Considerations for iPhone Program Design

Software for the iPhone presents some usability challenges and opportunities that you don't have with software design on the Mac. Let's run through some of the main points.

Form Factor

The most obvious difference between a program running on the Mac and one running on the iPhone is that you have much less real estate to work with on the latter. A consequence of this is that you need to be much smarter and more disciplined about layout and use of screen space. Another is that you can't present as much information as you might in a Mac OS X program. This is actually a nice discipline, since it forces you as a designer to be clear about the purpose of each part of your system and prevents you from building overly complex interfaces.

Only One Window

Your Mac programs have the luxury of space and the potential of multiple moveable windows. This means that you can provide secondary windows, configuration windows, and toolboxes to handle some features of the application while still being able to see the main window. On the iPhone you need to be more creative about how you handle secondary input. This usually comes down to having a tabbed interface, or a screen flip or similar mechanism for temporarily parking the main user interface while carrying out some other task. The consequence is that you need to design the iPhone application with the awareness that the user will have to work temporarily in another context and won't be able to refer to information in the main interface.

One Only Application

With very few exceptions, there is only one active application on an iPhone at any one time. Unlike in Mac OS X, you are not able to change back and forth between active applications. This means your application either has to be able to maintain its state by archiving it when the user moves to another application, or it needs to be designed so that state doesn't matter.

Direct-Manipulation Interface

An application running in Mac OS X on a notebook or desktop Mac has a disaggregated design: that is, the program is presented on the screen in one or more windows and the input is handled via the keyboard and mouse. The iPhone, by contrast, has everything in the same place: the display *is* the user interface. If you want to click a button you push it directly, and if you want to move a slider you put your finger directly on it and slide it. The only exception to this is where you have text- or number-entry fields, since you use a virtual keyboard to do this (and to me this is the only slightly jarring usability note in using the iPhone). The consequence for you as a developer is that you need to be aware of the shortcomings of the virtual keyboard and avoid asking the user to type too much. Apart from that, the direct-manipulation features offer great usability benefits, providing a very natural mechanism to manipulate controls, together with excellent feedback.

Gesture-Driven Interface

Despite the availability of rich gesture-based input mechanisms such as the multitouch trackpad on recent notebooks and the Magic Mouse, this is a major area of difference between Mac OS X applications and iPhone applications. The iPhone is both more limited (keyboard-type inputs using stubby (at least in my case) fingers can be a little clumsy) and more sophisticated (with the ability to slide, spin, pinch, and expand objects using gestures). As you will know from the enormous variety of applications on the App Store, the availability of a direct-manipulation, gesture-driven interface has released a huge wave of creativity in developers. The usability of the resulting software varies from the incredibly intuitive to the, frankly, obscure. Looking at how other developers have implemented their solutions for the iPhone can be very instructive when you are designing your own.

Accessibility in Mac OS X

Accessibility and usability go hand in hand. Writing a piece of software to be easy to use takes you a long way on the road to being accessible to users who need additional help in using the software. You tend to think carefully about the mental model your user has of the software, you think about how the user interacts with the controls, and in doing so you are naturally going to make more accessible software. But that's not enough—building usability and accessibility into your software involves subtly different disciplines and requirements.

Probably no one nowadays needs to be persuaded about the importance of writing accessible websites. In many countries now it is a legal requirement for computer systems to meet minimum standards of accessibility, particularly if you are targeting public-sector customers. It's curious, therefore, that so little attention is paid to accessibility factors in many desktop applications. And that is a shame, since on the Mac in particular there is excellent built-in support for users with sensory impairments, and as a developer you have a fairly easy job of creating your software to be accessible to all of your potential users.

In this section I'm going to cover some of the things you need to consider when writing an application for accessibility, and describe some of the developer support for the tools.

Accessibility Considerations

Let's start with the terminology: what exactly does *accessibility* mean? In short, accessibility is about ensuring that your software can be used by the widest possible range of users, regardless of any sensory impairments they may have. It means providing tools and design features within your software that allow users who are visually impaired, have limited mobility, or have hearing difficulties to get just as high-quality a user experience as any other users. The main topics to consider are display factors and keyboard operation.

Display Factors

Support for users with restricted vision in desktop applications comes down to a number of fairly simple rules:

- Avoid using combinations of color that are difficult to see for users with limited vision. If you stick to the standard color combinations used in Xcode, you won't go far wrong.

- Maintain a good level of contrast between text and backgrounds.

- Don't rely on color alone as a source of information in your interface. Users with color blindness, for example, may not be able to distinguish between certain colors.

- Avoid unusual typefaces or text effects such as shadows that may detract from readability.

- Use titles for all controls where possible so that it is clear what a control is for (and also to help with VoiceOver control, as you will see shortly).

Keyboard Operation

Your application should allow the user to control its functions with the keyboard. This means ensuring that you can use the keyboard to navigate and control the application. You can control the tab order to make a logical progression around the user interface, and can bind crucial controls and menu items to keyboard combinations. There is a wide range of reserved key combinations for keyboard navigation: these are listed in the Developer Documentation article "Accessibility Keyboard Shortcuts."

While doing so, you should ensure that you don't subvert any existing key combinations: this is as much a usability consideration as an accessibility consideration: your user will have an existing Mac experience that convinces her that, say, ⌘C is used to copy content, so if your application does something quite different you will definitely have an unhappy user!

You should also look closely at system key combinations that are used in accessibility support tools such as VoiceOver or Mouse Keys. VoiceOver uses the Control and

Option keys together with keys such as the arrow keys, K, C, R, D, M, U, H, and the spacebar. If you think your users are likely to use VoiceOver, then you obviously need to avoid using these key combinations for any other purpose. Mouse Keys allows you to use the keyboard to move the mouse around. There are some predefined keys for moving in different directions, and for clicking, holding and releasing the mouse button (see Table 14–1). The main concern is to not risk using these keys for navigation purposes in your application.

Table 14–1. *Mouse Keys keyboard shortcuts*

Purpose	Shortcut Key	(Equivalent Without a Numeric Keypad)
Up	8	8
Down	2	K
Left	4	U
Right	6	O
Diagonal NE	9	9
Diagonal SE	3	L
Diagonal NW	7	7
Diagonal SW	1	J
Button click	5	I
Button hold	0	M
Button release	.	.

Testing Accessibility in Your Software

Xcode includes a tool that helps you to design accessible software: Accessibility Verifier (the Xcode Developer Tools installation also includes an Accessibility Inspector, but personally I find Accessibility Verifier the more useful of the two tools).

Let's take a look at both of these tools now with the DailyJournal application. First, open the Xcode project for the DailyJournal application and Build and Run. Then find and run Accessibility Verifier (it's in /Developer/Applications/Utilities/Accessibility Tools/).

Once open, choose DailyJournal from the popup and click the **Verify** button. After a brief pause you will see the report (see Figure 14–5):

Figure 14–5. *Initial report from Accessibility Verifier*

There is some really valuable information in this report. First, the report shows all of the user interface features in that window, with a hierarchy indicating their relationships. It shows that there are no serious accessibility problems. However, it does indicate warnings against some of the controls. In each case it says "Missing AXTitle with no AXDescription or AXTitleUIElement attribute." This means that some important information is missing from the user interface. We'll come back to exactly what is missing in a short while. On a related theme, notice in the lower panel that for each of the controls the current displayed content or the title is shown. Notice that the three Manage... buttons are indistinguishable; that is a poor accessibility feature, guaranteed to irritate your visually impaired users. As you will see shortly, we can do better than this in providing accessibility information about these controls.

There is also some information here that is not so useful. You will see that there are 51 warnings against the **Role Verification** entry (if you are following this on your own computer you will see a different number, depending on the **Services** menu setup of your Mac). These are related to the Text View control, and if you open up this entry using the disclosure arrow you can see that most of these relate to the **Services** menu options available when text is highlighted in this control. Try it: choose a journal entry that has some content, highlight the text, and choose the **DailyJournal Services** menu. See Figure 14–6 for an example, though as noted previously what you see here will vary depending on your own **Services** menu setup.

Figure 14–6. *The Services menu is the source of most Role Verification warnings.*

This is all very well, but it has no obvious bearing on the accessibility of the Text View control, and the value of this to improving the accessibility of your software is not obvious.

VoiceOver

Any discussion of accessibility on the Mac should focus on VoiceOver. You have probably seen the VoiceOver Preferences in the **Universal Access** preference panel, but you may not have explored what you can do with it. This preference panel allows you to set up your Mac to provide assistance with a range of access issues, but our main focus in this section is on assistance for visual impairment. Somewhat unusually, the actual preferences for VoiceOver (and there is an enormous number of them) are handled in a separate utility, accessed from the preference panel. See Figure 14–7.

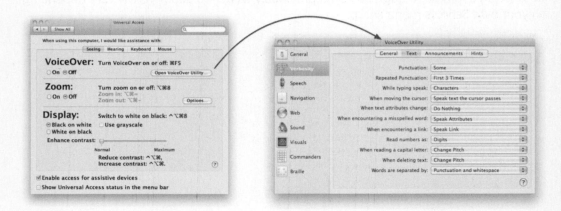

Figure 14–7. *VoiceOver preferences and VoiceOver utility*

In a nutshell, VoiceOver produces a spoken commentary describing the features that it recognizes in the application you are currently using, and it also provides a variety of key combinations that allow you to control applications using just the keyboard.

When you turn on VoiceOver you can click the **Learn VoiceOver** button in the **Welcome** dialog to run a short tutorial. I would heartily recommend exploring this application, as it provides an excellent tutorial to help understand how the end user can make use of VoiceOver (if you choose not to show the message again and decide later that you want to run the Learn VoiceOver application, you can reinstate this dialog from the VoiceOver utility).

Try Learn VoiceOver now, then take a look at a couple of typical applications on your Mac with VoiceOver itself. I would suggest trying an Apple application like Mail and then another application from a different vendor. Use the VoiceOver navigation keys (Ctrl+ +arrow keys) and note what you hear as you move around the user interface.

Well, that is pretty sophisticated, isn't it? Looks like it would be a lot of work to build those features into your application. Actually, no: the good news is that if you have created a piece of software using Xcode and Cocoa frameworks, that software will already work well with VoiceOver. Let's take a close look at one of our projects.

Open Xcode and choose the DailyJournal project. This is the most complex application we have worked on in this book and should be quite revealing in terms of its accessibility. Once the project is open, turn on VoiceOver (use ⌘+F5) and then Build and Run the application.

You will see a window like that in Figure 14–8. Notice the heavy border highlighting the search field, and also the HUD at the bottom of the screen.

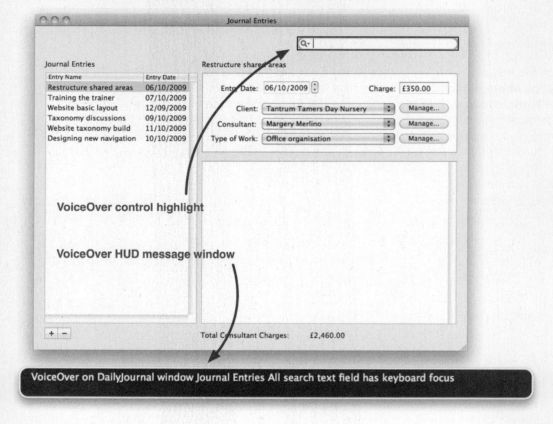

Figure 14–8. *VoiceOver overview*

The VoiceOver voice (you can choose from any of the built-in Mac OS X voices using the VoiceOver utility) will identify the control, and after a short pause will let you know how you can interact with that control. Try moving around the window using Ctrl+⌥+arrow keys, and VoiceOver will oblige you with a message as it highlights each one. Try adding and modifying records and opening the secondary windows. If you're feeling brave, try this with your eyes closed: it will give you a flavor of the user experience for someone with a visual impairment.

It's great that you can do this, and control the application so easily with the keyboard, but the interface as it stands has some problems. Take the three buttons that are entitled **Manage...**. It might be obvious to a sighted person that each button is associated with the popup adjacent to it, but for someone with a visual impairment these buttons are indistinguishable. VoiceOver doesn't have the necessary information to let the user know which is which. Similarly, if you move to the rich text field that this window uses for the journal content, VoiceOver can't tell you anything about it other than that it is a text area and you can type in it. Refer back to the results we had from the Accessibility Verifier; those showed the same problems.

Fortunately, there is something we can do about this. Quit the application and load up the NIB. You might like to turn off VoiceOver temporarily, or you will find it will give you a running commentary on your work in Interface Builder! Open up the **Journal Entries** window and select the **Manage...** button next to the client popup. Now find the **Identity** tab in the Inspector, and in particular the **Accessibility Identity** section. In the **Description** field type **Manage clients** and in the **Help** field type **Click here to bring up the Manage Clients window**. Add the appropriate information for the entryContent Text View (ensure that you select this view rather than its parent Scroll View) and then all of the other user interface controls that were mentioned in the Accessibility Verifier report: the search field, the Journal Entry table (see the following note about tagging tables), the three pop-up buttons, the other two "**Manage...**" command buttons, the **Add** and **Remove** buttons, the **Charge Text** field, and the **Total Charge** label.

> **NOTE:** In the case of the Journal Entry table you have a couple of options about what you tag. You can choose the Table View, in which case the title and description will be read out when you navigate to the table. You can choose an individual table cell, in which case VoiceOver will read out the text only when you navigate into the table and are on a particular cell. Note also that adding a title and description to the table column doesn't have any result—in practice the user will never select a column.

Save the NIB, press ⌘F5 to turn VoiceOver on, and in Xcode Build and Run. This time, when you navigate to this button VoiceOver will say "Manage Clients button" and after a short pause will follow this with "You are currently on a button. To click this button, press Control-Option-Space. The help tag is: Click here to bring up the Manage Clients window." Both of these spoken messages are backed by a HUD-type message window at the bottom left of the screen (see Figure 14–9). If you navigate on to the Text View then you will get the relevant messages there too.

> You are currently on a button. To click this button, press Control-Option-Space. The help tag is: Click here to bring up the Manage Clients window

Figure 14–9. *VoiceOver HUD window*

Once you have finished, turn off VoiceOver and then run Accessibility Verifier against the DailyJournal application again. This time you should see a more healthy report (see Figure 14–10). The figure shows the section of the report dealing with the controls where you have added **Help** and **Description** tags. Notice that the report has picked up these tags rather than the content of the control (see, for example, the **AXDateTimeArea** and compare this with Figure 14–5).

```
▼ AXGroup - "Consultant popup button"
        AXPopUpButton - "Consultant popup button"
        AXStaticText - "Consultant:"
        AXStaticText - "Entry Date:"
        AXStaticText - "Charge:"
        AXTextField - "Entry charge"
        AXStaticText - "Type of Work:"
        AXPopUpButton - "Type of work popup button"
        AXStaticText - "Client:"
        AXPopUpButton - "Client popup button"
        AXDateTimeArea - "Entry date picker"
        AXButton - "Manage Clients"
        AXButton - "Manage consultants"
        AXButton - "Manage Work Types"
```

Figure 14–10. *An improved report from Accessibility Verifier*

So you can enhance the basic behavior of your controls for VoiceOver simply by adding these two tags to the Identity information for the control. It's a good accessibility practice to add **Description** and **Help** tags to all of the controls that your user is going to interact with, but particularly where controls could be confused. A similar situation exists for image buttons. If there is not even a title on the button, VoiceOver has nothing much to go on in helping the user. Adding those **Description** and **Help** tags will make all the difference between an accessible application and a frustrating one. Having said all that, your user may find it annoying to have VoiceOver droning on interminably on every control, so keep the messages crisp and to the point.

Summary

There is a lot of competition in the software market. If you are writing software for the Mac or iPhone, you are targeting a very sophisticated audience and one that is frequently looking for high quality before low cost. "Pile it high and sell it cheap" won't work here—you will know from your own user experience that an application that delights you as well as doing the job you bought it for will be a more satisfying piece of software to use. You can make your product stand out from the crowd by taking care of the human factors in your system design.

Mac OS X provides probably the best support of any consumer computer operating system for users with sensory impairments. As a developer you can capitalize on and build on this support through a few simple steps to make your application work better for these users. The effort is minor, and the benefit is major: what's not to like?

In the final chapter you will be addressing an issue all developers face at some point: your product release. As always, Apple has provided some great support for helping you to create slick, efficient installation kits. You'll also be looking at options for delivering your iPhone applications.

Chapter 15

Packaging and Distribution

There comes a point where you have done all of the testing you can do. All of the bugs you know about are squashed, the icon has been polished to perfection, the help files written. It's time to share your product with an eager and soon-to-be grateful public.

In this final chapter, you'll be covering that last step. You will take the working application running in Xcode and turn it into the package you need to deliver to your end users. We're going to deal with simple and more advanced tools for doing this. We'll also be looking at iPhone distribution and what you need to get started on the road to getting your iPhone application to market.

Build Configurations—From Debug to Release

The first thing to be aware of is the Active Build Configuration. We haven't really come back to this since the early days back in Chapter 2, where you learned about the Xcode Workspace. All through the book your project has been in a Debug Build Configuration, as you can see if you take a look at the **Overview** popup in the Xcode Workspace toolbar (see Figure 15–1).

The Debug configuration causes your application to be compiled along with the debug symbols. The Release configuration removes the debug symbols and also carries out some optimization of the code during compilation. In the unlikely circumstance that you want to create a custom build configuration, you can do this via the **Project Info** window.

The fact is that the most likely thing you will do as a developer, at least to begin with, is to change your project from the Debug to the Release Build Configuration. The most visible consequence of this is that when you build the application, your application file (strictly speaking it's not a file, but a package folder, but you knew that, didn't you?) will appear in a different location. Go into Finder, open up the project file for a project such as Text Pal, and look in the build folder. If you have used only the Debug configuration then you will see two folders, called `Text Pal.build` and `Debug`. The first is used just for temporary files during building. The Debug folder contains your application executable, Text Pal.app. If you have built your project at any time against the Release Build Configuration then you will also have a Release folder in your top-level build folder. The Text Pal.app executable in that folder is the one you will be sending out to your users.

Now that you have the application, let's look at the options for distribution.

Figure 15–1. *Choosing the Active Configuration*

Using a Disk Image

The easiest way by far to distribute your application is simply to package it up in a disk image (dmg) file. You will be familiar with these if you have been using Mac OS X for any time: a dmg file is a highly portable archive file that you can easily move around using FTP, website upload utilities, and even email. When you receive a dmg file you can double-click it to mount it as a volume on your computer. If the dmg file contains an application, you can usually just drag the application file out of the mounted volume into your /Applications folder, or wherever you normally put programs. You can then eject the volume.

In addition to your application, a disk image can contain other files, such as readme files, user guides, and so on.

Let's try it out. Suppose you wanted to distribute Text Pal (the simple word processor from Chapter 3). Open up the project and set the Active Configuration setting (in the **Overview** popup in the Xcode toolbar) to Release. Choose **Build Clean All Targets**. Then choose **Build** (⌘B). Now you have your compiled application ready for packaging. Remember that the application will be below your project folder, in build/Release/.

Now to create the disk image. Start up Disk Utility (in /Applications/Utilities/).
Choose File New Blank Disk Image.... The New Blank Image configuration window comes up
(see Figure 15–2).

Figure 15–2. *Creating a new blank disk image*

Use the navigation panel to choose a suitable location for the image file. Give it both a
filename and an image name (in Figure 15–2 these are respectively Text Pal and Text
Pal v1.0). Choose a size that suits the space your application needs—in practice the
minimum size Disk Utility says it will use for a blank disk image is 10.5 MB, even though
it shows in the Figure as 10.2 MB. Leave the image as unencrypted, the partition map as
Single Partition – Apple Partition Map, and the Image Format as read / write disk image. Click on
the Create button and in a few seconds you will see the disk image mount on your
Desktop as Text Pal v1.0 (the disk image file itself is called Text Pal.dmg and will be in
the location you specified). Double-click the image icon to open up the disk image,
which at the moment is empty. Now drag the application file out of the Release folder
into the disk image window (see Figure 15–3). You can also drag in any readme or other
documentation files you want to distribute as part of your application.

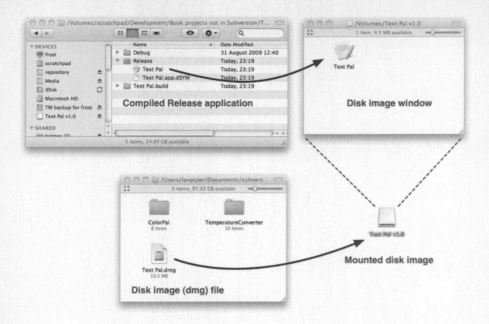

Figure 15–3. *Adding the Text Pal application to the disk image*

Now close the disk image window and eject the image from your desktop. The Text
Pal.dmg file (wherever you created it) is now ready for you to distribute.

Let's try something a little more polished. Many applications that are distributed in this
way have nice images and the ability to drag the application icon onto another icon
within the disk image window in order to install it. This takes a little bit more work, but is
quite straightforward. Let's enhance the appearance and behavior of the disk image for
Text Pal. There are basically three things that you need to do: add an alias for
/Applications, add a background image to the disk image window, and set the position
and size of the icons.

Start with the background image. Use a suitable graphics package to create a
background image: I used Photoshop, but there are many different options available, so
just use your favorite program. To make my image I did the following:

 ■ I took a screenshot of the Text Pal icon blown up to 512 × 512 pixels
   (you can use the **View   Show View Options** menu, or just use the slider
   control at the top or bottom of the window).

- I opened the image in Photoshop, cropped it to 537 × 336 pixels to fit the size I wanted in the disk image window, and reduced the opacity to 20%—as a background image it shouldn't overwhelm the icons. I also added a couple of boxes as placeholders for the icons, an arrow, and a message to the user. The final Photoshop image looked like Figure 15–4 (the **Layers** window is also shown so you can see how the image went together).

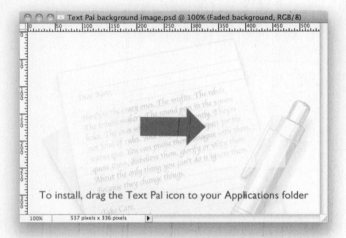

Figure 15–4. *Photoshop image for disk image background*

- Next I saved the image out as a PNG file with transparency.

Once you have your background image, reopen the Text Pal dmg file. Use **View Show View Options** to bring up the options for the disk image, and set them as shown in Figure 15–5. This involves dragging the new PNG file onto the image well near the bottom of the options window. Also set the icon size to 128 pixels, tell Finder to open it in icon view, and set **Arrange By:** to None (so that you can position the icons properly).

The final step is to add an icon as a target for the user to drop the application in order to install it in the /Applications folder. To do this, mount your disk image file again. It appears on the Desktop. Next, open a terminal window, change to the folder of the disk image and create a softlink pointing to the /Applications folder (see Listing 15–1).

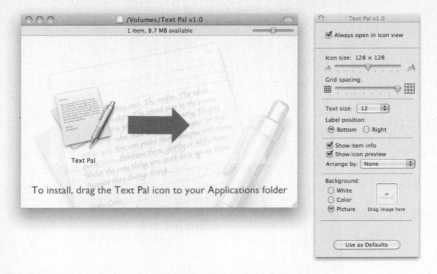

Figure 15–5. *Using View Options to set up the disk image window*

Listing 15–1. *Creating a Softlink for the Disk Image*

```
$ cd /Volumes/Text\ Pal\ v1.0/
$ ln -s /Applications/ ./Applications
```

The syntax for this command means "create a softlink for the location /Applications and put it in the current folder with the name Applications.

This softlink appears in the Finder window with an icon similar to an alias. Here's how the final disk image window looks (Figure 15–6). Now your user can simply drag over the Text Pal icon and drop it on the softlink icon, and it will be installed in the /Applications folder.

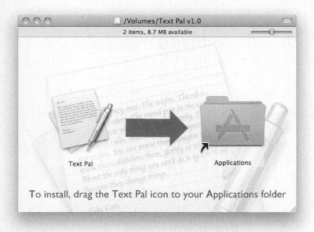

Figure 15–6. *Final Text Pal disk image window*

It may be that this is all you need for distributing your application to your customers. Many of the biggest and best-known applications in the marketplace are distributed in exactly this way. However, it's worth taking a look at the installation packaging tool that Apple has provided as part of the Xcode Developer Tools. If you want the user experience you are offering to your customers to extend to the installation process, then you might like to try out PackageMaker. Let's take a closer look.

PackageMaker

When you install one of Apple's own applications (including the Xcode Developer Tools), or Parallels, or any of hundreds of other applications, you'll be using an installation package produced by PackageMaker. PackageMaker is really the tool of choice if you want to give your user maximum control over the installation process, or if your application has to do something out of the ordinary (such as running pre- or post-installation steps).

What's in Store

Here's a quick thumbnail sketch of the PackageMaker process. PackageMaker collects the assets that you want to provide in the installation package and the rules that you want to apply to the installation process (for example, don't install on a version below Mac OS X 10.4 or if there is less than 10 GB of available disk space, and so on), and allows you to choose options like the location of the installation and whether and how you will handle upgrades as opposed to new installations, and to define scripts to run before or after the installation. It's a sophisticated and comprehensive installation tool.

Creating an Installation Package with PackageMaker

In this section you will be creating a distribution package for DailyJournal. The first thing you need to do, having opened up the DailyJournal project, is to set the Release Build Configuration. I won't go into detail here since you did this just a few pages back. Check that the application builds and runs OK, just to be sure nothing has gone awry.

Starting PackageMaker

You will find PackageMaker in /Developer/Applications/Utilities. Open up the application. The first things you are asked for are your organization and the minimum OS version you are targeting. The organization value is used to set the names of preferences and similar files in Library/Preferences and other folders. See Figure 15–7.

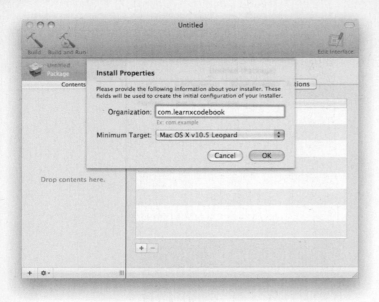

Figure 15–7. *Setting the organization and minimum OS version in PackageMaker*

Once past that initial window, you need to start setting up the installer project. There are essentially two files that you need to think about here: the PackageMaker document, which is your collection of configuration options that are used to create the installation package, and the installation package itself. The various options that you'll be setting here will be stored in the PackageMaker document file (stored with a .pmdoc extension) and that document is used to provide the data to build the installation package file (stored with a .pkg extension). You can save the PackageMaker document file any time you want, and like any file it's worth periodically saving your work in case things go wrong. Start now and save the document file in a convenient location with a sensible name. I chose DailyJournal installer as the name.

Adding Content

The first thing to do is to add the payload—the application itself. Find the DailyJournal.app that you recently built (it will be in the project folder, in build/Release) and drag the application file into the left pane of the PackageMaker window. The icon and title appear in that pane (Figure 15–8).

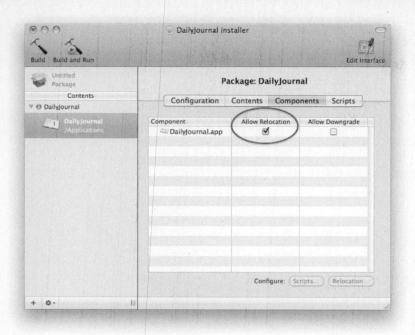

Figure 15-8. *Adding the content payload*

> **CAUTION:** Notice the **Allow Relocation** option circled in Figure 15–8. This should *not* be checked, though it is by default. Leaving it checked will result in your installation failing—and failing silently, which is even worse. So unchecking this option is a high priority!

Package Content Configuration

Turn to the **Configuration** tab. In most cases you won't need to change these settings, but understanding them is crucial. The **Install:** setting specifies the location of the payload—the app file that you just added to the package. The destination is /Applications by default. If you keep this option you should also make sure that **Require admin authentication** is also checked (because most Macs require admin privileges to install into /Applications). It's also a good idea to leave the **Allow custom location** option checked, since this gives the user some flexibility if she wants to install the application elsewhere. For most applications, you should not require the user to restart her Mac. See Figure 15–9.

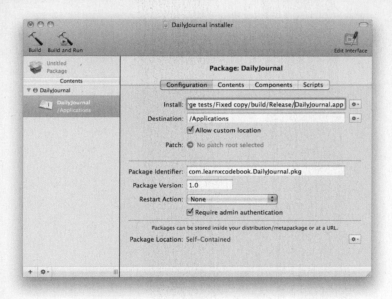

Figure 15–9. *Package content configuration*

Package Content Ownership

The next tab is the **Contents** tab, and this is used to set the owner, group, and privileges for your application. The advice in the Apple Documentation is that these should all be set to root as owner and admin as group (if you take a look at a typical application in /Applications and open the Package Contents, this is how they tend to be set). Given that, it seems a bit odd to me that these values are not set this way by default in PackageMaker. Be that as it may, it's a good idea to set them now. Use the disclosure arrow to open up the entire file tree and select all of the files. Set the owner to root and the group to admin, and check the **Group Write** flag if it is not already checked. See Figure 15–10 to see how things should look now.

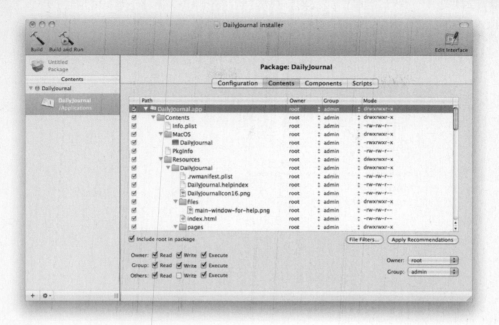

Figure 15–10. *Configuring owner and group settings*

The **Scripts** tab allows you to define scripts that need to run either before or after this content component (your application may have a number of components and you may want one or more of these to have pre- or post-installation steps). You don't need to change anything here.

So really, so far, all you have had to change was file ownership. And since there is just one component in this installation, that's it, right?

Offering Choices for Custom Installations

Well, not completely. That has set up the installation package for that component, but there are also some wider settings that you need to consider. Save for now and then click on **DailyJournal** (above the DailyJournal icon, where you see a disclosure arrow and a blue button). This shows the **Choices** tabs. You would use these if you had a custom installation that allowed you to make choices about what components to install. Think about the installation of Xcode, or Mac OS X itself. If you choose a custom installation then you get to choose what components are installed and what components are left out. This part of the PackageMaker program lets you add, remove, and configure the choices available to the user. For the DailyJournal application there are no choices, so you don't need to make any changes here.

Package-Level Configuration

The next piece of configuration is Package-wide settings. Click on the PackageMaker icon at the top of the left pane. This shows you the Package settings: see Figure 15–11.

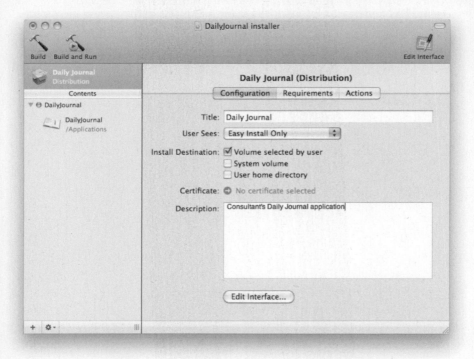

Figure 15–11. *Package settings for the DailyJournal installation package*

This section of PackageMaker deals with settings at the package level. In Figure 15–11 I have already added the Title and Description. For this installation you will specify **Easy Install Only** rather than offering a custom installation (if you had some choices to consider then you would set this to **Custom** or allow the user to choose between **Custom** and **Easy Install** values).

In the **Requirements** tab you can define conditions for the installation to proceed. If your application needs a lot of disk space or memory, here is where you can define the conditions. As an example, this package has a condition set that will result in failure if the destination disk has less than 10 MB of disk space available. Be careful to get your pass, fail, true, and false settings right here, by the way: this can be less than intuitive! See Figure 15–12.

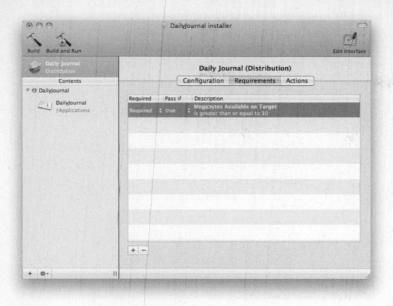

Figure 15–12. *Setting installation requirements for DailyJournal*

The **Actions** tab allows you to set a variety of pre- and post-installation tasks for your installation package. Simply click on the **Edit...** button for either pre- or post-installation actions. This gives you an interface reminiscent of Automator (see Figure 15–13). As in Automator, you simply drag actions across from the list into the workspace. You can chain actions together, too. Here I have asked PackageMaker just to show me the location of the application file in the Finder once installed.

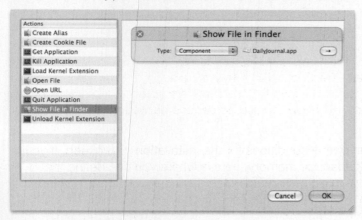

Figure 15–13. *Creating a post-install action*

Clicking **OK** takes you back to the **Actions** tab with the post-install action in place (Figure 15–14):

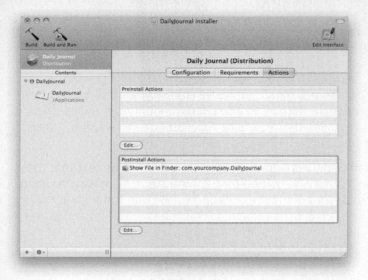

Figure 15–14. *The Actions tab with the post-install action in place*

Polishing the Interface

There is one more thing to do before you build the package. The user interface provided by default, while pleasant, is not customized to your application. Let's do something about that. Click on the **Edit Interface** button at the top right. This gives access to the user interface design assistant (see Figure 15–15).

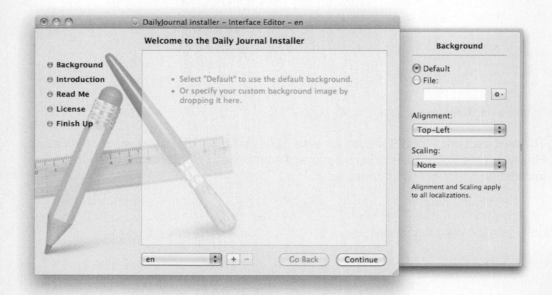

Figure 15–15. *The assistant for designing the installer user interface*

You can navigate through this in much the same way that you would if you were running the installation, using the **Continue** and **Go Back** buttons (I consider this assistant to be a fine example of a highly usable design for this and similar reasons). In this first section you will specify a different background. Recall back in Chapter 13 I created a 512 × 512-pixel icon image for the DailyJournal. Well, thinking ahead, I also created a version of the same image with 20% opacity so that it would sit nicely in the background. If you have downloaded the files for this chapter, find the image called `DJPackageMakerImage.png` and drag it into the user interface. Set the scaling to **To-Fit** and your nice partly opaque image will sit across the background.

Now move on to the Welcome Panel configuration. You can choose the text that the user sees—by default this is "You will be guided through the steps necessary to install this software." but you can write your own here or drop in a file with the text. If you create an RTF file in TextEdit you can include different fonts, weights, and colors. Let's stick with the standard. Move on to the **Important Information** section, and the same kinds of features are available. Try creating an RTF file in TextEdit and dropping it in here (see Figure 15–16):

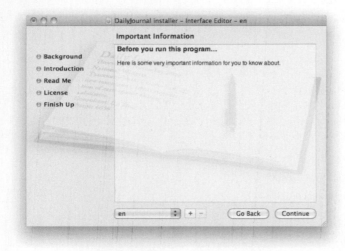

Figure 15–16. *Important information added from an RTF file*

The next section is for a Software License Agreement and offers the same options. Finally, on the **Finish Up** section you can add some text to be displayed when the installation has successfully completed.

When you have finished making changes to the various sections, close the assistant window. Save the PackageMaker document. That concludes the setup and configuration. All that is left now is to build the installation package itself.

Building the Package

After closing the user interface design assistant window you will be back in the main installer setup window. Just click on the **Build** button. You will be prompted for a name for the package. This is the name that the user will see below the **Package installer** icon when he comes to install your program. Click **OK**, and the build process will begin. This should take a few seconds, and all being well, you will see a message confirming success (Figure 15–17).

Figure 15–17. *The installation package built successfully*

So it looks like a successful build. Click on Return and close PackageMaker. You can actually run the installer packer from inside PackageMaker (see the buttons in Figure 15–18) but I prefer to run it from the Finder because it more properly reflects what a real user will be doing.

Testing the Installation Package

Ready to test the installation? OK, let's go and find the installation package. It will be where you chose to save when you click the **Build** button. In the Finder it will look like Figure 15–18:

DailyJournal

Figure 15–18. *The DailyJournal installation package*

Double-click this, and off we go. Assuming all goes well, you will be taken through the steps I set out earlier, and will end up with a window confirming a successful installation. Notice also (see Figure 15–19) that the post-install action has run correctly, as the newly installed DailyJournal application is highlighted in the /Applications folder. Job done!

Figure 15–19. *A successful installation!*

So that brings us to the end of this tour of installation tools for Mac OS X. Most developers, as I mentioned earlier, take the option of creating simple disk image files, but I hope this section has shown that it doesn't take a lot more effort to make really polished and flexible installation kits that could enhance your users' perception of your products.

Distributing your iPhone Application

If you are writing iPhone applications, then you will have been testing using the iPhone simulator, but you won't have been able to put any of your applications onto a real iPhone or iPod Touch. Likewise, there is no equivalent to the methods you have on Mac OS X for bundling your application into an installation package.

Like it or not, unless you are going to resort to "jail-breaking" your device, you have only one option for distributing your application, even to your own iPhone, and that is to join the iPhone Developer Program.

Belonging to the iPhone Developer Program is not the same as being a registered iPhone Developer (confusing, isn't it?). Registering as a developer, which you looked at back in Chapter 4, simply gives you access to the Developer Tools and the ability to run applications on the simulator. Anything beyond that requires joining the program.

At the time of writing there are two levels of membership in the iPhone Developer Program. You can register either in the Standard Program (aimed at individuals or companies who want to use the App Store) or the Enterprise Program (aimed at corporations who want to distribute applications in-house). The chances are that you will be using the Standard Program, but both cost you money, so it is worth careful consideration of which program is right for you. Here is where you start: http://developer.apple.com/iphone/program/apply.html.

> **NOTE:** In the Standard Program you are able to register as a company or an individual (the cost is the same either way). The main distinction comes from the name that appears as the seller in the App Store listing for your application. However, if you do register as a company you will need to provide evidence of your company—basically the program needs to know that you are able to act as an authority on behalf of your company. It also takes longer, since there is more work involved in the validation.

Once registered you are entitled to distribute your application through the App Store. So how does it work? In summary, there is some planning, including deciding what you are going to charge for your application. The App Store takes a cut of anything that you earn for your application, so you need to take that into account if you are planning to make money from your work! You need to set up both your Mac and your iPhone. Once you have done those things, you submit your application to the App Store for approval. You will hear back from the App Store in due course and, all being well, your application will be approved for distribution through the App Store.

Preparation Steps

A key part of the process of getting your application onto a real iPhone is to prepare the iPhone itself. You need to register your iPhone with the iPhone Developer Program Portal. There are also some preparation steps that you need to take within Xcode. It's all a little bit involved, but this section will set it out clearly. The workflow comes down to the following process:

- Information gathering (on your Mac and iPhone)
- Registration and information generation (on the iPhone Developer Program Portal)

Information Gathering

There are three pieces of local information that you need to gather: your iPhone Device ID, a Certificate Signing Request, and an Application ID description. To get your Device ID, attach your iPhone to your Mac using the USB cable, then open up the Organizer, as shown in Figure 15–20 (use the Window ➤ Organizer menu or use ^⌘o).

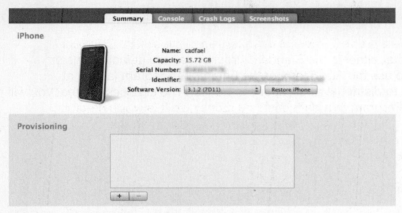

Figure 15–20. *iPhone Device ID and other information in the Xcode Organizer*

You may see a message telling you that you need to use a different version of either the iPhone SDK or the iPhone OS: both are under continuous and rapid development and for some features it may be important to update one or the other.

The piece of information you need to pick up from here is the Device ID (labeled **Identifier**). Copy this and paste it into a text file somewhere—you'll need this a bit later. Actually, this will be a useful place for you to come back to once you are set up. You can use the other tabs in the Organizer to grab screenshots of your application running on a real iPhone, to check crash logs, and other useful stuff.

Next, you need to generate a Certificate Signing Request. You do this using the Keychain Access utility (it's in /Applications/Utilities). Essentially you will be asking Apple for a certificate that you will use to confirm you as the developer. The process will generate public and private keys: Apple will hold the public key and the private key will go into your Keychain.

Start Keychain Access and choose the menu item **Keychain Access   Certificate Assistant   Request a Certificate From a Certificate Authority** (see Figure 15–21):

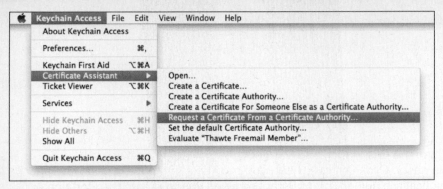

Figure 15–21. *Initiating a Certificate Signing Request*

This takes you through a setup process. In the first window, add or select your email address, choose the **Saved to disk** option, and check the box to specify key pair behavior (see Figure 15–22):

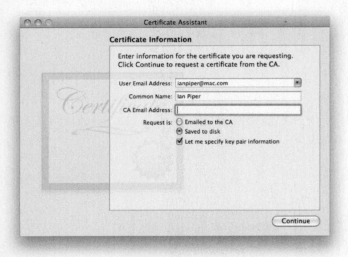

Figure 15–22. *Setting up the Certificate Signing Request*

Accept the suggested filename and location (it will be something like CertificateSigningRequest.certSigningRequest). Take the suggested options of RSA and 2048 bits. Finish the assistant process, and your certificate request will be saved. The final piece of local information that you need to think about is an Application ID. The ID itself is generated on the Developer Program Portal website (I'll be covering this momentarily), but it is based on an ID description that you provide. That ID description is also used widely to describe your Application ID, so it needs to be memorable. For the Show Message application let's use the name telluraApps. It's probably a good idea to store this along with the Device ID that you stored earlier.

Registration and Information Generation

Having gathered the Device ID, Application ID description, and Certificate Request, you can move to the iPhone Developer Portal. Use your web browser to sign in at http://developer.apple.com. If you are a member of the iPhone Developer Program you will see a link to the iPhone Developer Program Portal.

On the main portal page, click on the **Launch Assistant** button. This starts the provisioning process. The first thing you will need to provide is a description for your Application ID. This is where you use the description that you thought up a while back (I used telluraApps in this case). Click **Continue**. Next, you provide a name for your device and its Device ID. Click **Continue** again. The Assistant reminds you to create the Certificate Signing Request—you've already done this, so click on **Continue** again. On the following page use the **Choose File** button to find the Request file and upload it.

Next (this is a bit of a marathon, isn't it?) you reach the point of generating the Provisioning Profile. This is the name given to the collection of bits of information that are generated in this process and that you will download to finish setting up your Mac and iPhone. You can create other, specific Provisioning Profiles for other applications, or simply use one to cover all of your applications. Give the Provisioning Profile a suitable name (such as telluraProvisioningProfile1) and click the **Generate** button.

You will see a spinning wait icon and then a summary of the Provisioning Profile (see Figure 15–23). Use the **Download Now** button on the next page.

Figure 15–23. *The Provisioning Profile has been generated.*

The result of this is a file with the extension .mobileprovision. You're not done with the Developer Program Portal yet, so don't close the browser window, but briefly go to the Finder and install the provision file; make sure that your device is attached, and then drag the .mobileprovision file out of your Downloads folder (or wherever you keep downloads) and drop it in the Xcode Organizer window (see Figure 15–24). If your Application ID description specified an application and company ID in the form com.skeyn.ShowMessage (reverse domain name format), you need to use the same value in the bundle identifier in the info-plist file.

Figure 15–24. *The Provisioning Profile installed in Xcode*

Back in the browser, continue to the next stage, which is to download the certificate. Click on the **Download** button, and you will find a .cer file in your Downloads folder. Double-click this to install it into one of your Keychains (choose the login Keychain). Open up the Keychain Access application again and check the **Keys** category to confirm that you have public and private keys for this certificate (see Figure 15–25).

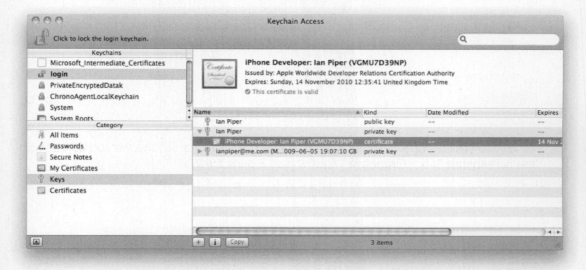

Figure 15–25. *The Developer Certificate in the Keychain Access application*

Back to the browser again. The last couple of pages remind you to check that the certificate is correctly installed and confirm that the process has successfully completed.

Checking That It All Works

You should now be able to test your application on your iPhone. Back in Xcode, set the correct SDK and device (at the time of writing, this is iPhone Device 3.1.2). See Figure 15–26.

Figure 15–26. *Choosing the iPhone Device SDK*

While you are here, change the **Active Configuration** to **Release**.

You're nearly done. Now just Build and Run. Assuming all went well with installing your certificate, you will see a prompt asking for access to it. Click on **Always Allow** (unless you want to see this every time!). The status bar will tell you that Show Message is wending its way to your iPhone. The application will start up on your iPhone, as you can see from the screenshot in the Organizer window (see Figure 15–27).

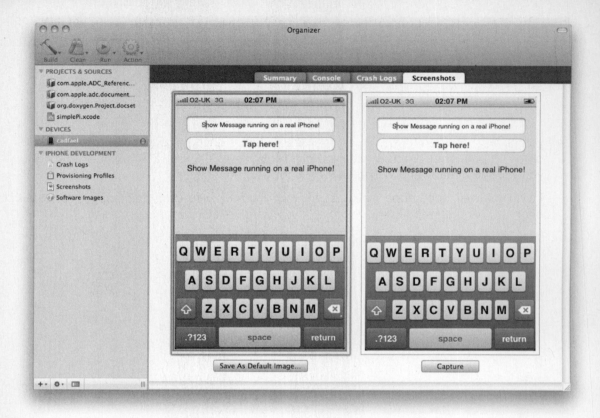

Figure 15–27. *Show Message running on a real iPhone*

You are also able, once you have done all of your testing and bug-fixing, to deploy your application to the App Store. Sadly, discussion of the process for doing that is beyond the scope of this book, but once you are registered you will find all the information you need for this on the iPhone Developer Program Portal Developer Program Portal.

Ad Hoc Distribution

You also have the ability to do Ad Hoc Distribution, which is a mechanism by which you can distribute your application in a limited fashion via email or a website. The idea of this mechanism is to allow you to conduct beta testing with a nominated group of testers, or to distribute your application to a small nominated group of people. Each of the proposed beta testers or users needs to register their Unique Device Identifier (UDID) in your Ad Hoc Distribution profile. You register these UDIDs at the iPhone Developer Program Portal. From this you will be able to download an updated .mobileprovision file, which allows you to distribute your application to the iPhones with these UDIDs. You can currently store up to 100 UDIDs in your profile, which limits the number of beta testers you can have.

If this is of interest to you, take a look at Erica Sadun's Ad Hoc Helper (free from the App Store). This tool makes it easier for your beta users to get their UDIDs to you.

Summary

Beginnings and endings are important. You started your journey through this book, perhaps, as a newcomer to development using Xcode Tools. I hope that it is ending with you as an enthusiast for using these tools to create exciting new products for Mac OS X or the iPhone. They are truly excellent platforms for development, and if you get it right you will find a ready and willing user base for your software.

I wish you well, and I hope that you use what you have learned in these pages to create effective, usable, well-tested, accessible, and, above all, enjoyable programs.

If you have questions or comments about the book, please feel free to send them to feedback@learnxcodebook.com or leave feedback at the Apress website, www.apress.com.

Index

You Need the Companion eBook

Your purchase of this book entitles you to buy the companion PDF-version eBook for only $10. Take the weightless companion with you anywhere.

We believe this Apress title will prove so indispensable that you'll want to carry it with you everywhere, which is why we are offering the companion eBook (in PDF format) for $10 to customers who purchase this book now. Convenient and fully searchable, the PDF version of any content-rich, page-heavy Apress book makes a valuable addition to your programming library. You can easily find and copy code—or perform examples by quickly toggling between instructions and the application. Even simultaneously tackling a donut, diet soda, and complex code becomes simplified with hands-free eBooks!

Once you purchase your book, getting the $10 companion eBook is simple:

❶ Visit **www.apress.com/promo/tendollars/**.

❷ Complete a basic registration form to receive a randomly generated question about this title.

❸ Answer the question correctly in 60 seconds, and you will receive a promotional code to redeem for the $10.00 eBook.

233 Spring Street, New York, NY 10013

Offer valid through 4/10.